The Georgia Open History Library has been made possible in part by a major grant from the National Endowment for the Humanities: Democracy demands wisdom. Any views, findings, conclusions, or recommendations expressed in this collection, do not necessarily represent those of the National Endowment for the Humanities.

NATIONAL
ENDOWMENT
FOR THE
HUMANITIES

CHARLES-HENRI, COMTE D'ESTAING

This carara marble bust by Jean-Antoine Houdon is owned by Frederick Boucher of New York City.

STORM OVER SAVANNAH

*The Story of Count d'Estaing
and the Siege of the Town
in 1779*

ALEXANDER A. LAWRENCE

THE UNIVERSITY OF GEORGIA PRESS
ATHENS

COPYRIGHT 1951
THE UNIVERSITY OF GEORGIA PRESS

Reissue published in 2021

Most University Press titles are available
from popular e-book vendors.

Printed digitally

ISBN 9780820359472 (Hardcover)
ISBN 9780820359465 (Paperback)
ISBN 9780820359458 (Ebook)

PRINTED IN THE UNITED STATES OF AMERICA

TO MY FRIEND AND FORMER PROFESSOR

E. Merton Coulter

DISTINGUISHED HISTORIAN, TEACHER, AND EDITOR

Foreword to the Reissue

The Franco-American siege of British-held Savannah from September to October 1779 was one of the pivotal events of the War for Independence. A year earlier, having been thwarted in their attempts to subdue the American rebellion by launching campaigns in New York and Pennsylvania, British officials decided to shift their efforts to the South and captured Savannah in December 1778. The intended second phase of the British southern strategy, the occupation of South Carolina, depended on the retention of Savannah. The unexpected arrival of a French fleet and army, soon joined by American forces, threatened not only the city and its garrison but also put at risk the entire British plan for their southern campaign.

Given the importance of the siege, it is surprising that historians have devoted so little attention to it. When Alexander Lawrence published *Storm Over Savannah* in 1951, only two previous volumes had addressed the topic: Franklin Benjamin Hough's *The Siege of Savannah*, a collection of documents that appeared in 1866, and Charles Colcock Jones's brief 1874 work, *The Siege of Savannah, in 1779*. Lawrence was thus the first historian to undertake a comprehensive study of the siege, and since he wrote, no updated accounts have appeared. Benjamin Kennedy's *Muskets, Cannon Balls, and Bombs: Nine Narratives of the Siege of Savannah in 1779* (1974), provides a useful supplement to Lawrence's work in the form of French, British, and American documents, and a few articles in the *Georgia Historical Quarterly* that focus on narrow aspects of the siege likewise enhance the story,[1] but none of these match the thorough narrative and analysis found in *Storm Over Savannah*.

Lawrence stated that his purpose in writing was to present an objective account of the French participants in the operations at Savannah. He accomplished this task admirably, producing informative sketches of the lives and careers of the French commander Charles-Henri, comte d'Estaing, and his most important subordinates, including the comte de Grasse, the marquis de Vaudreuil, the comte de Noailles, and Louis-Antoine de Bougainville. Lawrence also explored the political machinations at the French court that made or destroyed officers' careers and the internecine quarrels among officers that plagued the French forces at Savannah. Nevertheless, he made clear that despite the political maneuvering necessary to achieve high rank in the French military, all the officers involved in the siege were bold leaders. They willingly shared danger with their troops on the battlefield, even if in camp the class-based system created stark differences between the difficulties faced by common soldiers and the comforts enjoyed by their aristocratic commanders.

Had Lawrence focused only on these topics, his work would have been a valuable contribution to the literature on the siege. However, he went well beyond his declared intention; Lawrence also devoted extensive attention to the American and British participants at Savannah, from officers such as American commanding general Benjamin Lincoln and British colonel John Maitland to ordinary soldiers and the tribulations they faced, whether as besiegers or defenders, in the trenches around the city. The result was a detailed history of the military campaign, though Lawrence also discussed the plight of civilians in the besieged town. Furthermore, while most historians of his era, and many since, showed a distinct pro-American (and pro-French) bias when writing on the Revolution, Lawrence's work is remarkably free of such favoritism. Readers become acquainted with the siege not only from the French and American perspectives but also from those of the British and their supporters.

Although Lawrence wrote more than a decade before the "new social history" that emerged in the 1960s brought fresh attention to the historical roles of marginalized groups such as women, African Americans, and Native Americans, he did not ignore these people in his account of the siege. Lawrence described the contributions of the Afro-Caribbean soldiers, who made up a substantial portion of the French land force, along with those of the African Americans in British service. The latter labored alongside Loyalists and British soldiers to construct fortifications, guided crucial reinforcements from South Carolina past French warships and into the city, and even bore arms to defend Savannah. Lawrence noted that African Americans faced prejudice from those they aided as well as their enemies, regardless of the cause they served. He addressed the hardships women experienced during the siege as they endured bombardment from French artillery and noted that Britain's Native allies also participated in the defensive efforts, though the coverage of their contributions is brief. Lawrence's writing on these groups reflected the conventions and prejudices of his time, however, and some of the language he used when referring to them is considered offensive today.

Another noteworthy aspect of the siege that Lawrence addressed, and that still remains largely obscure, was the strained relationship between the French and Americans. He noted that when American forces reached Savannah, d'Estaing wrote almost apologetically to the British commander, General Augustine Prevost, that he had been unable "to refuse the Army of the United States, uniting itself with that of the [French] King," which Lawrence observed was a bizarre comment from an erstwhile ally. Lincoln and d'Estaing quarreled over several matters: the comte granted Prevost's request for a twenty-four-hour truce without consulting Lincoln and was forced to apologize. When he learned that d'Estaing had earlier demanded that Prevost surrender the city and its garrison to the French, Lincoln took offense at the lack of any mention of the Americans. That dispute had barely been settled when the allies learned that Maitland had succeeded in getting his eight hundred troops from Beaufort, South Carolina, into Savannah to reinforce the defenders. This sparked a series of accusations and recriminations between French and American officers over whose mistakes had enabled Maitland to reach Savannah, with each side attempting to blame the other for what Lawrence asserted was the failure of both. Relations between the rank and file of the French and American armies verged on outright hostility, and the failure of the October 9 assault on the British defenses further strained relations as each ally criticized the other's performance. Lawrence's discussion of the tense and tenuous alliance, an issue he noted was glossed over in contemporary press reports and other public statements, provides a valuable insight into the true nature of the Franco-American relationship.

The attention to detail in Lawrence's work further enhances its value. He pointed out that the pressure the French felt to conclude their operations at Savannah as rapidly as possible arose not only from concern about traversing the Atlantic Ocean during the hurricane season but also because the allied forces lacked provisions, whereas the defenders of the town were adequately supplied. Lawrence provided an insightful analysis of the death of Polish count and American general Casimir Pulaski; traditionally believed to have been mortally wounded while leading a cavalry charge, Lawrence noted that the terrain where Pulaski fought was unsuited for mounted troops and that Pulaski likely was struck at some distance from the British positions, a more accurate if less dramatic version of events.

Yet Lawrence's work does not lack drama. His account of the allied attack on the British lines succeeds in capturing the spirit of the action without sacrificing accuracy, and his writing throughout the volume is engaging and accessible. Evidence of Lawrence's thorough research is found on virtually every page, with quotations from American, French, British, Hessian, and Loyalist participants appropriately interspersed. A significant number of quotations in French, untranslated, may frustrate some readers.

JIM PIECUCH

Note

1. See, for example, George Fenwick Jones, "A Note on the Victor at Springhill Redoubt," *Georgia Historical Quarterly* 63, no. 3 (Fall 1979): 377–79; Richard C. Cole, "The Siege of Savannah and the British Press, 1779–1780," *Georgia Historical Quarterly* 65, no. 3 (Fall 1981): 188–202.

Preface

EARLY in September in the year 1779 a great French naval armada appeared suddenly off the coast of Georgia. Aboard the fleet were four thousand troops of His Most Christian Majesty Louis XVI come from the West Indies to cooperate with the Americans in destroying in the Southern colonies Britain's military power, which was then centered upon Savannah.

Much has been written about our French Allies in the North during the American Revolution, of Rochambeau and Lafayette, and of how the army and navy of France took part in the great victory of Yorktown. A score or more books deal with that phase of the War of American Independence. But no one has ever essayed to write the history of the French at the Siege of Savannah. For that matter, little enough is known of the Siege itself. For some reason there has been a tendency to overlook an event that possessed qualities of drama and color rarely matched elsewhere in American history.

Charles-Henri, Comte d'Estaing, who commanded the French land and naval forces that came to Georgia in 1779, has been a mere name in American history books. He was, as these pages reveal, an extraordinary individual. If the portrait of the Count, who is the central figure of this study, is at times unflattering, I can only reply that he has been painted as his contemporaries saw him.

A galaxy of soldiers and sailors of *l'Ancien Régime* accompanied d'Estaing. They numbered famous French sea fighters, celebrated global navigators, noblemen with thousand-year-old names, elegant *beaux* of the Petit Trianon, future generals and admirals of the Republic and the Empire, and youths destined for prominent parts on the political stage of France in the turbulent times that lay ahead. They were a brave and entertaining, if sometimes unharmonious, lot. The Siege of Savannah would have been a far less lively episode without them.

The failure of the bloody assault by the French and American forces upon the British lines on October 9, 1779, affected the whole course of the American Revolution. Contemporaneous British sources attest the significance of the defeat of the Allies. "I clearly saw," wrote the Royal Governor of Georgia at the time, "that if this Province then fell, America was lost and this I declared on every occasion." General Prevost's troops "have preserved the Empire," exulted the Chief Justice of New York when he learned of the victory. Colonel John Maitland of the Seventy-first Regiment of Scotch Foot, a martyr of the Siege, had "heroically re-established," to quote a writer of the time, "the declining glory of the British arms, in one of those most important and critical moments which decide the fall or the rise of nations." If any partiality for this son of the Sixth Earl of Lauderdale seems reflected in these pages it stems from my desire to rescue from oblivion a great soldier of the Empire.

With good cause the defeat of the Allies at Savannah was celebrated in London by the firing of the Tower guns and at New York with parades. Had Georgia been lost, the only foothold remaining to George III in his American colonies would have been the city of New York. British morale was tremendously boosted by the victory at Savannah which steeled the Ministry in its decision to continue the effort to subdue America. The victory permitted the transfer of the main theatre of war to the lower South. General Clinton who had embarked some of his troops for the projected attack on Charlestown returned to New York when he heard that d'Estaing's fleet was off Savannah, advising Lord Germain that "Should Georgia be lost I shall have little hope of recovering that Province and also of reducing and Arming South Carolina." Three years of cruel civil war that followed in Georgia and in the Carolinas might have been spared if Savannah had fallen to the Allies in 1779.

When I began my researches for this book, which was first published in 1951, I suspected that the key to the proper telling of the story of the Siege lay in France. Little in the way of source materials in that country had been utilized by historians at that time. The French version of the event was practically an unknown chapter. My research was pointed toward France, along trails which, as far as d'Estaing's Savannah campaign was concerned, were then untravelled by American scholars.

The Archives Nationales and the records in the Library of the Service Hydrographique de la Marine in Paris proved a veritable Pandora's box of manuscript material relative to d'Estaing's expedition: some 2,000 pages of military and naval records, letters, orders, journals, reports, logs, and returns. Routine in the main, they offer many revealing items. A surprising number of French journals or diaries were located. The most important of the manuscripts is the "Observations" of Count d'Estaing which he wrote aboard the *Languedoc* after the Siege. They consist of his notes or commentaries upon the journal kept by a French officer named O'Connor. Though not given to serious analysis of America the Count wrote interestingly and frequently well, with a continuous thread of sarcasm on the subject of the *"Insurgents."* If the bibliography appended at the end of this book seems unduly long, my justification is that it may be useful to those who labor hereafter among these and the other source materials I utilized.

I said Pandora's box by design. For to one whose schooling

in French lay nearly a quarter of a century in the past, the task of reading several hundred pages of eighteenth century manuscript material, to say nothing of a mass of published writings in that language, loosed a plague of worries. Translation offered no serious difficulties where the writing was legible, but oh the penmanship of some of the French officers! Where assistance was needed it was kindly supplied by Abel Doysié of Paris. It was Monsieur Doysié who located for me the d'Estaing-O'Connor manuscript in the Bibliothèque de Service Hydrographique. Mary Catherine Mauduit of Savannah also deserves my acknowledgment for the assistance she gave wherever proper translation was a problem.

I am indebted to no one more than to Lilla M. Hawes, Director of the Georgia Historical Society, whose familiarity with Southern archives is extensive. My indebtedness to the various libraries, historical societies, and individuals that made materials available to me is a considerable one. This blanket acknowledgment is a poor medium of repayment. Whether in this country, or at Paris, London or Edinburgh where my research was vicarious, I found a readiness to assist and a courtesy that truly lightened my labors.

In the Preface to the first edition in 1951 my thanks were extended to my efficient secretaries, Barbara B. Kehoe and Norma B. Meehan, who typed and retyped many drafts of the original manuscript. It is with pleasure that seventeen years later I express a like obligation to them in the typing of the revision.

Since the publication of the first edition of *Storm Over Savannah* additional source materials, including the journals of several French officers, have come to my notice. I have drawn on them in the new edition. Numerous minor revisions in the original text and a few corrections have been made.

ALEXANDER A. LAWRENCE

I

Imperiled City

Savannah sprawled indolently in the September sun atop its great sand bluff. Below the town, the slow-tided river coursed round the big crescent bend and out to sea. The top-sails of the brigs that crowded the harbor scarcely reached the level of the houses on the Bay, for the height of the bluff was such as to "put a man out of breath before he can reach the Top," remarked a visitor of the day. From it there was a sweeping view of the luxuriant rice fields and savannas that stretched as far as one could see toward the north and the east.

"Let the English reader picture to himself a town erected on the cliffs of *Dover,* and he will behold *Savannah,*" wrote a British traveller. There, however, comparison with the old country both began and ended. More than four decades had passed since Oglethorpe had come and time had moved on to 1779 and the nineteenth year of the reign of George III. But Savannah was still a frontier community standing in a tiny clearing in the endless pine forests—a remote seat of British rule at the edge of the vast wilderness called Georgia whose chief link with the outside world was still the river that emptied into the Atlantic eighteen miles eastward.

Three highroads connected the town with the country around. The Augusta or Ebenezer Road with its South

Carolina connection at Zubly's Ferry wandered off westward through the pine-barrens and across the piedmont country to lose itself finally in regions where the sound of the ax of the first settler was yet to echo through the virgin forests. The Ogeechee Road struck southward down the coastal plain along ancient trails of the Guale Indians past Midway to Darien. The Sea Island Road crossed the swamp southeast of Savannah and forked out toward Thunderbolt, Beaulieu, and other settlements on the inland waters, that fantastic lacework of sounds, rivers, and creeks that nature had woven along the seaboard of Georgia and Carolina.

The population of Savannah, which was ordinarily about 750 whites, had been greatly swollen by war. The people crowded into what the British army had not commandeered of the town's four hundred and fifty houses and spilled over into the nearby hamlets of Yamacraw, Trustees' Garden, and Ewensburg. The Georgia capital received few compliments from visitors of the period. The scarcity of buildings in the town made it hard for them to perceive the symmetrical plan of streets and squares of which the residents boasted. It was "very straggling built," wrote a traveller. "The Houses lie Scattered, and are poorly built mostly of wood—in Short the whole has a most wretched miserable appearance," was a British officer's description of the place.[1]

The streets, which were wide and unpaved, were either incredibly sandy or quagmires, depending on the weather. It was "white sand so deep" that "it is just like walking through fresh fallen snow a foot deep," complained a Hessian.[2] On windy days "A man runs no small risk of being chocked [sic] by the clouds of sand and dust," observed another visitor of the day who imagined that in the summer Savannah, "what between Sand Flies (of which even now there are Legions) Musquettoes, etc. *must certainly be a most agreeable place* to reside in."[3]

The public buildings were as little impressive as the dwellings. Pierre Colomb, who was at Savannah in '78, could later recall "no one building I can describe." His only lasting impression was of the "vast rice plantations" that surrounded the town, requiring "a perpetually flooded soil, and whenever the waters are drained off, give forth a noxious air full of disease. . . ." The largest structure was probably "Y^e great or English church" on Bull Street about which the traveler John Bartram (more interested in botany than architecture) had found nothing worth recording beyond the fact that the edifice was "80 foot long & 48 or 50 wide." Other landmarks in the town were the Governor's Mansion, the Market, the old silk-house called the Filature, the big new military barracks, and several public taverns in at least one of which patrons found wines "good and plentiful" and dinners "chosen and served with taste." The omission of a Court House from this chronicle of the town's sights deserves a word of explanation. Recently the Chief Justice had returned to Savannah to find the erstwhile seat of royal justice "filled with Soldiers & their Wives, and in a very disagreeable Situation." The "Soldiery" had even used the "Bench & Bar" for firewood, complained that dignitary to whom the sacrilege must have seemed a perfect symbol of the disrespect the military establishment paid the civil government His Majesty of late had been "graciously pleased to re-establish" in the Province of Georgia.

But if there was little to admire in the architecture of the town, a visitor might be impressed by Savannah's "delightful society" as was Elkhannah Watson of New England who passed that way in 1778. The gay balls and dinners in Savannah homes and after Major Habersham's marriage a morning reception where the guests enjoyed "a collation of fruits, wine, and salt fish, etc." would never be forgotten by a young American soldier from Virginia named Brooke.

Officers fortunate enough to be invited to the homes of the wealthy merchants were "sumptuously" entertained, he reminisced—"breakfast in the morning, luncheon at eleven o'clock, dinner at two, tea and coffee in the evening, and a hot supper at night."[4]

This Whig society had been supplanted a few months before by a Tory regime. State had reverted to Province. The social and political life of the little capital now centered about the Governor's House on St. James Square. There astute Sir James Wright lived in state and there most of the public business of the Province was conducted. The Royal Governor had returned in triumph a few weeks before to the wooden mansion in which the rebels once held him captive. The bullet marks were still discernible where the "Western" riflemen who guarded him had fired at the building while he and his family were prisoners there. Eight months had now passed since the day a slave named Quash revealed to Colonel Archibald Campbell the route that led across the swamp southeast of the town—a path which Colonel George Walton had once frequented "with young ladies, picking jessamines," as he testified at the court-martial of General Robert Howe. By some oversight that ill-starred American commander failed to fortify the approach. Turning Howe's right flank, the British had stormed into Savannah on the heels of the fleeing Americans. That night the Rebel Governor, John Houstoun, paused long enough in his westward flight from the capital to dash off a note informing General Benjamin Lincoln that the day had been lost. Thus had been restored His Britannic Majesty's dominion over this realm of palmetto and pine.

Though war had dried up most of Savannah's once flourishing export trade in rice, lumber, pitch, hides, and indigo the port remained a place of great strategic value to the King. It was "the key of the southern provinces, and the Gibraltar of the Gulf passage," wrote Chief Justice Stokes, explaining that "to the south of this province there is not a port on the continent that will receive a sloop of war."[5] It was a dagger at the back of South Carolina. "What barrier have we to secure us from the conquerors?" asked Charles C. Pinckney, Jr., in discouragement after Savannah fell. It was the keystone in the master English plan of invading Carolina and salvaging the Southern colonies out of the Revolution—that wicked rebellion in which, complained a charming Tory female in Savannah, "everywhere the scum rose to the top."[6]

The revolt in America was now in its fifth weary year and Seventeen seventy-nine had dragged through a long summer to September 8th. A strangely accelerated tempo pervaded the drowsy Georgia town that day. Startling news was filtering back from Tybee Island at the mouth of the river. Unwonted activity was noted at the headquarters of General Augustin Prevost on Broughton Street. Couriers wheeled away, the horses leaving trails of dust as they clattered out the highways. His aides-de-camp had not been so busy in months. In the face of grave emergency, however, they maintained their solid English composure. At least Captain Alexander Shaw of His Majesty's Sixtieth Regiment did. In phrasing an important dispatch sent that day to St. Augustine Shaw summed up the situation as "the little hurry we are now in." Red-coated regulars, Provincials from the North, and Wissenbach's Hessians were moving out into assigned posts. There was a stir and bustle at the Governor's House where a special meeting of Council had been convened. Wagons filled with slaves bringing shovels and tools were rolling into Savannah from the plantations around.

Something portentous was in the air that the town could be shaken in any such manner as this from its summer doldrums. Even the Indians in the service of George III had roused themselves from the torpor of grog and tobacco. His Cherokee and Creek allies, the Governor soon discovered, were not nearly "so hearty in the Cause, & so Warmly attached, as I Expected." Like the Hessian auxiliaries they left an impression on the English that while they were not at all averse to taking the King's shilling they were at heart quite indifferent as to which side ultimately triumphed. The principal contribution of the redskins to the British war effort was the plundering of slaves from the Carolina plantations. They brought their booty into over-crowded Savannah, scaring the women-folk of the town out of their wits with the shorn heads, gaudily painted faces, and the tomahawks which they threw with inconceivable skill.

The monotony of life in this outpost of British empire had been broken by something more exciting than the "Dancing Assemblies" or the dramas at the little theatre on Broughton Street with "characters by gentlemen of the garrison" or even the Jockey Club events in which hard-riding Stephen De Lancey of New York usually captured the purse—gala afternoons topped off at night by "a very genteel ball" where the ladies "made a brilliant appearance." Such was "the spirit of the Turf, and Entertainment" during this summer that the *Royal Georgia Gazette* had recently extolled it as *"An happy presage of happier days."* The editor proved something less than oracular.

Before daybreak on this Wednesday, September 8th, 1779, Governor Wright had been awakened by a note from General Prevost. Sir James' face must have blanched as he read it. The message confirmed the worst fears of the past few days. Off Tybee bar "There were 42 Sail of French Ships of War in Sight, most of which appeared to be large Ships." It was now plain that an attack on Savannah was intended. "No Man could have thought or believed" such a thing, said the Governor.[7] It was almost incredible. Everyone knew that Monsieur d'Estaing's fleet was hundreds of miles away, preoccupied with France's lush possessions in the West Indies and by no stretch of the imagination interested in this poor, remote Province. Nothing seemed further from Savannah than England's hereditary enemies, those giddy opportunists who had taken the side of the Americans for no better reason than to avenge Britain's rape of the Bourbon empire.

Yet here these light-minded people were—come with a fleet of 22 sail of the line, 10 frigates and other ships, carrying 4,000 troops. At the stormy season of the year, too! It was still hard for Prevost to believe Savannah was the real enemy objective. "It is not improbable but his serious views are to the Northward of this—Perhaps Rhode Island, or New York—but I can only conjecture," the British commander was saying as late as the 9th.[8]

Several strange sail had been sighted off Tybee Island a few days before. The flotilla consisted of two large two-deckers, two frigates, and two small sloops. When Lieutenant Lock went out in the pilot boat to investigate they immediately weighed anchor and stood out to sea, indicating an "inclination not to be discovered." However, the French uniforms could be plainly distinguished on one of the frigates. In a dispatch heavy with misgivings General Augustin Prevost had reported their appearance to Sir Henry Clinton. To the relief of the British the vessels disappeared. But those ships were merely the faster sailers of Admiral d'Estaing en route to Charlestown to inform the Americans of the arrival of the French off Georgia. The main body of the fleet had now come up.

For this sudden turn of affairs the British were ill-prepared. Reports had previously reached Prevost that a "French Squadron with land Troops on Board were . . . destined to this Quarter."[9] But the news had not been seriously credited. His forces, General Prevost apologized in a hasty dispatch to Admiral Byron, were "somewhat disjointed." The flower of the army was at Beaufort. Nine hundred troops, consisting principally of the Seventy-first Regiment of Scotch Highlanders, had retired to that port after the failure to capture Charlestown a few months before. Another garrison was at Sunbury. Scarcely a thousand men could be mustered at the moment in the Georgia capital.

The route by land was cut off by the Americans. Beaufort was all of fifty tortuous miles from Savannah by water. And now the *puissance* of France had come up out of the Caribbees through the Windward Passage. The cause of George III in America was in mortal peril.

II

The Pomp and Glory

A MIGHTY French armada lay at anchor in the open sea. To the west stood the coast of Georgia, with the low, long shoreline of the Tybees necklaced by the white sand beaches. From the mastheads of the great ships-of-the-line streamed the fleurettée banners of the Bourbons. "They stretch," wrote General Prevost, "from off Beaufort North, as far to the Southward as we could see from Tybee Light." [1] Most of them were two-deckers though some were of the triple deck class. Some were old ships that had fought in the naval battles of the seventeen-fifties. Others were modern and Nelson was to know the thunder of their guns in the days of Napoleon. Like song from the lips roll the names of these giants of the deep—*Languedoc, Diadème, Annibal, Zélé, Vengeur, Dauphin Royal, Fantasque, Guerrier, Tonnant, Robuste, César, Vaillant, Sagittaire, Provence, Magnifique, Fendant, Hector, Fier Rodrigue.*

The officers were for the most part members of the nobility which formed a close corporation in the French navy of that day. "You may think it incredible," wrote John Paul Jones at the time, "but it is a fact that a royal ordinance is in force, not long ago promulgated, requiring that candidates for promotion from lieutenant to captain must first of all produce proof of noble lineage for at least four generations back of their own, or must be members by heritage of the order of the Chevalier of St. Louis!"

Great names were to be found among these officers. There was the Comte de Grasse, a hulking man with a thousand-year-old patronym whom undying fame at Yorktown and then bitter defeat in the West Indies awaited during the next three years. No less famed was the name borne by the Marquis de Vaudreuil who commanded the *Fendant*. Of the family of Louis de Barras, another of these mariners, a French proverb said, "Noble as the Barras, as ancient as the rocks of Provence." A self-effacing veteran of forty-five years' service in the navy, Count de Barras was, like de Grasse and de Vaudreuil, to have a prominent role in the great victory at Yorktown.

One of the ablest of these seafaring aristocrats was the Comte de La Motte-Piquet, a small, thin, ugly man who had been the first officer of a European power to salute the flag of the young American republic. Gui-Pierre, Comte de Kersaint, captain of the famous frigate *Iphigénie*, and the Marquis de la Prévalaye belonged to two of France's most illustrious naval families. The latter was destined to have the privilege of delivering to Congress the treaty of peace recognizing the independence of the United States. Among the most popular and capable of the Bourbon sea captains of the day was Comte d'Albert de Rions, commander of the *Sagittaire*. "If you had given me him when I asked you, we should now be rulers of India," the great de Suffren was to tell the Ministry two years later.

Pierre-André de Suffren, now fifty years old, commanded the flotilla of five ships which d'Estaing ordered into the Savannah River to seal the entrance. Visitors aboard the vessel of this son of the Marquis de Saint-Tropez got a royal welcome. The Chevalier de Pontgibaud tells how he was compelled to drink such a quantity of punch on one occasion that he nearly fell into the sea in leaving the ship. The captain of the *Fantasque* was extremely corpulent. While dining with Hyder Ali in India he experienced such difficulty in sitting on a carpet that the ruler ordered cushions brought for him. "Etiquette was not made for such as you," observed the understanding Nabob.

Suffren could boast of an interesting career in the navy, commencing at the age of fourteen. It included service in the caravans of the Order of Malta. But his greatest fame lay ahead. Largely upon the recommendation of d'Estaing, who recognized his genius, he was placed in command of a squadron sent two years later to the Indian Ocean. His fighting record in those waters during 1782–83 would rank Bailli de Suffren as the greatest French naval officer of his time.

Another interesting figure among these officers was the Comte de la Pérouse, captain of the frigate *Amazone*. Watching the big September sea moons come up off Carolina, the thirty-eight-year-old mariner must have brooded during these weeks over the ever faithful Creole girl he could not marry because of the disapproval of his ambitious parents. A smile perchance displaced the pensive mood of M. de la Pérouse when he thought of Thomas MacKenzie, commander of the sloop *Ariel* which his frigate captured off Beaufort. The plucky battle this young Englishman put up and his attractive personal qualities "inspired a bit of enthusiasm" among the French, said d'Estaing.[2] Their enthusiasm was understandable. For here was a man who made war in a way a Frenchman well might envy! Strange cargo was found aboard H.M.S. *Ariel*. Her complement included the mistress of Captain MacKenzie. "One is able to say that he has vigorously defended her," the witty Louis-Antoine de Bougainville remarked in his Journal at the time.

One day the long romance of Count de la Pérouse was to end in marriage. Then he would sail off to explore the blue immensity of the Pacific where he found uncharted isles, the strait north of Japan which bears his name, and a mystery-shrouded fate on a coral reef in the New Hebrides.

Men of scientific renown were along, including the Marquis de Chabert who was widely known for his work as a nautical astronomer and hydrographer. The researches of the Chevalier de Borda in the metric system field and in the measurement of the inclination of the magnetic needle were no less applauded in Europe. Comte de Chastenet de Puysegur had discovered mummified remains while exploring a cave at Teneriffe which permitted archeologists to connect the extinct Gauches with the Indians of South America. Puysegur would later prepare and publish the massive *Détail sur la navigation aux côtes de Saint Domingue*.

Other well-known names in the fleet included those of Comte de Broves whom Admiral d'Estaing was to leave in command of the squadron when he went ashore; the Comte de Bruyères-Chalabre, captain of the *Zélé;* Marquis de Poype-Vertrieux, captain of the *César;* Comte de Bernard de Marigny; Marquis de Pontèves-Gien; the Chevalier de Capellis; and two young officers with great French names —Comte de Colbert and the Marquis de la Galissonière.

But the most famous of these sea captains was not of the nobility. Louis-Antoine de Bougainville belonged to the faction in the French navy known as the "blue" as distinguished from the "red" party—one who had not entered the naval service as a career man and ascended through the grades. Bougainville was one of the more interesting figures of his time. In his youth he had written a brilliant treatise on integral calculus. Abandoning the law for the profession of arms, he secured the influence of Madame de Pompadour in becoming an aide to Montcalm with whom he served with considerable distinction in Canada. After a turn as a diplomat at London he had successfully colo-

THE POMP AND GLORY 13

nized the Falkland Islands. But it was as one of the greatest of global navigators that M. de Bougainville is celebrated. In his interesting book describing his voyage around the world aboard the *Boudeuse* from 1766 to 1769 he wrote with discernment and humor of the strange peoples who inhabited the far-away islands in far-away seas he had visited. His name is preserved by the flaming tropical flower called Bougainvillea and by a well-known island in the Solomon group.

During the sojourn of the French fleet off the Georgia coast we shall hear more than once from the captain of the 74-gun *Guerrier* whose embittered soul was to give vent in his meticulously kept journal to many a choice insult of Vice-Admiral d'Estaing.

It was the late afternoon of September 9th. From the deck of the *Languedoc* the coast was a haze which faintly rimmed the oriflamme west. The French long boats had gathered near the great flagship. They were crowded with the troops who were to be moved down the coast a few miles southward for the landing. A place on the Vernon River called Beaulieu had been selected as the point of debarkation. Some of France's best regiments were represented. There were detachments from the Armagnac, Dillon, Agénois, Gâtinais, Foix, Hainault, Auxerrois, and Cambresis Regiments. Among them were grizzled veterans of Rossbach, Minden, and even Fontenoy.

The launches bearing the troops of *Sa Majesté très-Chrétienne* rolled sickeningly in the ground-swells of the Atlantic. As many as a hundred men were in some of the boats. They were immensely uncomfortable in their tight-fitting linen breeches, leggings that reached above the knee, and stiff collars which regulations required to be hooked. Broad cross belts supporting heavy cartridge-boxes and tri-cornered hats that shaded ears but not eyes added to their miseries. The lot of the French foot soldier of the era was a bad enough one under any circumstances. Often he was not even known by his own name. Rosters of d'Estaing's army contain such *noms de guerre* as *Vive L'Amour, Bien-Aimé, Jolicoeur*—euphemisms which perhaps helped to hide the "filth, vermin and misery" that Marshal de Saxe said was to be found beneath their façade of "well groomed, white powdered hair." There was much grumbling. Since arriving off Georgia the commander-in-chief never seemed quite certain what he was up to. Such delays!

Tall Charles-Henri, Comte d'Estaing—Vice-Admiral of France, Lieutenant General of the Armies of the King, Chevalier of the Orders, Commander-in-Chief of the Forces of His Most Christian Majesty in America—might well feel the sense of personal power as he reviewed the troops in the boats gathered near the towering *Languedoc*. His sensitive face, almost feminine in its grace (its weaknesses unable to escape the chisel of the famous Houdon), was creased with care. The past few days had been hard ones. He had just returned from a fatiguing foray on Tybee Island. The General was never one to spare himself, "working night and day," said a French naval officer—"sleeping only an hour after dinner, his head resting upon his hands, sometimes lying down, but without undressing." [3]

No empty words were those of official documents which styled him *"un très haut et très puissant seigneur."* A unique privilege had been gained for the descendants of Dieudonné d'Estaing when that hero sacrificed his life to save King Philip Augustus at the Battle of Bouvines in 1214. As a result the d'Estaing family was entitled to wear the coat-of-arms of France. A darling of the French court from boyhood, Charles-Henri d'Estaing could boast that he was "brought up about the person of the dauphin who distinguished me."

Despite his fifty years he possessed, according to one of his naval officers, "the enthusiasm and the fire of a man of twenty." With the blue ribbon of the Order of Saint-Esprit worn across his white jacket in the shape of a cross he had made a gallant figure a few weeks before at Grenada leading his troops to the breach and cheering them on with *"Soldats, en avant, suivez-moi! Vive le Roi!"* It must have been comforting to Louis XVI to know that the throne was supported by stalwart descendants of the men who in olden days had defended the marches with their battle axes and their lives. "The King never had a subject who loved him better, and who is a more worthy citizen," wrote John Paul Jones in 1778.

M. d'Estaing was more than a courageous fighter. He was a man of considerable intelligence and a tireless worker. A fluent writer, his pen could be turned to poetry and even to a tragedy in verse (*Les Thermopyles*, 1791). His manners were elegant. He was unstinting in his praise of deserving officers and relentless in his efforts to secure recognition for them. But grave faults offset these better qualities. This favorite of Versailles, whether in the day of Madame Pompadour or of Marie Antoinette, possessed the weaknesses of the courtier. He had wasted much of his wife's fortune in gambling and high living. The Comtesse had been compelled to bring litigation to separate her estate. A faithless husband, Count d'Estaing was the father of a bastard son in Auvergne and the reputed sire of another in Paris.

He was, above all, inordinately ambitious. His career had been and would continue to be one long pursuit of personal advancement. To that end he was forever intriguing in the antechambers of Versailles. "No mind," General Henry Lee would write in scathing judgment, "was more obedient to the calls of duty, connected with the prospect of increasing his personal fame, than that of the French admiral." [4] Not a few of the latter's colleagues agreed. "The ambition of Count d'Estaing is easily excited," complained an anonymous naval officer who described him as *"avide de gloire."* Bougainville and others were bitterly to inveigh against "the ambitious vice admiral" while the fleet was on the Georgia coast.

In the Seven Years' War d'Estaing's restless quest for glory led him to follow the letter rather than the spirit of the parole he had given after being wounded and taken prisoner at Madras. Turning privateer after his release, he had ravaged the English settlements on the Persian Gulf, satisfying his sense of honor by removing himself to a small boat and becoming a mere spectator in time of actual combat. Admiral Boscawen threatened that if he ever got the "villain" in his power he would "chain him upon the quarter-deck and treat him like a baboon." The Count had the misfortune to be captured on his way home. He was held for a time under close surveillance in a dungeon at Portsmouth, an experience that did not increase his love for *la perfide Albion.* "May Heaven grant," he is supposed to have exclaimed on one occasion, "that before my death I may see the moment when these proud islanders shall not possess either continent or island in the new world."

Tired as he was on September 10th, the Vice-Admiral could take time to pen a polite note of encouragement to one of his "young heroes," exhorting a promising officer to continue his study of the regulations pertaining to the infantry service. Louis-Marie, Vicomte de Noailles was among the most engaging of the youthful noblemen who had accompanied d'Estaing to Georgia. The accomplishments of this handsome, well-built soldier included that of being one of the best dancers of his day. He had been the *beau idéal* of the Marquis de Lafayette, his brother-in-law. One might easily guess from the colonel's insigne of this twenty-three-year-old soldier that he was a scion of some great feudal family. He was indeed. His father, the potent

Duc de Mouchy, was a Marshal of France. "I love him, I esteem him," Count d'Estaing had recently informed the Duke. His young Colonel possessed, he reported to the Minister of Marine, *"l'amour pour la guerre."* "The troops of his division love him. *Oui, Madame la Maréchale,* his division—for I beseech you to believe that Vicomte de Noailles commands one." [5] So the ever politic General d'Estaing had written to this nobleman's mother after the capture of Grenada. *Madame la Maréchale* was none other than the celebrated *"Madame Étiquette,"* well known in French history as the strict and ceremonious lady-in-waiting to Marie Antoinette.

Equally prominent in the *après nous le déluge* set in France was the commander of the Dillon Regiment—Arthur, Count Dillon, twelfth in his line in the peerage of Ireland. Colonel Dillon's great-grandmother had been the natural daughter of Charles II and Barbara Villiers. For generations the Dillons had served the rulers of France. They were bright luminaries in the firmament of Versailles where the Comtesse de Dillon was a particular favorite of the Queen. Another Dillon who had come with the Irish Regiment was Théobald-Hyacinth Dillon. Édouard, the famous *"le beau Dillon"* of the careless, profligate days at the Petit Trianon and a reputed favorite of the impressionable young Queen, did not accompany the Regiment to Georgia though some French records indicate that he was there. "The beautiful Dillon" had been badly wounded in a sea battle off Grenada in July. For one hastens to add that those titled dandies of Old France were no mere carpet-knight warriors. In battle they were bold as lions, ready to die with their men though perhaps not always as willing to share their sufferings.

The roster of highborn officers of *la Vieille France* reads with the sonorous cadence of Shakespeare's catalogue of the French chivalry at Agincourt. Besides Comte d'Estaing,

Vicomte de Noailles, Comte Dillon, and the Vicomte de Fontanges, there were the Marquis de Pondevaux, a nephew of the great Vergennes; Comte d'Hervilly; Vicomte de Béthisy; Marquis de Rouvray; Comte de Villeverd; Marquis de la Roche-Fontenilles; and Baron Curt von Stedingk. One hardly passes over the last named without a word more. This handsome Swedish officer was a grandson of Frederick's famous field marshal, von Schwerin. The close friend of King Gustave III and welcome guest at the levees of Louis XVI, Stedingk would be a special favorite of Catherine the Great in the days to come. He was to have an important role on the diplomatic stage of Europe in the years ahead.

But others in d'Estaing's army besides these aristocrats would make names for themselves; for example, a bright-eyed, ebon-skinned boy from the West Indies by the name of Christophe. Henri had come to Georgia either as a volunteer in the colored Chasseurs from Cap François, as some say, or as the serving boy of a French officer, as others contend.[6] Be that as it may, the time would come when this unruly youth was to wear a title greater than any of these beribboned noblemen. For Christophe would one day be King of Haiti and build the fabulous mountain citadel of Sans Souci. A dusky volunteer named Beauvais, and André Rigaud, a mulatto, were two of the several other future generals of the black revolt in San Domingo who learned their first lessons in war and freedom at Savannah.

One does not have to be discerning to detect beneath these spangles and *fleurs-de-lis*—behind the glitter of sounding titles and ancient names, germinations of coming revolution in France itself. High command in the French army, as in the navy, was the patrimony of the well-known and influential. Opportunity had come so easily to some of these young aristocrats—so much easier, for instance, than to Lieutenant Blandat of the Regiment d'Agénois, who was in one of the landing boats. Twice wounded during the War of the Austrian Succession and severely cut on the head by a sabre in the Seven Years' War, Blandat had served his King faithfully for nearly thirty-five years. But he would still be a lieutenant if he served another lifetime. Perhaps, however, we should use some other example than poor Mathieu who in two weeks' time would be lying in an unmarked grave outside Savannah, far from the hills of Franche-Comté in the land of his fathers.

Another day would dawn for France—a day when some of the youths serving in the rank and file of this French army would be found at the head of her armies. Among them were a young corporal in the Auxerrois Regiment named Jourdan, former apprentice to a silk merchant, and a strapping twenty-five-year-old private in the Hainault Regiment, one Claude Dallemagne. The time would come when Jean-Baptiste Jourdan was to be a Marshal of France and Dallemagne one of Napoleon's bravest generals.

Privilege under the Bourbons was no wide dispensation. There were layers of French humanity into which it did not extend in any shape or form. Consider the half-naked seamen who manned these ships. Many of them had not been ashore since the squadron left Toulon. They had not been paid in months. Few could read or write. It made little difference for letters never seemed to reach either them or their homes. D'Estaing had complained to the Ministry about the delivery of mail but there was a widely-credited rumor in the fleet that all letters were ordered thrown overboard. The scurvy was bad. The skin of the sailors was "livid" and they had "the marks of death painted on their faces," wrote a French naval officer.[7] Masses were said and there were frequent religious processions aboard the ships. But somehow the health of the crews did not improve.

Such were the forces of King Louis XVI of France that had come to help the Americans recover Savannah.

III

The Americans

THE unexpected news of the arrival off Georgia of the French fleet which Viscount de Fontanges brought to Charlestown on the third of September had produced an electric effect in South Carolina. With little deference to military security the newspapers of the city heralded the event. "The same Night," reported *The Gazette of the State of South-Carolina,* "arrived here M. le Vicomte de Fontanges, from His Excellency the Count d'Estaing, who is not far distant with a very powerful Fleet and Land Forces of our great and good Ally, His Christian Majesty, come purposely to the Relief of these invaded States. We expect important intelligence every hour!" Information useful to the English but lacking here was furnished by another Charlestown newspaper the same day. "Late last night," read an item that greatly irritated the French, "the Lieutenant of Marines of the armed brig Bellona, came up to town with intelligence of His Excellency Count d'Estaing's fleet, consisting of 25 sail of the line, 20 frigates and 3 courvettes or sloops at anchor on Thursday noon, in 14 fathom water, off Tybee; on board the fleet are 5000 land forces."[1]

The *Bellona* had violated d'Estaing's orders by leaving the fleet. One of his chief virtues, as a general, said du Petit-Thouars, was that "of covering his projects with the most impenetrable veil." He had carefully guarded his secret as to this expedition. To be sure, the cleverer officers in d'Estaing's squadron, seeing the Negro troops being embarked in San Domingo, had promptly deduced that their objective lay no further north than South Carolina. But the only living soul in the West Indies to whom the Vice-Admiral had confided his plan of touching at Charlestown for the purpose of aiding the Americans before proceeding home via Halifax and Newfoundland had been the Governor of Hispaniola. The Count was bitter on the subject of the American press. "It is a terrible thing," he reported, "The American newspapers, as little truthful as the English gazettes, are even more imprudent and nearly always tell their lies at the most inappropriate time." [2]

For months the Americans had been urging the French to come, if only to show their faces off the coast. D'Estaing had been repeatedly told, he explained to his superiors, that "the American cause was in great peril and that all their hopes were based on my early arrival." A Frenchman serving in the Continental army had been especially active in persuading him to come. "Never has this country been in greater need of help. It is necessary to defend it against itself and against the enemy. All here is in frightful confusion; very few regular troops, no help from the north, a feeble and badly disciplined militia and the greatest friction among the leaders." So Colonel Brétigny had written from Charlestown, adding that South Carolina could look "in truth to you alone, Monsieur le Comte, to save her from peril." [3]

Such eloquent appeals had proved irresistible to Count d'Estaing who explained later to the Minister of Marine, M. de Sartine, that "the cruel task" of the Georgia venture was "irrevocably imposed by national honor and by an irresistible train of events." Whatever may have been the motives of glory his enemies attributed to him, the expedition against Georgia possessed immense implications for the cause of American freedom. With the British army in the South destroyed, Savannah again in American hands, and a French squadron on the coast, Lord Germain's new overall strategy of war would die in the borning.

Major General Benjamin Lincoln, commanding the Southern Department, had hastily concentrated all his available forces to collaborate in the projected attack upon Savannah. "It has been proposed to the Count to land three thousand troops—I hope he will do it," he wrote Samuel Huntington, assuring Congress that "every exertion will be made to cooperate with him." [4] Lincoln and Rutledge had been forced to confess their weaknesses to the French. "Most of our army is disbanded, the time for which they engaged to serve having some short time since expired." Nevertheless, they had promised that "barring accidents" one thousand men would be in the field on the Georgia side of the Savannah near Ebenezer by the 11th "ready to cooperate with your Troops." [5]

Interspersed by ammunition and baggage wagons and a few field pieces, the Americans strung out on the long road to Purysburg above Savannah. The elite of Carolina were marching—John Laurens ("The Bayard of the Revolution"), conspicuous in his regimentals and long-plumed hat; unprepossessing little Francis Marion, later immortalized as the "Swamp Fox"; Charles Cotesworth Pinckney, Jr.; Thomas Heyward, Jr., a signer of the Declaration of Independence; General Isaac Huger; Colonel Peter Horry; Dr. David Ramsay, the historian; Hezekiah Maham whose "Maham tower" would earn him a share of Revolutionary fame; and proud Pierce Butler, whose father was an Irish peer. Major Thomas Pinckney and a few other Americans had preceded them aboard the fast-sailing frigate commanded by La Pérouse.

As recently as September 1st, David Ramsay had despondently observed that "Most people expect the enemy here in October or November, and yet we are half asleep. . . . A spirit of money making has eaten up our patriotism." But overnight the situation had changed. The militia was turning out "in all parts of the state, with such spirit and alacrity," boasted *The Gazette of the State of South-Carolina*, "that the ferry-men at the several rivers cannot carry the men across fast enough." The way they responded "redounds much to their honour," attested another Charlestown editor.

They had come from the upcountry like General Andrew Williamson, who was accompanied by three nephews and three sons-in-law. They had come from the farmlands around Orangeburg as had William Thomson, a dead-shooting Continental veteran, bringing a son, a nephew, and his three sons-in-law. They had come from the great plantations of the tide-water region and from the mansions and counting-houses of Charlestown. They marched with light heart along roads matted with pine needles—"every one cheerful, as if we were sure of success; and no one doubted but that we had nothing more to do, than to march up to Savannah; and demand a surrender." Thus General Moultrie was to write later, regretful at the time that he could not be there to have "shared the glory" but anticipating the pleasure of hearing soon "the joyful news of the surrender of Savannah." [6]

Sickness and desertion had decimated the Continental establishment of South Carolina. Her six regiments were almost cadre organizations. Hardly a thousand men were left in the whole lot. Never zealous on the point of military etiquette, they insisted on unflapping their hats. They discarded gaiters and went bare-legged. They were the despair of officers with their long, uncombed hair and unshaven faces, which, as Colonel Marion of the Second Regiment complained in his Orderly Book, "makes them appear more like wild savages than soldiers." But these Carolina regulars possessed fighting qualities that were to win high praise from the French at Savannah.

Meanwhile Casimir Pulaski advancing ahead of the main American force had crossed the Savannah with a handful of his Legion. The famous cavalry officer dispatched a message written in French to Count d'Estaing on the evening of September 12th. He informed him that "General Lincoln with artillery and about 600 infantry will pass the most difficult place tonight. General McIntosh is on the march. I think at this moment our forces will consist of 1000 infantrymen, 8 pieces of cannon and 260 cavalrymen. . . . After tomorrow General Lincoln will be able to place himself some miles from Savannah. He awaits your decision." [7]

The tiny Georgia Continental detachment under Lachlan McIntosh (back from exile after the fatal duel with Button Gwinnett) was on its way down from Augusta. Three companies of Georgia militia were also en route. A number of these soldiers bore the names of future counties of the State—McIntosh, Twiggs, Jackson, Baker, Houstoun, Habersham, Meriwether, and White. There were also troops from Virginia. As usual that State had sent them off badly equipped. They had come to Georgia "without a Single Tent," complained General McIntosh who wished that he had "some liquor for them to keep their Spirits up." Discipline was often a problem in the armed forces of a burgeoning democracy. Among the several courts-martial convened at this period was that of Captain Belfield of the Virginia Light Dragoons who was charged with "ungentlemanly behaviour" in "associating with a private soldier." [8]

The Continental Line of Georgia had been practically obliterated as a result of a series of disasters during the past year. Its arms were described by Colonel Elbert as a "medley of Rifles, old muskets & fowling pieces." Dry moss was all that was available at times for wadding. Shoes consisted in many instances of moccasins cut from hides. Variety was the most distinguishing feature of the Georgia uniforms. One saw cocked hats, round hats, beaver hats, leather hats, and straw hats. There were breeches made of homespun, coarse white cloth, and buckskin. Black coats trimmed with red and blue coats edged in white were observed. Deerskin jackets were the nearest approach to uniformity of dress among the Georgians who made a sombre contrast to the brightly-garbed Frenchmen they would soon meet at Savannah—the Gâtinais Regiment with yellow collars and blue, yellow, and crimson pompons on their hats; the Foix with its distinguishing color of green; the Agénois of yellow; the Hainault violet; and the Auxerrois of black. Americans would gape at the spectacle of French generals and staff officers resplendent in royal blue coats with scarlet vests and breeches and high black boots.

It is unfortunate that the Marquis de Chouin and the Chevalier de Pontgibaud who so colorfully described the militia of New England were not along to record their impressions of the raw levies of Georgia and Carolina. An exception would have to be allowed, however, in the case of the Charlestown militia. Even Count d'Estaing did so. The militia of that city, he wrote, were "infinitely better armed and clothed than the others. Nearly all have cartridge-boxes, bayonets, stockings and shoes." [9] Among the American regulars only Pulaski's outfit was to impress the French. According to an officer in the Agénois Regiment, the hundred lancers they saw at Savannah were "well equipped and excellently mounted."

But other troops than those of Generals d'Estaing and Lincoln were trying to get to the town on which the finger of world history had suddenly come to rest. The scene shifts to Beaufort village.

IV

In Which Colonel Maitland Starts South

FROM beneath the oaks that fringed its graceful bluff Beaufort looked out across a Bay strangely alive with activity. It was September 12th and the 900 troops comprising His Majesty's garrison on Port Royal Island were pulling out. The armed ship *Vigilant* and the *Scourge* and *Vindictive* galleys were taking on cargoes of Redcoats. Britain's only stronghold between New York and Savannah was being hurriedly evacuated. Bagpipes commingled with Highland burr and German guttural to make a cacophony sadly out of character with the timeless languor associable with Beaufort. The Hessians particularly were glad to leave this Carolina Low-country. *Die grosse Hitze und die menge derer Sandfliegen in diesen Wohnplaz von Schlangen und Crocodillen!*

The gravity of the business he was about was sharply etched on the face of the commanding officer at Beaufort. It will be well to glance for a few moments at this forty-seven-year-old British soldier, for Lieutenant Colonel John Maitland of the Seventy-first Regiment of Scotch Foot is to play a large part in this drama of Revolutionary history. No family in Scotland was more illustrious than that of this youngest son of Charles, Sixth Earl of Lauderdale, a nobleman distinguished for "the sweetest disposition and finest accomplishments." [1] From Thirlestane Castle, the magnificent seat of the Maitlands at Lauder, had come some of the great men of that country, among them the first Duke of Lauderdale, who was the "l" in the famous "Cabal" of the reign of Charles II. Within its massive walls, "Bonnie Prince Charlie" had found refuge after his defeat at Culloden, when John Maitland was a boy. The lineage of Colonel Maitland was scarcely less distinguished on the side of his late mother, the former Elizabeth, Lady Ogilvy. Her father, who was Earl of Findlater and Seafield, had been Lord High Chancellor of Scotland.

Had he time for such musings, Colonel Maitland might well ponder the fate that had brought him from his seat in the House of Commons, where he represented the Borough of Haddington, to these climes. For the "easy fortune" and high station he enjoyed at home he had exchanged the hard life of a soldier in this rebellion-torn part of the world. An empty right sleeve attested the fact that he had already fulfilled his duty to King and country. A cannon ball had carried away that hand twenty years before during Admiral Boscawen's victorious action against the French in Lagos Bay, Spain, where Captain Maitland fought with the Marines, being "the only Commission Officer," he wrote, "wounded in that Ingagement." [2]

With the coming of the American Revolution he had re-entered the same branch of service with the rank of Major. In the fighting in the Jerseys in '78 he proved himself an alert, resourceful officer. Striking up the Delaware on one occasion, a British force commanded by Maitland and Captain John Henry of the navy had destroyed thirty-seven American vessels, including two frigates and eleven large merchantmen. During that year he was transferred at his request to the Seventy-first Regiment. He was "so beloved" among the Highland troops, it was said, that "they could have been put upon no service led on by him but what they would have gone with the greatest alacrity."[3] Colonel Maitland was in fact universally popular—admired by friend, respected by foe. When he communicated with General Moultrie it was not in the condescending manner some British officers affected toward the colonials. It was with the politeness of gentleman dealing with gentleman. He had earlier attracted, it was said, the "particular notice of General Washington with whom he was personally acquainted." The Scotch officer on one occasion had jocularly notified the American commander that in the future his men would wear red feathers in their bonnets so that he would know the Highlanders were to be credited with annoying his posts and obstructing his convoys. Until the end of the War the Seventy-first wore Maitland's red feather.[4]

He had had no hand in the fearful pillage that took place during the British incursion into South Carolina. "There will not be the least cause for censure on any part of the conduct of the hon. col. Maitland . . . and some few other officers, who did not come divested of politeness and humanity," said a Charlestown paper.[5] This was no ordinary compliment, coming from a Whig gazette.

Since his arrival in the South, Maitland had greatly increased his military stature. At Stono Ferry he had beaten off a strong attack by the Americans, displaying much skill in rallying troops and in the timeliness of his dispositions. General Prevost arrived as the battle ended, "only to applaud," as a Savannah newspaper put it, "the gallant behaviour, defence, and prudent disposition of Col. Maitland." His conduct did the Scotch officer great honor, declared Sir Henry Clinton, adding that he had but "acted very much like himself."[6]

The same news that had galvanized Savannah had set the Beaufort garrison in motion. Frenchmen on the coast! Prevost's attempts to communicate with Maitland had miscarried. On the fifth of September a barge with ten Negroes at the sweeps was captured in Skull Creek by a small party of Americans under Lieutenant de Treville. Captain Vardy had unsuccessfully tried to destroy the dispatch which directed Colonel Maitland to evacuate Beaufort and come to Savannah.[7] When the French ships first sighted off Tybee disappeared, Prevost had sent another dispatch. The original orders were countermanded. Maitland was to hold himself in readiness to move at a moment's notice. If intelligence should be obtained from any source that Savannah was the enemy's real objective he was to run no risk of being cut off. Eventually word had gotten through concerning d'Estaing's intentions.

The way by land was blocked. So was the route by sea. As Colonel Maitland was leaving Beaufort on the 12th an English naval officer recorded in his journal, "At Sunset a French Ship anchored off Tybee; two more anchored in the South Channel, and one in the North."[8] The inland water passage south of Beaufort had in all probability been sealed by this time.

There were some eight hundred effective troops at Beaufort—the same soldiers General Robert Howe had once called "raw boys from the Highlands who would not fight." They had showed before what they could do. They would do so again, if Maitland could but get the Seventy-first to Savannah! By some sort of miracle he had to do so —soon.

If Colonel Maitland was at all distracted from that object, it must have been when his eyes fell upon the courthouse and the gaol as he looked up at the little settlement of thirty houses. The British had been using them as hospitals and the sick were being evacuated. There were many on the invalid list, for this was an unhealthy country—a land where "Even on the most beautiful days the air is not pure," complained the Hessians.[9] Yet these Carolina islands, wrote Prevost, were "reckon'd the Montpelier of this Country." [10]

There was a flush, too, on Colonel Maitland's face. It was not the flush of strong drink for which he was reputed to have a fondness. Somewhere on this malarial coast he had contracted what the physicians of the day diagnosed as "bilious fever." His health had been much impaired by the long and enervating summer during which the temperature had hovered for three straight weeks between 90 and 98, reaching 103 at one point. But if the thought occurred to this officer that he should be with the sick instead of at the head of his troops he instantly dismissed it. . . . The vessels moved away. The tabby-frame house which had been the headquarters of the Honorable John Maitland for the past two months faded around the bend in the deepening twilight of the September afternoon. To the south thunder rolled through heavily overcast skies.

> *"Haste on, ye brave! Your Country cries;*
> *Fierce wolves of France and faction wait:*
> *The FREEBORN, chains, shame, death defy;*
> *Your swords decide an empire's fate."*
>
> (From *Savannah, a Poem in Two Cantos to the Memory of the Honourable Colonel John Maitland* by Robert Colvill, London, 1780)

V

Prevost Gets a Summons

Scarcely had Maitland's flotilla left Beaufort when the initial contingent of French troops began to disembark at Beaulieu thirteen miles below Savannah. About ten o'clock on the night of September 12th Count d'Estaing leaped ashore at the head of a few men at this bluff on the Vernon River which had been recommended by Philip Minis, a former resident of Savannah, as "the best place for landing, on account of its facilities both for disembarking and for forming any number of troops." [1]

Fortunately the French encountered no opposition. "A hundred men would have been sufficient to drive us back," said Jean-Rémy de Tarragon, an officer in the Armagnac Regiment.[2] The spot was "very badly chosen," complained d'Estaing who declared that "a post of a hundred men would probably have repulsed us" while "fifty soldiers with two small pieces of artillery would have killed many." [3] But the only casualties of the landing proved to be two infantrymen who were wounded when muskets went off by accident as the troops scaled the steep river bank in the dark "like blind men," to use M. de Tarragon's words. A hundred paces beyond, they discovered the next morning, an easy ascent was located.

Their first nights on the American mainland was an eerie experience for these Frenchmen. Overhead the moss drooped from the great oaks like the grey pennons of a spirit world. If Beaulieu was lovely, its beauty was a brooding, melancholy sort. The haunting cry of the whippoorwill never found more appropriate setting. Locating a large copper pot on the Morel plantation, the troops built big fires and feasted upon soup and *"très bonne viande"* to the enjoyment of which "the appetite we had contributed no little," wrote Captain Séguier de Terson of the Régiment d'Agénois.[4] Beyond the light of the campfires, for all one knew, lurked the redskinned allies of the English, the *"sauvages"* called *"Cheroquais."* But only the shades of Indians stalked this bluff which once had been a favorite camping ground for the coastal tribes. No enemy was near. Carefully husbanding his slender forces, General Prevost had withdrawn his outposts into Savannah.

The French were fearfully weary. Getting across the bar in front of Ossabaw Sound had involved "unheard-of difficulties." Colonel Curt von Stedingk wrote that some of the troops were in open boats for three straight nights.[5] "One is not able to undergo anything more cruel," declared Séguier de Terson in describing his experiences. Content to understate things, M. de Tarragon reported that they had been *"fort mal à leur aise."* The passage of the bar was "infinitely dangerous," according to d'Estaing. Considering the poor quality of the American pilots, a touch of bad weather would have sufficed, he said, "to end the expedition in a single hour by the drowning of all the landing troops."

They had had trouble enough even in finding Beaulieu after entering the river, what with the multitude of creeks and islands along this coast. There had been frequent delays. The story of one of the diversions has a theme worthy of the pen of Cervantes. A French naval officer tells us that General d'Estaing landed on one of the islands with two hundred grenadiers—his mission, the capture of 500 beef cattle which he had been informed were guarded by a detachment of British troops. Several hours later the expedition returned empty-handed. The French had traversed the length and breadth of the island in the course of which they crossed bogs where "one sunk to his knees." But they had found, wrote Meyronnet de Saint-Marc, "neither beef nor English." [6]

Weary as the men were, much needed rest on reaching land proved what Séguier de Terson called a "vain hope." There were no tents. The second evening ashore a squall came up and there was rain all night. Morning found the troops in "a pitiable state," this officer reported.

The day after coming ashore d'Estaing sent a message to Casimir Pulaski, whose cavalry, probing ahead of the main American force, had reached the environs of Savannah. Complimenting the Polish soldier's "sublime bravery and activity" that made "nothing impossible," he expressed the hope that Pulaski would be "the first one who joins me." [7] They did not meet until the 14th or 15th. Meanwhile, however, Pulaski had made contact with the French army. From the Habersham plantation on the Ogeechee Road he forwarded a dispatch to General Lincoln on the early morning of the 14th. He wrote in faulty English, but it was good news he conveyed. "I give myself the pleasure," Pulaski said, "of sending you the expedition of Count d'Estaing, & shall do my utmost for to join the Count as soon as possible with my Detachment." [8]

When d'Estaing and Pulaski met near Beaulieu they "cordially embraced," according to Captain Paul Bentalou. It was a rainy day and there was much to talk about. Pulaski spoke French well. No doubt the Polish hero unburdened his heart to this understanding Frenchman about the treatment a foreigner received at the hands of the Americans. "Nothing Less than my honour, which I would never forfeit," he had recently complained, "retains me in a Service, which ill treatment makes me begin to abhor."

It did not take d'Estaing long to gain an unfavorable impression of what he called the *"américains de la georgie."* On the road to Savannah lay the orphanage founded by the celebrated George Whitefield. While reconnoitering, the Count stopped at Bethesda which was then serving as the residence of George Baillie. On entering the house he observed in a conspicuous place an elegant, life-size painting of what he took to be "Liberty" represented, he said, in the person of "Milady Abbington" who carried a wreath of thorns in her hand and trampled upon a crown. It was evident that it was not hanging in its accustomed place. During the absence of Mrs. Baillie (who "did not show the least American zeal") Count d'Estaing inquired of two small children when the portrait had been placed there. "Last night," they informed him, divulging in the innocence of youth that they were all *"Royalistes."* [9] Actually what the French General saw was Russell's allegorical portrait of the Countess of Huntingdon, patroness of Bethesda. The crown upon which her foot rests in the painting is a symbol of things temporal, the thorns of those spiritual. At best this devout English dowager was a dour model for "Liberty" and the Right Honourable Selina would no doubt have been greatly perturbed to learn that her portrait was being palmed off in Georgia as a symbol of American freedom.

Led by General d'Estaing astride a "large Chair Horse" borrowed at the Orphan House, the French began to move up toward Savannah in force on the 14th. On the night of the 15th they camped four miles from the town. The Count was superbly confident. The main idea now was to beat the Americans to Savannah. So, at any rate, it seemed to Major Thomas Pinckney. Had not the American general Sullivan furnished d'Estaing with a precedent at Newport the year before? Soon the city would be his, a brighter feather in his cap than Grenada. There would be a *Te Deum* at Paris and a triumphal return to the *Oeil-de-Boeuf!* The very thought was calculated to make the General's sensuous mouth curl in a smile of anticipation—Condé, Turenne, Saxe, d'Estaing.

There was much pillaging along the way. The better disciplined among the French troops went hungry, said Captain de Tarragon, while the others lived off the fat of the land, slaughtering "poultry and sheep under the eyes of their officers, who were too feeble to make any opposition." It was as though a locust plague had passed through the countryside. From Bethesda the French took 13 steers, 10 cows, 5 sheep, 39 hogs, 50 fowl, and 20 gallons of Jamaica rum. The Morel plantation at Beaulieu was ransacked, d'Estaing's troops carrying away 9 horses, 23 cows, 30 hogs, 13 sheep, 3 hens, 5 wagons and a carriage, crystal goblets, candles, and many other things. The widow Morel promptly submitted a bill for £267.[10] But despite the good Whig background of this daughter of the patriotic Jonathan Bryan, there is little likelihood that her losses were made good.

On the morning of September 16th the French, 2000 strong, were at the Minis house three miles from Savannah. Advancing at the head of one hundred and fifty grenadiers to within a mile of the city, Count d'Estaing sent in a flag. The emissary bore a summons to surrender. In haughty phrases General Prevost was called on to capitulate *"aux Armes de Sa Majesté Le Roy de France."* The British General was informed that he would be held personally responsible for attempting a defense characterized as "manifestly vain and ineffective." There were ill-veiled threats. When d'Estaing stormed Grenada it was impossible for him "to be happy enough to prevent the whole being pillaged." "Humanity obliges the Count d'Estaing to recall this event to his memory; having so done, he has nothing to reproach himself with."[11]

Captain Séguier de Terson thought the summons *"très honnête et fort bien écrite."* But most observers considered it a vainglorious display. Captain Joseph O'Moran of the Dillon Regiment, who spoke both French and English without trace of accent was the bearer of the letter. He was instructed to look and listen closely in order to observe the real reactions in the English camp. The better to fool the enemy, he changed his uniform to one other than that of the Dillon Regiment.[12]

Instead of being deceived the British became deceivers. Time was a precious commodity. From little Fort Charlotte at the eastern end of the bluff the English could look far out across the marshes toward the sea. Somewhere out there were Maitland and his men.

General Prevost stalled. Before he answered the summons he had to confer with the Royal Governor. "I hope your excellency will have a better opinion of me and of British Troops," he finally replied, "than to think either will surrender on a General Summons without Specifick Terms." He requested the French to offer conditions that might be honorably accepted. D'Estaing had replied, refusing to propose terms, that being the "part of the besieged." (Was not Maitland bottled up in Beaufort?) By this time it was afternoon. Every hour the British gained was solid gold.

Prevost then suggested a truce of twenty-four hours for the purpose of considering the question of surrender. "There being various Interests to discuss, just time," he said, "is absolutely necessary to deliberate." It was nine P.M. when his letter reached the French camp. The British had gained a whole day. Meanwhile they were busy entrenching themselves, a fact of which d'Estaing was not ignorant. "It is a matter of very little importance to me," he had informed General Prevost, requesting the English for "form's sake," however, to desist while the conferences were going on.

VI

The British Dig In

WHEN the French first arrived nearly everyone at Savannah despaired of hope. "Deep and universal despondency prevailed within the Garrison, and the only deliberation was, how to render submission as little disgraceful as possible," said Alexander Garden.[1] The British had hardly twelve hundred troops to man a semi-circular line over 12,500 feet in length connecting the eastern and western ends of the long river bluff. Because of the nature of the terrain it could not be narrowed.

Prevost himself seems to have shared the prevailing pessimism. "We are not afraid of any one of them," he said in a dispatch to Admiral Byron, "but both together may be too many for us, if they should be able to effect a Junction and the French Land Forces is anything considerable." A similar air of resignation is sensed in a message he hurried off to St. Augustine. "The Season seemed to promise us that we had nothing to fear this year from such Forces, but so it is," wrote the British General, "and this is to advise you of it. We will defend ourselves as long as we can. If we are abandoned, it will be so much the worse."[2]

There was brave official talk, to be sure. The British were to defend the redoubts "with the bayonets till the last extremity." Prevost expressed confidence that they would "exert themselves as usual in that required for their own honour and the honour of the King's Arms." Their spirits were bolstered by his assurance that the enemy, being "mostly Carolinians, are not expected to be very determined."[3]

But apparently there was serious thought of surrender at one point. As the days passed the possibility of the arrival of Maitland became "to all thoughtful persons more and more doubtful," declared the *Georgia Gazette*. Writing to General Clinton on September 8th, Prevost said, "I hope Colonel Maitland will be here this day with the detachment from Beaufort." The next day in another letter to Clinton, he expressed the same hope, regretting that the Seventy-first had ever been left at Beaufort. It was a decision, however, that had been concurred in, he explained, by every one of his field officers. "If Lieu^t. Col^o. Maitland arrives safe, all will be well," he added.[4] Two days later (the 11th) Sir James Wright was confiding to Governor Tonyn of Florida that "If we do not hear something of him today I shall be in great pain about him." General Prevost and Governor Wright would have been pained, indeed, had they known that Maitland had not even left Beaufort.

Fear was felt for the safety of the populace of Savannah if the town were stormed. There were "bloody menaces," according to Anthony Stokes; while Colonel Cruger of New York said that the enemy "talk'd of nothing but putting all to the Sword." "What furious people intended, and humane persons expected" was illustrated, declared the *Georgia Gazette,* by the case of Charles Price of Sunbury. This young attorney, who was regarded by James Jackson as "one of the best lawyers in the United States," had come to Savannah with the Americans. The Tory editor had an explanation as to why this son of an English official was serving with the enemy. His sole purpose in coming, it was explained, had been "to save his father from the general carnage." Since Price was killed during the Siege of Savannah, no one will ever know the real answer.

But some American militiamen undoubtedly came to Savannah with the main idea of protecting the populace when the town was captured. For example, there was Andrew McLean, who claimed that he was regarded by the "Rebells as a Person inimical to their Party." He was induced by General Lachlan McIntosh to march with the American militia, he later explained to the Royal Council. The Rebel leader had come to him and suggested that the "Prospect of being presently in Possession of Savannah was so certain" that, since McLean's "Principles were regarded in an unfavorable Light," he should "come down with the Army" merely to save himself. McLean had been thus induced to accompany the Americans, but he had gone with what he called "a firm Resolution to take no active Part in Favor of Rebellion, but to use all his Endeavors to assist the Inhabitants of Savannah, in Case that Place had been taken."[5]

The case for the belief that little quarter would have been given is bolstered by an affidavit furnished the English authorities by John Murray, a loyal subject of the King who was captured on his way from Florida. Murray claimed that he was taken aboard the *Languedoc* where he saw a number of American sympathizers, including John Glen, the Rebel Chief Justice of Georgia. In a conversation between the two on September 8th, the latter expressed confidence that Savannah would soon be in the hands of the Americans. Murray thereupon ventured the hope that if the city fell they would be lenient to the Loyalists. To this Glen replied, "It was not now a time to use gentle & moderate measures, but to make reprisals and to retaliate for the injuries which had been done to their persons & their properties."[6] The Americans had not forgotten how Savannah was sacked a few months be-

THE BRITISH DIG IN

fore. "The finest furnishings, *comptoirs,* tables and chairs of mahogany were smashed and lay around the streets," wrote a Hessian officer. "It was a pity to see," he added. There had been more than looting, according to Pierre Colomb who served with the Americans. "Robbery, incendiarism, rape, and murder were the fruits of that unhappy day," this French volunteer recorded in his Journal.

Major General Augustin Prevost, who in appearance resembled George Washington, was a soldier of experience and personal courage—"brave as Caesar," in the words of one of his aides-de-camp at Savannah. He had been wounded at Fontenoy and still bore near his temple the unsightly circular scar from a wound received while serving under Wolfe at Quebec. His reputation in Georgia was not that of a very forceful individual. According to a letter of a Scotch merchant at Savannah published in *The Scots Magazine* in December, 1779, the General was "very diffident" and possessed "no opinion of his own." During the same year Lieutenant Colonel Archibald Campbell, one of the abler British soldiers of his day, had appraised him in terms somewhat less than enthusiastic. "Prevost seems a worthy man," he wrote, "but too old & inactive for this service. He will do in Garrison, and I shall Gallop with the lighttroop." [7] For some months the general had been requesting to be relieved of his command in Georgia, where his wife and children were with him. His successor was even now on the high seas. The rigors of war in Florida, Georgia, and South Carolina had undermined his constitution. "I begin to feel the effect of age," he confessed, "and find that this campaign necessitates the greater physical powers of a younger man." [8]

In significant italics Governor Wright was to inform Lord Germain that he had "some *strong* Reasons to apprehend & fear" that Savannah would be surrendered. "The enemy's soldiery were much dissatisfied, and though it was pretended that Savannah would be defended, even the officers gave their opinions publicly that it would capitulate," reported a Charlestown paper.[9] A French naval officer recorded in his journal that Prevost announced at the parleys that he "wished only to save his honor by the appearance of a defense." But the British General was at the time engaged in a desperate game of dissimulation and such statements must be received with a good deal of skepticism.

Any thought of surrender found a stout antagonist in Sir James Wright. But for the Governor's efforts, claimed friends, the decision would have been otherwise. He is even credited by some with casting the deciding vote in the Council at a time when the others were equally divided. "I thought myself happy in being here at the time of Siege," the Governor informed Lord Germain, "For I Clearly Saw that if this Province then fell, America was Lost and this I declared on every occasion & urged the Necessity of every Exertion Possible to Defend the Place."[10] His Chief Justice backed him strongly. "I did all that I could to support those who desponded, and I would not suffer the language of fear to pass my lips," said Anthony Stokes.

Strange at times are the ways of the English. Since the capture of Savannah few measures had been taken to strengthen its defenses. There was only a gesture in that direction. "We had been repairing the Old Redoubts and raising New Works," claimed Governor Wright in extenuation. But little enough had been accomplished before the French arrived. "All this would have been considered unforgivable negligence had not the whole affair turned out favorably," opined Captain Johann Hinrichs.

But if the English are given to complacency, they are equally capable of extraordinary exertions in time of peril. A critical moment in the fortunes of the Empire was at

THE BRITISH DIG IN 43

hand—one that "might materially have affected Great Britain not only with regard to her colonies, but even as a nation," said the *Royal Georgia Gazette*. The defenders rose to meet the challenge. England was to experience at Savannah one of her finer hours.

Fortunately for the garrison, it possessed in James Moncrief a brilliant army engineer. Though related by blood or marriage to Whigs of high station in the North like Governor Livingston, General Montgomery, and John Jay, he had remained loyal to his King. Moncrief was now to win "immortal honour." "There is not one Officer or Soldier in this little Army," Prevost would inform Lord Germain, "capable of reflecting or judging—who will not regard as personal to himself any mark of Royal favour graciously confer'd thro' your Lordship on Captain Moncrief." [11] Sir James Wright was to add a strong endorsement to these views. "Now my Lord give me leave," he asked, "to mention the great ability & Exertions of Captain Moncrief the Chief Engineer who was Indefatigable day & Night."

Between four and five hundred slaves were put to work on the defenses around Savannah. Many of them were from the Royal Governor's eleven plantations. The barn, rice machine, and other buildings on his property adjoining the town common were dismantled and the materials utilized for making platforms for the works. Houses near the town which might give shelter or cover to the enemy were burned. Among those destroyed was the two story dwelling of Josiah Tattnall, called "Fair Lawn," together with the "large Kitchen Store House, Stable and Chair House . . . Barn and Fodder House." Drafts were placed upon slave-holders who were ordered to furnish "Hoes, Axes, and Spades, also cooking Utensils." [12] Formidable works began to rise, admirably adapted to a force which was insufficient to man the whole of a closed line. The four redoubts which were in existence when the French arrived eventually became thirteen. The ten or twelve cannon that faced the Allies when they first appeared were to become more than a hundred. The works consisted of a chain of redoubts between which horse-shoe batteries in embrasure were erected. Supporting them to the rearward were epaulements and traverses. The whole was surrounded on the front by an abatis of cedar and pine. A chain of sentries provided communications between the redoubts.

The British vessels retired to Savannah. Cannon were removed and the seamen assigned to batteries. The marines were incorporated with a battalion of the Sixtieth Regiment. Vessels were sunk across the channel and a boom stretched across the river to prevent fire rafts being floated down. The old cables of the *Fowey* were cut up into wads for the guns and her sails were utilized for tents. Able-bodied civilians were sent into the lines. The clergy itself pitched in. Reverend John Joachim Zubly who had once announced in the Continental Congress that "A Republican government is little better than a government of devils" became Chaplain to the Provincial troops. His Independent meeting house was turned into a Hessian hospital. "Every officer, Soldier and Sailor worked with the utmost Cheerfulness," declared Captain John Henry of the British navy.[13] "Perhaps never did troops and militia join more generally and heartily in the defence of any place," said the *Royal Georgia Gazette,* a view in which Chief Justice Stokes concurred. "The conduct of the Militia and Volunteers, who went into the lines to defend the town, would do honour to veteran troops," he informed a Grand Jury. "It proves," Stokes said, "how well men will behave when they are fighting in a good cause." [14]

However, there was to be a seamy side too. In bitter terms a British officer was later to complain of the men who in the hour of peril had "feigned themselves sick,"

"inhabited deep cellars" or had taken refuge "in dens and caves under the Bluff and at Yamacraw" and on the shipping in the harbor. Among the troops in the lines these "skulkers" were the subject, he said, of "many murmurings, councils, and conversations." [15]

But it is time to turn back now to follow the fortunes of the troops who had left Beaufort on the evening of September twelfth.

VII

Maitland Finds a Way

MAITLAND's little fleet meanwhile had inched its way southward along the inland waterways of Carolina—across Port Royal Sound on whose shores ("one of the goodlyest, best and fruitfullest cunteres that ever was sene") Jean Ribaut's dreams of French empire had long since become ashes of roses—past islands wild with beauty and big with romance—past Spanish Wells where centuries before, the tide of Castile had rolled and receded—on through the wide sea marshes and into the waters of Callibogue where the imaginative might still espy the dugouts of the vanished Yamassee caciques silhouetted against the headlands of Dawfuskie.

Why had not this way been closed? A man-of-war posted at the mouth of Skull Creek where Prevost's first express had been intercepted would have sealed it. The Americans knew that Maitland would try to reach Savannah through these waters. A newspaper in Charlestown reported that the Beaufort garrison had embarked "rather hastily, on board the Vigilante, the gallies, and some other small craft, with an intent to push through Skull Creek, and join General Prevost at Savannah, but it is doubted whether he has been able to effect that junction; it is rather believed that his vessels are blocked up in Skull Creek." [1] Apparently d'Estaing and Lincoln were less accurately informed of the enemy movements than the Charlestown press.

There was to be acrimonious controversy over the failure to cut off the Beaufort troops. Lincoln for his part maintained that the French had agreed in the Council of War at Charlestown that they would "block up the enemy in Port Royal." He had warned d'Estaing as early as September 5th that "it will be necessary that the mouth of the Savannah, Broad River, Ogeechee and the inlet to Sunbury be soon effectually guarded." [2] The Americans contended that M. de Fontanges had promised to send a fifty gun vessel up the Beaufort River. Though the Viscount warmly denied having made any such commitment the French Archives contain a copy of an order which d'Estaing sent on September 7th to d'Albert de Rions in which that officer was directed to "block Port Royal and anchor at the entrance of the Broad River" in order to keep any ship from "entering or leaving there." He was charged with preventing the nine hundred troops of the Beaufort garrison from availing themselves of that route.

The Vice-Admiral explained to his Ministry that the order sent to d'Albert de Rions was given independently of any promise to the Americans to send a vessel to Port Royal. In any event, its prompt execution would have driven an impenetrable wedge between Beaufort and Savannah. No officer in the fleet, said d'Estaing, was "more bold, more anxious to get things done or a better sailor than M. D'Albert." [3] But the captain of the *Sagittaire* found himself unable to carry out his instructions. The Charlestown pilot refused to carry the ship over the bar. Captain d'Albert pleaded with him in vain.

Not without irony was it that through a channel never less than four fathoms at high water a more venturous French navigator named Ribaut had entered these same waters in 1562 to pronounce the Sound "one of the greatest and fayrest havens of the worlde . . . where without daunger all the shippes in the worlde myght be harbored." Two hundred and seventeen years later it would "admit Ships of a Considerable Draught," according to General Prevost who on September 6th informed Clinton that if the French were "so minded, we had no Naval force to prevent their Entering Port Royal River. . . . and cutting between the division of our little Army."

For his part, the French commander insisted that the Americans were to blame. Colonel Brétigny told him, he said, that at the Council in Charlestown Lincoln was personally charged with preventing the junction of the Beaufort detachment. Though he at first blamed, d'Estaing later exonerated Vicomte de Fontanges. "It is beyond comprehension," he informed M. de Sartine, "that a high ranking officer, as experienced and as informed as he is intelligent, could have forgotten the principal object of a mission as important as the one I confided to M. de fontanges." On September 18th Fontanges would write to M. Plombard, the French consul, to obtain his version of what had taken place at the meeting at Charlestown. Plombard informed him that Lincoln and Rutledge were both convinced that if the French made themselves masters of the several sea passes, any junction would be impossible. If the Americans were ignorant of the existence of an interior route, it was no fault of his, he consoled.[4]

Everybody's business had become nobody's. Too much had been taken for granted. It should have been realized that an officer as resourceful as Maitland would stop at nothing in attempting to reach Savannah. The blockade of Beaufort was the key to everything, demanding as General Henry Lee said, "primary attention." D'Estaing fully realized it. "To prevent any sort of junction," he wrote, "was the basis of the plan." The failure to cut off that garrison, declared Thomas Pinckney, was the "first great error" of the Allies. If the troops from Beaufort had been "prevented from getting into the Town (& wh'ch was practicable) they would have Capitulated without firing a Gun," claimed Colonel Joseph Clay.[5] With that statement there was general agreement.

But Maitland's men were still far from their goal. By this time they had been transferred to small craft, the *Vigilant* and the other vessels being left in a fortified anchorage off Buck Island on the southwestern side of Hilton Head, where the convalescents were disembarked. The critical point in the operation had now been reached. The British were nearing the Savannah. To enter it they had to cross Tybee Roads, but far across Callibogue Sound the top-gallants of French frigates could be seen in the Savannah. That channel was barred. If the lower South—if America itself was to be saved to the King—Maitland somehow had to get his troops through twenty miles of marsh and swamp that lay between them and beleaguered Savannah. Unless the French were dawdling more than one dared hope it was too late, even could they find a way.

At this crucial moment fortune threw some Negro fishermen in the path of Maitland. In their strange Gullah version of the English language they told the British about an obscure waterway behind Dawfuskie Island. In serpentining through the marshes a creek looped within a short distance of another. A shallow cut had been dug to connect the two. This passage, which was called Wall's Cut, could be used only at high tide. But once in the creek to which it led, the English with luck and hard work might get into the Savannah above the point to which the French vessels had advanced. Lieutenant Goldesbrough, who was in charge of the boats, was prompt to take advantage of the opportunity.

Poems would be written about this exploit. "With rapid wing, but not before untried, From BEAUFORT'S banks the gallant MAITLAND flew." [6] So went a line in one of them. Fever and all, the Colonel would have managed a smile had he read that. Closer to the truth was the version of an incredulous Charlestownian who supposed that the British "must have plunged through swamps, bogs and creeks which had never before been attempted but by bears, wolves, and run-away Negroes." [7]

A long stretch of shoal creek lay between Wall's Cut and the Savannah. The men struggled through mud and marsh up to their waists. The boats were dragged through the narrow creek by main force. But suddenly the British were looking out upon the waters of a great river. Along the marsh-bordered banks of the Savannah one could see "multitudes of alligators lying in the mud like old Logs." That was all, for no enemy vessels were that far up the stream. American pilots ("pilots more in word than in deed," d'Estaing described them) had informed the French that by becoming masters of Tybee Island they would effectually block the route from Beaufort. On September 11th the French Admiral had ordered Chevalier Trolong Durumain to proceed with three vessels (already in Tybee Roads) up the Savannah and as close to the city as possible. The purpose was not to intercept Maitland, but to pursue and destroy the English ships and, in the end, establish a communication with the French land forces.[8] But numerous difficulties had been encountered. Cannon had to be taken on. The channel was narrow. There were several mud banks, and the Comte de Chastenet de Puysegur, who commanded the *Truite*, had to take soundings nearly every foot of the way upstream.

The only men-of-war Maitland encountered in the Savannah were the *Keppel* brig and the *Comet* galley which had been sent down the river from Five Fathom Hole to cover his approach. Before long there was a glimpse of a church steeple. It was September 16th, around noon. The summons to surrender had been received only a short time before.

The English are sometimes accounted an undemonstrative lot, but this was drama to warm the hearts of even the most reserved, the sight of these long-awaited reinforcements—veterans of Brandywine, Fort Montgomery, Brier Creek, and Stono Ferry—filing up the bluff and marching off to their posts in the lines. Even rough British tars were so moved that they gave three cheers. "Brave Fellows," applauded an elated English naval officer—"Savannah in the highest Spirits." The arrival of Maitland brought "inexpressible joy," said Sir James Wright. After reviewing the troops in the lines that day General Prevost described them as "all in high spirits, and the most pleasing confidence expressed in every face." [9]

In ponderous phrases an English historian of the time described the occasion. "The safe arrival of so considerable a reinforcement," wrote Charles Stedman, "and that too of chosen troops, but above all, the presence of the officer who commanded them, in whose zeal, ability and military experience so much confidence was deservedly placed by the army, inspired the garrison of Savannah with new animation." [10]

Half the Beaufort troops were still on the way up the river. But time enough for that! Shortly before midnight on the 16th a flag had come in from d'Estaing. "I consent to the Truce you ask," said the Count magnanimously, announcing that the sounding of retreat the next evening would signalize the "Recommencement of Hostilities."

Possibly General d'Estaing had not yet received the message Fontanges had sent that night from Brewton Hill advising him of the arrival of the Beaufort troops. Perhaps he had heard that ominous news and knowing that he was in no position to carry out his threat of an assault was merely trying to save face. Whatever were d'Estaing's motives, the English had reason to be pleased. By the evening of the 17th, Maitland's troops, to the last effective man, would be in Savannah.

Boats had been observed on the way up the river on the 16th. Fontanges learned of the fact when the French established a post at Brewton Hill that day. At nine o'clock on that evening he scribbled a hasty note conveying the bad tidings to d'Estaing. "The Americans have assured me," he reported, "that they saw pass today 14 boats, each filled with at least 25 men who ascended the river and reached Savannah." [11]

The following morning d'Estaing personally investigated. On a murky day he and Lincoln watched from Brewton Hill the last of Maitland's soldiers enter Savannah. "I have had the mortification," the chagrined Frenchman said, "of seeing the troops of the Beaufort garrison pass under my eyes." What was almost as bad, the "indifferent" Lincoln, after witnessing this "doleful sight," promptly "fell asleep in a chair." [12] The Count was being a bit unfair in branding as indifference what was actually the American General's remarkable habit of "somnolency," which was such that he would even nap between sentences while dictating dispatches.

The arrival of the reinforcements was *"au grand contentement des Anglais,"* reported Séguier de Terson who sadly added, *"et à nos grands regrets."* Through the scattered pines they could see, just across the British lines, the big barracks—*"un très bon corps de caserne,"* as he described it. Yesterday the building seemed so close the French could almost reach over and touch it. Now it was as though it were a thousand miles away. The steady rain which set in on the 16th did not improve Allied tempers.

Nor were spirits helped by the northeaster that blew the ships from their anchorage, depriving d'Estaing of all communication with them for several anxious days. The landing of his troops ceased for the time.

There was one comic touch that helped relieve the gloom in the French camp. While the negotiations were being conducted, the Vicomte de Cambis, an aide-de-camp to d'Estaing, took the wrong road on his way back to Beaulieu. He encountered a British outpost. The young officer jumped from his horse and tried to escape by running into the woods. He was taken prisoner but was given his freedom the next day on parole after a pleasant meal with General Prevost at Savannah. Fearful of the wrath of his querulous commander, the French officer went around repeating over and over, in the tone of Géronte, a famous line from one of Molière's plays: *"Mais que diable allait -il faire dans cette galère?"* ["But what the devil was he doing on that galley?"] [18]

VIII

The Allies Resort to the Spade

THE arrival of the Beaufort garrison "made us about 2,000 strong and so very saucy," said an English officer, "as to refuse to let *Monsieur* and *Jonathan* in."[1] The British strength was actually greater. Records show that 2,360 men were present and fit for duty. The French overestimated the number of the troops in Savannah, fixing the total as high as 3,790. According to a summary compiled from information furnished by British deserters, Prevost's troops were composed as follows:

Regulars

The 1st and 2nd battalions of the 71st Regiment	650	
Grenadiers of the 6th [60th?] Regiment	100	1,350
Marines	50	
Hessians	550	

Corps partly raised in the country

Colonel Skinner's Corps	100	
De Lancey's Volunteers	200	
Carolina Volunteers	270	
Light Infantry	200	1,240
Brown's Volunteers	200	
York Volunteers	150	
Dragoons nearly all militia	120	

THE ALLIES RESORT TO THE SPADE 55

Militia

Company of English Volunteers	150	
Company of Tory Volunteers	150	
Citizens serving the batteries	200	1,200
Sailors serving the batteries	500	
Negroes armed	200	

Against the British defenders the Allies could muster an effective total of around 5,500 regulars and militia. The Americans numbered approximately 1,000 Continental troops and 1,100 militia while the French forces consisted of 3,182 European soldiers, 545 Negro troops from San Domingo, and 156 West Indian volunteers.[2] D'Estaing's army was made up by regiment or detachment as follows:

Armagnac	338	Martinique	87
Champagne	95	Port Au Prince	156
Auxerrois	216	Dragoons	49
Agénois	97	Marines	359
Gâtinais	99	Volunteers of Valbel	21
Cambresy	188	Artillery	151
Hainault	360	Grenadier volunteers	
Fois	292	of San Domingo	156
Dillon	373	Volunteer Chasseurs	
Walsh	27	of San Domingo	
Le Cap	102	(mulatto and blacks)	545
Guadeloupe	172		

While there was still a sizeable difference between the two armies, the arrival of the reinforcements resolved any question of surrender. At the British Council of War on the 16th it was the unanimous opinion that Savannah should be defended to the last extremity. It was convened merely for "form's sake" after he received d'Estaing's summons, the view of the army being already well known, wrote General Prevost. But there is another version. Garden's *Anecdotes of the American Revolution* states that when Colonel Maitland arrived at Savannah the deliberations were taking place at the Governor's council chamber. "With hurried step" he approached the table. "Striking the hilt of his claymore against it," Maitland spoke up in his Scotch dialect, mincing no words as usual. "The man who utters a syllable recommending surrender, makes me his decided enemy," declared Maitland; "it is necessary that either *he* or *I* should fall." "So resolute a speech, at a moment so critical, produced the happiest effect on the minds of all," said Garden, who added that "Hope and courage regained their influence in every mind."

Garden's work is hardly the most reliable evidence of the past. But the story finds contemporary support elsewhere. According to an account that reached New York after the Siege, the Council of War before which Colonel Maitland appeared upon his arrival at Savannah was deliberating the answer to the French and even the matter of surrender itself. When he heard that term mentioned "the gallant Colonel arose though almost quite worn out with fatigue." He "abhorred" the word *"Capitulation,"* declared Maitland, who in a firm tone warned that "if he should survive and go home to Britain, he would report to the King the name of the first officer who should dare to propose a capitulation." [3]

A similar account came back to England. The Reverend Colvill wrote in a preface to his poem "Savannah" that "The council of war were on the very brink of signing a capitulation, when COLONEL MAITLAND gave his voice for a most vigorous resistance, and threatened to report the officer of his SOVEREIGN who should propose such a cowardly surrender." To like effect was a letter published in December, 1779, in *The Scots Magazine* wherein a merchant of Savannah declared that this "most determined brave officer, could not hear the word *capitulation* with any degree of patience; but took every opportunity of openly declaring what he thought a man deserved that could think of it."

A passage from the journal of a French officer is entitled perhaps to weight. Meyronnet de Saint-Marc says that some British deserters on being interrogated by the French about affairs in the town reported that at the outset the garrison was little disposed to a serious defense. However, the whole situation changed, they said, upon the arrival of Colonel Maitland. "That brave officer had engaged them in a vigorous defense, putting them to work on the fortifications *tout de suite*."[4]

Shortly before the expiration of the truce General Prevost's answer was delivered. "The unanimous Determination has been made," he informed d'Estaing, "that though we cannot look upon our Post as absolutely inexpungable, yet that it may be and ought to be defended." To the stilted phrases of military diplomacy the oral reply said to have been given by the blunt-spoken Prevost is a sharp contrast. "The King, my Master, pays these men to fight, and they must fight, and we decline your terms," he is quoted as telling d'Estaing's emissary.[5] In his orders of the day the British commander expressed his "Unlimited Dependence" on the "known Stedyness & Spirit of the Troops . . . Doubting Nothing of a Glorious Victory should the Enemy try their Strength."

Meanwhile General Lincoln's forces had come up during the 16th, encamping west of Savannah. "I have not been able to refuse the Army of the United States, uniting itself with that of the King," d'Estaing informed Prevost in one of his communications that day—strange sort of talk about an Ally. One sometimes needs to recall Choiseul's statement several years before. "M. d'Estaing in whom I thought I saw a superior talent is a fool," that Minister had remarked, "and a dangerous one." Monsieur le Comte was evidently flushed by his recent successes in the West Indies. He had quaffed the heady wine of Grenada and St. Vincent. "Caesar and Alexander were nothing to him," said a critic who described d'Estaing as the "Wonder of the Age." [6]

The Count had been lulled into overconfidence by the total lack of opposition to his landing and to the march from Beaulieu. "I am at the moment of persuading myself that the resistance of Savannah will be very feeble," he admits in his Notes. Meyronnet de Saint-Marc quotes him as remarking to one of his aides on the way to Savannah from Beaulieu, "I am convinced that if we march right on the city sword in hand, we will take it in spite of our small number." To this complacency the Americans had contributed their share. General Lincoln and Governor Rutledge had assured the French that "Confessing ye insufficiency of the works about the Town of Savannah, and the small number of Troops to support them—we think that there can hardly be a doubt but if the British were closed in by the French and American Troops they would be forced to surrender immediately." [7] Colonel Brétigny and the Americans had even informed the Count (the latter reported to his Ministry) that "two fifty-gun ships and some mulattoes" were all that were needed for the job.

The failure to attack at once was surprising to many observers. "Why did he not on the 13th, or at least on the morning of the 16th, storm and take this miserable sand pile with fixed bayonets?" asked the Hessian officer Hinrichs, to whose dispassionate military eye it was "inconceivable" that d'Estaing permitted the "slightest delay after the 12th." "It is amazing," wrote General Prevost two years later, "that a man of the ability and recognized reputation of Count D'Estaing should have delayed his attack long enough for us to complete our works and batteries and to permit Lieutenant-Colonel Maitland to enter the town." "Any four hours before the junction," said General Lee, "was sufficient to have taken Savannah." Ten minutes was all that was required, claimed British officers.

"I hope you approve the truce I have granted the enemy," d'Estaing blandly inquired of General Lincoln on the 17th. He apologized for his failure to accord the Americans an opportunity to look over his letter granting Prevost's request for time. "It did not seem to me to be worth disturbing you about after the fatigue of a long march."[8] What Lincoln thought about all this is not recorded. But if one story be true, there was wrath in certain quarters. To Colonel Francis Marion the respite given the British was incomprehensible. "I never beheld Marion in so great a passion," Colonel Horry is quoted as saying. "I was actually afraid he would have broken out on General Lincoln." "My God!" the usually taciturn South Carolinian is said to have exclaimed when he learned of the truce, "who ever heard of any thing like this before!—first allow an enemy to entrench, and then fight him!"[9]

To these criticisms d'Estaing could reply he was not prepared for an attack in force. "We would not be able to undertake anything much in the way of an offensive today," he informed Lincoln on the 17th. Many of his troops were not ashore. The Americans had agreed at Charlestown that, "barring accidents," one thousand men would be in Georgia by the 11th. The "accident" had happened. General McIntosh had not sent down flats from Augusta on time. At Zubly's Ferry only one canoe was to be found. A flat had to be built. Lincoln's troops were unable to complete the crossing of the Savannah until the 13th, two valuable days being lost there.

The addition of the Beaufort reinforcements made a frontal attack a doubtful and costly proposition. The French had two other alternatives—they could either depart or they could lay siege to the town. But the French had to stay now. The American alliance itself would have been jeopardized if d'Estaing went away. "London, America and even Paris," he said, "would have worse than dishonored me." "One would have supposed," he argued, "that I had secret orders not to aid the Americans. It would have been a never-ending source of complaints, of suspicions between the two countries." [10]

The Count remembered only too well how close he had come to disrupting the alliance the year before when he sailed off from Newport to fight an English squadron and found himself unable to resume the operations there on account of the damage sustained by his vessels in a storm. As a result the siege had to be raised by the Americans. "The devil has got into the fleet," wrote the exasperated Nathanael Greene. General Sullivan had publicly insulted France. "Heroes of Flight," Samuel Barrett angrily called the French, exclaiming, "if this is Gallic faith we have formed a sweet and hopeful alliance!" Such accusations had imposed on the Vice-Admiral what he called the "painful but necessary law of profound silence." They still rankled. John Sullivan, to be sure, was a *gauche* pettifogger. But Count d'Estaing could not afford to have the charge of deserting his Allies lodged against him a second time.

Under the direction of the French engineer, Captain Antoine O'Connor, trenches were commenced near the English center on the night of the 22nd. The next morning the British awoke to find that on a moonlit night (*"très beau clair de lune"*) the enemy had entrenched themselves "up to the chin" less than three hundred yards from their principal works. Lack of tools proved a handicap, but as time passed the Allied trenches were advanced to within two hundred yards of the British lines. "The Monsieurs" could be heard "working like Devils every Night," said an

THE ALLIES RESORT TO THE SPADE 61

Englishman. Captain O'Connor was the only engineer d'Estaing had brought to Georgia. The Count was highly pleased with the services of this young officer at Savannah. He had had to double, d'Estaing said, in many jobs, including "the most dangerous reconnaissances, laying out trenches, superintending the workers and service in the trenches from which one was able to get him away only by express order." In spare moments O'Connor found time to write a journal of the Siege, a hum-drum affair which was to serve, however, as a basis for the Vice-Admiral's more interesting commentaries.

No breach of the English works by the conventional system of approaches and parallels was planned, said d'Estaing. It was to be no regular siege. He had in mind only a support for his batteries. "A trench against an entrenched camp defended by a force as numerous as that of the attacking one would seem absolutely chimerical," he explained in his Notes. "All my proceedings would have been so," he added, "if I had had any other object in view than that of establishing and of supporting batteries as close as possible." The hopes of the Allies were now staked on intimidating the defenders into surrender by a bombardment of Savannah.

With great difficulty cannon and mortars were brought from the fleet via the new depot established at Thunderbolt, which was closer to the town than the Beaulieu base. The troops were rewarded with 100 crowns for each 18 pounder delivered on trucks hastily built by American carpenters. Four batteries were erected. As an example to his men, d'Estaing himself assisted in the work. The battery on the Allied left was composed of six 18 pounders and an equal number of 12 pounders. On the right a second battery of five 18 pounders and seven 12's was erected. Behind the trenches another French battery of nine mortars was commenced. The Americans established a battery of four 6 pounders, representing their entire artillery strength.

Despite the unhappy turn affairs had taken the Americans remained optimistic. It was in their nature "to promise much and to have little," said d'Estaing who complained that "This nation always counts on having what it lacks." The *"hauteur"* of Prevost's refusal to surrender proved a "little surprising" to General Lincoln but nevertheless, wrote the Count, the American commander remained confident that the British would capitulate. Dipping his quill deep in venom, d'Estaing described Lincoln's reactions to the turn of events. *"Mon tranquile Confrère, heureux dans Sa quiétude inébranlable, ne Doutoit de rien"* ["My tranquil colleague, happy in his indomitable placidity, entertained no doubts"]. Despite all that had happened General Lincoln was convinced, continued the French commander, that the enemy would capitulate at "the first sound of large cannon and the first bomb thrown into the city." [11] The mortars were what the Americans really relied on and believed in. "In American eyes," the Count wrote in his Notes, "the mortars represent the ark of the covenant and the sure way of making the walls of Jericho fall." "I hoped so," added d'Estaing, "but I doubted it."

It required no small amount of gall on his part to accuse Prevost of *"hauteur"* or Lincoln of complacency. We learn, however, from other sources about the optimism of the Americans. On September 27th Colonel Joseph Clay wrote to a friend that "General Lincoln is very well and tho' undergoing great fatigue in fine spirits. . . . We are so forward with our Approaches as to have reason to expect we shall be able to carry the place in a very few Days." The following day in a letter to Gervais he said, "I hope my next will Congratulate you on the Reduction of Savannah." He continued to be optimistic although that event remained as remote as ever. "A few Days I am hopeful will put us in Possession of [the] Town," Clay was writing three weeks after the arrival of the Allies before Savannah.[12]

All this suited the British. Had not the great Moncrief assured them that "if the Allied army would once resort to the spade, he would pledge himself for the success of the defence"?

IX

Seeds of Failure

THE lull of bringing up cannon and opening batteries presents a favorable moment to look in on the camps of the French and Americans. What one saw there did not augur much in the way of success.

Among the French themselves the essentials of cohesion were lacking. The presence of so many noblemen in the army and navy hardly contributed to real discipline. The noble-born officer was inclined to consider himself on the same level with his fellow aristocrats even though they might outrank him. The courtier class in the service looked down on the provincial nobility and both lorded it over the commoners. The *esprit de corps* that existed was surprising for an army in which nobles became colonels in less than four years and lieutenants as young as fifteen while the ordinary soldier was fortunate to reach the grade of petty officer after twenty years.

The army that d'Estaing brought to Georgia was a heterogeneous affair, made up of regulars drafted from no fewer than fourteen different regiments and of volunteers recruited in the West Indies. According to Captain de Tarragon, the regulars were "prejudiced against the militia uniform." They did not relish fighting beside militiamen. Matters were not made any less difficult by the presence in the army of several hundred free Negro troops from San

Domingo, that fantastic isle of sugar plantations and voodoo where the witch doctors of racial unrest were stirring a horrible brew for the future. In Count d'Estaing's elaborate printed orders concerning the expedition, pointed reference was made to the fact that the "people of color" would "be treated at all times like the whites." "They aspire," he said, "to the same honor, they will exhibit the same bravery." A generous "emulation between the mulattoes and blacks" was predicted.

Things did not turn out exactly that way. Between the mulattoes and the blacks existed wide social distinctions. Among mulattoes themselves there were varying degrees of privilege. As many as thirteen distinct subdivisions were recognized by the whites. Mulattoes and blacks stood on equal footing only in the matter of their common objection to heavy labor. An official roster of the French forces at Savannah contained a notation that the corps of free Negroes was "capable only of employment on trenches." However, their commander insisted, d'Estaing complained in his Notes of the Siege, that they be treated as *"des mousquetaires."* During the march from Beaulieu the Count had to put his own shoulder to a field piece in order to demonstrate, as he sarcastically put it, that these "musketeers" were "quite able to perform that work without dishonoring or tiring themselves too much." The truth was that the cannon were of little use at the moment. In the confusion of the landing and the march, Meyronnet de Saint-Marc tells us that "one found no ammunition." The Comte de Truguet, who was serving as an aide to d'Estaing, was hurriedly sent back to Beaulieu to take over the functions of chief of artillery.

The French commander was unpopular with a considerable group of his officers. His rapid promotion had aroused much jealousy in the navy where he was thought to favor the *"officiers bleus."* Originally an army man, he was regarded in naval circles as *"un intrus,"* being referred to as *"pousse-caillon"* or "infantryman." To such detractors d'Estaing replied, what of Duquesne, Tourville, Duguay-Trouin, and Jean Bart? They had not passed through the lower grades in the navy either. "If I ever come to imitate them in anything," said the Vice-Admiral, "it will be glory for me to have had the same disadvantage that they had."

It is safe to say that no such glory awaited Admiral d'Estaing. Intrepid on land, he was hesitant and overcautious on sea. The choleric Suffren complained after the brush with Admiral Byron off Grenada that if his commander-in-chief had been "as good a sailor as he was brave, we should not have allowed four demasted vessels to escape." The opposing admirals were a "well-matched" pair, said du Petit-Thouars—"Byron lacked activity, d'Estaing judgment."

It might have helped if there had been more co-operation by some of d'Estaing's naval officers. If accounts are to be believed, the lack of it amounted at times to sabotage. Nathanael Greene, who was familiar with the situation (although he would never reveal the source of his information), is quoted as authority for the statement that "A party had been formed against this admiral . . . resolved to thwart, and if possible, disgrace their commander." The same sort of thing occurred off Grenada that had been experienced the year before at Newport. There, to quote the author of the *Journal d'un officier de la marine*, "The general gave the signal all day with cannon shots to put on all sail. I cannot hide that some captains were neglectful and others in the rear took in sail."[1]

The French officers were an independent and voluble lot, seldom hesitating to speak their Gallic minds on any and all subjects. Somewhat wistfully in his report to M. de Sartine, d'Estaing compares them with the English, who were "so reserved, adroit and among whom each individual is ceaselessly occupied with the general interest." Captain Séguier de Terson recounts that shortly after arriving off the Georgia coast M. de Bougainville and the Chevalier de Dampierre attended a dinner given by the Comte de Grasse aboard the *Robuste*. He tells us that during the meal *"On a beaucoup parlé politique."* Always there was "much political talk" it seems. Later Colonels de Noailles and Dillon joined the group and there was a discussion of approaching events. The *"Messieurs de la Marine,"* reported Séguier de Terson, were agreed that affairs were by no means *"à notre avantage."* Admiral d'Estaing had been ordered to return to France with the Toulon squadron. "Without any orders from my court," he confided to George Washington, he had raised this army and brought it to America. A story was going the rounds in the navy that the real reason he had taken the best Colonial troops and de Grasse's squadron to Georgia was his fear that if he left them in the West Indies his rival, the Marquis de Bouillé, might reap the glory of retaking Saint Lucie.[2]

In the French army one did not like the way things were run any better than in the navy. The lack of ammunition for the batteries was proof of "the little order that exists in our army," said Séguier de Terson, whose early apprehensions were realized. "I fear," he had written at the beginning of the campaign, "we are going to be poorly cared for." It was more than the matter of food and of ammunition. "Unhappily," d'Estaing reported, "drog"—that "American nectar" as he termed it—had to serve as "wine for most officers and all of the soldiers." The Count must have shuddered as he described the recipe for the American concoction, this *"mélange* of sugar, water and fermented molasses."[3]

The French were at times a backbiting lot. On the morning of September 24th the British Light Infantry under Major Colin Graham made a sortie in force against the newly-opened Allied trenches in order to gain an idea of the strength of the forces which manned them. The French fell into a trap by coming out of the trenches in pursuit. They approached too close to the fortifications and the British cannon "galled them severely." As a result three officers were killed and nine wounded while eighty-five men were officially listed among the dead and wounded. According to Jean-Rémy de Tarragon, the French found themselves in a dilemma. Colonel O'Dune shouted " 'Forward' with all his might" while at the same time Colonel de Rouvray ordered "the retreat beaten." This was hardly a surprise to Captain de Tarragon who early in the campaign had perceived that "M. de Rouvray was no soldier." He believed that if the French had not "played into their hands by ordering out the six companies" they "would not have lost a man." Another Frenchman blamed O'Dune. The Colonel was "drunk," said an officer who asserted that the "excitement caused by the wine carried him beyond the proper limits." [4]

The mercurial qualities of these Frenchmen contrasted sharply with the more restrained temperament of their English foes. Consider, for example, an anecdote about John Skinner of the Sixteenth Foot, well known later in military annals as Lieutenant General Skinner. The conduct of this Oxford-educated officer on a certain trying occasion after the sortie was in the best British tradition of stout fellowship. The young Lieutenant arrived late that day, it seems, at the mess-tent after duty elsewhere in the lines. His friends were eating and chatting away as he proceeded into a separate compartment of the tent to leave his sword and hat. There he was shocked to see laid out the body of his most intimate friend, who had been killed that morning in the sortie. Skinner joined the company and finished dining without either asking or learning how his companion had died. A British officer could not violate the rule that prohibited any allusion to such subjects.[5]

Drinking on duty seems to have been a vice not altogether unknown among the French. For example, there was the case of Major Thomas Browne, or "de Browne" as he styled himself, of the Dillon Regiment. According to the Vicomte de Noailles, he was "one of the best officers the King had in his service." D'Estaing himself entertained the "greatest respect," as he put it, for "all the military qualities" of this veteran campaigner. But he was not long in discovering that the Major possessed a weakness—an "unfortunate fondness for the bottle," or to use the Count's own words, *"malheureux penchant pour le vin."* A few weeks before at Grenada, Browne had forgotten to withdraw an advanced post prior to the attack with the result that a calamity was narrowly averted at the very outset.

One night while Major Browne was in command of the trenches before Savannah his failing evidenced itself again. To the alarm of the Allied camp a lively fusillade began at the front. Thinking that his lines were under attack, d'Estaing hurried over the intervening two-thirds of a mile with six companies of grenadiers. It was all a mistake. The enemy proved purely a figment of somebody's imagination. "Without any motive and against no object had all this powder been wasted," complained the General.[6] D'Estaing had a long, heart-to-heart talk with Browne, who renounced the habit whenever he should be on duty in the future. Poor, brave Major Browne! So little time left to test the strength of this resolve!

D'Estaing was peculiarly fitted for office work, which he found "a recreation," according to an observer in San Domingo. A vast amount of paper work went on under him. Yet things remained disorganized. Sometimes the situation wore a comic opera aspect as when the French landed on Tybee Island to take the little fort at the mouth of the

Savannah. General d'Estaing believed it was occupied by the enemy. After proceeding some distance toward the fort the Count looked back and to his surprise saw but a handful of soldiers following him. Much irritated, he complained to his Adjutant General. M. de Fontanges replied that no orders had been given to him to bring along more troops. D'Estaing seems to have forgotten that the men were in the landing craft. He had neglected to send orders to disembark and, according to de Tarragon, they had passed a miserable night. Major Thomas Pinckney, who had gone ashore with the Count's staff, witnessed the incident. "This extraordinary occurrence," said the South Carolinian (no admirer of d'Estaing) showed "something of the manner of the proceeding of the commander-in-chief of the expedition, and of the footing on which he stood with the officers under his command."[7] The *"peu d'ordre"* observed by Séguier de Terson in General d'Estaing's army was equally true of Admiral d'Estaing's fleet. "One is not able to see anything more beautiful than this squadron," wrote that officer, adding, however, that it sailed "always without any order."

Things did not go smoothly between the Allies. There had been a minor diplomatic crisis when the Americans learned that d'Estaing had summoned the British to surrender in the name of the King of France, something they did not learn until the Count sent Lincoln a copy of the correspondence. Not a word about the Continental Congress! General Lincoln was much put out—*"mécontent,"* to use the expression of Count d'Estaing who might well have inquired how the British could surrender to an army that had not yet arrived. Lincoln says that he "remonstrated" with the French on the subject and that "the matter was soon settled."[8] But the tom-toms of English propaganda continued to thump the controversy for some time.

The French were little impressed by the grave New Englander who commanded the Americans—a *rara avis* among soldiers who neither cursed nor drank. The Count frequently complained about General Lincoln. His pen became a stiletto whenever he referred to the American commander, who possessed, he said, "no opinions of his own." "Although very positive in his proposals [he] was entirely cold-blooded and extremely indifferent in carrying them out," d'Estaing informed M. de Sartine. To be sure, he was a brave man. *"Il ne craint point les coups de canons"* ["He is not afraid of cannon fire."], the Count conceded after making a reconnaissance tour with the rebel leader who still limped from a wound received at Bemis's Heights. But d'Estaing hastened to qualify this tribute to Lincoln's courage in the face of English cannon. "I wish he had preferred those of Beaufort," he wrote in his Notes with what must have been a sigh. "This junction accomplished, this misfortune arrived, this fatal and decisive mistake committed —I never ceased to repeat to General Lincoln the dim outlook I had as to our operation," the Count informed M. de Sartine. But the Americans "never stopped begging, even demanding, our perseverance," d'Estaing added by way of explanation of why the French stayed on after Maitland's arrival.

Benjamin Lincoln was a patient soul. "In his character," wrote an army surgeon of the day, "is united the patient philosopher and pious Christian." According to his friend Governor John Brooks of Massachusetts, Lincoln possessed "great benignity of disposition" and though he may have "often disappointed others, he seldom offended them." Such virtues stood the American commander in good stead at Savannah, for Monsieur le Comte, the sharpest tongued of men, must have sorely tried him at times during these weeks. Among his complaints was the fare at General Lincoln's table. The American chefs had no flour and when the Count dined with the *"Insurgents"* he was served only what he described as "a massive cake of rice and corn cooked under the ashes on an iron platter." "Southern generals could never be placed in the *de luxe* class," reported d'Estaing whose Continental palate was not at all tempted by such delicacies as hoe-cake. "I absolutely forbade my two brother commanders [Noailles and Dillon?] to put themselves for more than a year on General Lincoln's diet," he quipped to M. de Sartine. "It would have been bad enough," he added, "for young courtiers to be reduced to such a diet but it would have been infinitely worse if for an indefinite time it should have become the diet of all the troops."

Little love was lost between the French and Americans. The Charlestown press might report during the Siege that the "most perfect unanimity and concord subsisted between the officers and men of both armies." D'Estaing might send word to John Laurens when the French fleet arrived off Georgia that "Esteem, friendship and confidence are sure presages" of success. Colonel Laurens might tell the Count that his "presence at this particular moment is like that of a guardian angel. You are going to destroy the common enemy and spread joy and gratitude in every heart." [9] But actually there was little esteem or mutual confidence among the Allies. There was to be still less, it might be added, of anything in the way of success.

The Americans were "so much despised by the french as not to be allowed to go into their Camp," asserted Colonel John Harris Cruger.[10] One may readily discount such a statement as Tory propaganda and up to a point it undeniably was. There was, however, a part truth in Cruger's remark. According to the Order Book of Major John Faucheraud Grimké of the Continental Army, there were certain limits beyond which American troops could not stray without a written permit. When they went into the French area without a pass they were promptly arrested. Evidently

SEEDS OF FAILURE

a number of Americans suffered this fate as General Lincoln formally notified his troops that in the event any violation of his order as to going off limits without a permit resulted in an American soldier being "taken up & confined in the French Camp, he must not expect his Interposition to get him Liberated."

A strange quirk of fate had thrown together as companions in arms the *jeunesse dorée* of Old France and up-country settlers like young Sam Davis (father-to-be of a certain Jefferson) who had come down to Savannah with his rifle and his horse. Only the thin bond of mutual interests of the moment bound France and America. A not untypical viewpoint in d'Estaing's squadron was that held by the author of the *Journal d'un officier de la marine*. "The Americans," he said, "are easily deceived, indolent in character, suspicious; they always imagine that they see whatever they fear and do not take the trouble to examine the reasons which make them believe it." [11] A cadet on the *Guerrier* probably expressed a prevailing sentiment among the French concerning the campaign when he described it as an "ill-conceived enterprise without anything in it for France."

Relations were strained by the criminations and recriminations over the failure to prevent the junction of the Beaufort troops. D'Estaing blamed it all on the Americans, accusing General Lincoln (in his Notes) of having brought his army to Georgia, instead of containing the British at Beaufort, because of his selfish desire to be in on the capture of Savannah. He reported to his Ministry that on the part of the Americans there were "altercations, reproaches and false accusations which did not even begin to hide so glaring a mistake." Warm words had passed. Fontanges seems to have expressed himself in strong language on one occasion. D'Estaing describes the scene in his Notes. "Colonel Laurens, a superlatively brave officer who had fought a pistol duel with one of his generals because he had spoken in derogatory terms of his friend, General Washington, took no offence," wrote the Count, "at what Fontanges said." "It must be," suggested d'Estaing sarcastically, "that his conscience reproached him somewhat, imparting a gentleness not natural." What was Colonel Laurens (himself of Huguenot stock) to do? With Franco-American relations as touch and go as they were, was he expected to fight a duel with the chief of staff of his French allies?

Fontanges' nerves were on ragged edge. He was nearly in tears because his commander ("for whose glory I would give my life when the occasion arises") at first blamed everything on his inattention—"a dreadful thing to me," he confessed to M. Plombard, considering all the pains taken in connection with his mission to Charlestown. Had not the Adjutant General carried with him twenty-two pages of carefully prepared questions, requests, and points of agreement in respect to the joint operations against Savannah?

The French were unimpressed by the people, the troops and the generals they saw during the expedition to Georgia. Colonel von Stedingk informed the King of Sweden that the rebels were "so badly armed, so badly clothed, and I must say so badly commanded, that we could never turn them to much account." "It seemed," he said, "as if the Americans in general were tired of the war. Their troops were reduced almost to a band of deserters and adventurers from every country." [12] They played a feeble role at Savannah, reported another French officer who explained that "Their General, by his character, was not able to make them play any other." He admitted, however, that the Americans had showed "the greatest will" and that "their regular troops, which one should well distinguish from their militia, have conducted themselves in a superior manner at all times." [13]

SEEDS OF FAILURE 75

Colonel de Noailles sympathized so much with the unmilitaristic Americans that he was tempted to leave the French service and follow the example of the Marquis de Lafayette. "He has found their military qualities quite different from those of the Prussian troops," wrote d'Estaing in a sarcastic reference to his Allies. "Forgetfulness, lack of frankness, petty jealousy, incredible ignorance of their own country" were characteristics of American generals, the Count was to inform M. de Sartine.

Apparently there was only one person in America that Monsieur d'Estaing really admired. When the French fleet was at Boston John Hancock had presented him with a full-length portrait of General Washington. Never, wrote Lafayette at the time, had he seen "a man so glad at possessing his sweetheart's picture." The Vice-Admiral hung the portrait in a conspicuous place on the *Languedoc* and it was wreathed in laurel.

October had come and the maples in the swamps were blood red. The Siege, now two and a half weeks old, was about to enter a new phase. The French batteries were finally in readiness. "The town would immediately surrender," predicted a Charlestown gazette, "or be laid in ruins in a few hours."

X

The Bombardment

LATE on the night of October 3rd, Savannah was awakened by the crash of shells—"one of the most tremendous Firings I have ever heard," declared Major Moore. Anthony Stokes has left a vivid account of the bombardment in a letter to his wife. The building in which the Chief Justice was residing happened to be directly in the line of fire. He hurriedly dressed and left, "but a shell that seemed to be falling near me, rather puzzled me how to keep clear of it, and I returned to the house," he reported, "not a little alarmed." He decided to go to Yamacraw outside the danger zone, a place to which many of the populace were repairing. The chief judicial officer of His Majesty's Province of Georgia presented a somewhat undignified spectacle as he made his way across the town in the dark, darting from house to house as he went. "When I got to the common, and heard the whistling of a shot or shell," recounted this worthy bencher of the Inner Temple, "I fell on my face." The climax of ruffled judicial dignity came when he passed the camp of Governor Wright's Negroes. There, said Chief Justice Stokes, "I fell down into a trench which they had dug."

When the firing stopped he returned to his quarters. Hardly had he fallen asleep before the shelling commenced again. This time a "very heavy cannonade" was heard from

THE BOMBARDMENT

another direction—the river. It came from the *Truite* which had been armed with several 12 and 18 pounders and stationed in Back River off the eastern end of Hutchinson Island nearly opposite the town. When the *Bricole* was unable to ascend the river further, Lieutenant Durumain had transferred his flag to this bomb ketch commanded by Comte de Chastenet de Puysegur. Because of the extreme range the *Truite* inflicted little damage in the town.

According to Meyronnet de Saint-Marc, the firing had ceased by order of Count d'Estaing who feared that his supply of ammunition would soon be exhausted. But another Frenchman supplied a different version. The bombardment had stopped, he said, at the instance of Colonel de Noailles. A number of the mortar shells had fallen around the trench where that officer commanded. Investigation disclosed a serious error. Instead of beer, a ship's steward had supplied the French naval cannoneers with a keg of rum. When the bombardment was resumed they continued to fire with "more vivacity than precision . . . being still under the influence of rum," wrote an officer.[1]

In the next five days more than a thousand shells fell in Savannah. "They shook the ground, and many of them burst with a great explosion," declared Anthony Stokes. Four Negroes huddling in the cellar of Lieutenant Governor Graham's house lost their lives. Seven more were burned to death in a fire started by a shell that struck a residence near the Church. A daughter of a Mr. Thomson was almost cut in two by a missile. Two women and two children died when a ball passed through the Laurie residence on Broughton Street. A shell which fell in the provost killed two men instantly and wounded nine others. Major T. W. Moore lost what he described as "my fine valuable Negro Carpenter and a beautiful Mare that cost me 20 Guineas" and, what was almost as bad, "my Store of Wine."

A number of the "poor women & children," wrote Major John Jones on the 7th, "have already been put to death by our Bombs & cannon; a deserter is this moment come out, who gives an account that many of them were killed in their Beds and amongst others, a poor woman with her infant in her arms were destroyed by a Cannon Ball; they have all got into Cellars but even there they do not escape the fury of our Bombs, several having been mangled in that supposed place of security." [2] "A more cruel war could not exist than this," added Jones.

"Forty women or children of various colors" lost their lives in Savannah, said Chevalier de Tarragon, "but not a soldier." He was misinformed. Ensign Pollard of De Lancey's Brigade was killed by an 18 pounder in a house on the Bay. It was much safer at the front, and Governor Wright and the Lieutenant Governor took up residence in a tent next to Colonel Maitland's on the southwestern side of the town. A number of civilians moved to the same sector.

The thunder of the big guns could be heard as far away as the ships off Tybee. To nineteen-year-old Aristide-Aubert du Petit-Thouars, who had been brought up on adventure books, befell the pleasure of observing the bombardment at closer range. The experiences of this young officer at Savannah exceeded the fondest dreams of boyhood. Among them was the privilege "of steering a craft armed with four swivel guns and carrying a crew of sixteen men under the walls of a city ablaze." There he saw "the cannon balls and bombs which I had carried to the camp and to the vessels bombarding the port fall in the city." [3]

In the effort to destroy Savannah, "carcasses" or bombs filled with combustibles were thrown into the town by the French. "I suspect this night the whole will be in Flames— Count De Staign [sic] being determined that they shall now surrender at discretion," wrote Major John Jones on October 7th. But such was the diligence of the fire watchers that only two houses were burned during the Siege. One of them was the dwelling occupied by Captain Knowles. Its destruction would be unworthy of note had not the belongings of Anthony Stokes been stored in the cellar of the house. Much to the annoyance of the Chief Justice, a merchant had "inhumanly" insisted on placing twenty-five puncheons of rum in the already crowded quarters. During the bombardment the house was struck by a shell and caught fire. Four of Stokes' slaves were killed on the spot and four others "so much scorched, that they died in a few days." [4] That was not only hard on pocket-book but also on conscience, for "I have made no great hand of my trade in human flesh," confessed this English official who prayed "to be forgiven for the share I have had in it." It was not the only bad luck Stokes ran into on the night of October 6th. An explosion of the rum being momentarily expected, he was able to retrieve only two small trunks from the cellar. Up in flames went most of his papers, a loss that would be felt in some degree by posterity when he published his able *View of the Constitution of the British Colonies, in North-America and the West Indies*. It was to handicap him, too, in furnishing legal opinions to the Governor, "all the Chief Justice's Law Books, except 4 volumes, being burnt during the Siege," he apologized to the Council. They helped make a grand three-hour conflagration which Lieutenant Meyronnet de Saint-Marc observed far out at sea aboard the *Marseillais*.

As many as fifty shells struck some of the houses. Few buildings went undamaged. "The Town was torn to pieces," wrote Major Moore—"nothing but Shrieks from Women and Children to be heard." The people huddled in cellars and below the river bluff where the big wharf rats were hardly less terrifying than the cannon balls. Banks of earth were placed around houses and casks filled with sand were used to strengthen foundations. Mrs. Prevost and her children lived in a damp cellar which feather-beds helped make bomb-proof. Mrs. McIntosh, the wife of the American General, resided in similar quarters at Savannah, suffering "beyond description," according to Major John Jones, who was allowed to visit her. Many of the ladies, including the "prettiest woman of the city," "presented themselves of their own accord at the French camp," said a naval officer. "It was necessary for us to take good care of them as they were unwilling to return," he continued, repeating a current jest that "our gallantry could not be denied even in our manner of making war."

Gallantry to the fair sex, however, was conspicuous on neither side. The British refused a request by the Americans that Mrs. Lachlan McIntosh be permitted to leave the city. The Allies in turn declined Prevost's proposal that the non-combatants, including his wife and children, be allowed to go down the river on a ship "until the business is decided." Later Colonel O'Dune told the British that "the scoundrel Lincoln and the Americans" were to blame for their denial of the request for safe conduct of the women-folk. The Americans had their own version of the matter, a libelous one as far as Prevost was concerned. A Charlestown paper reported on September 22nd that the British commander requested that his wife be given passage to Florida along with his "plate and effects." To this petition d'Estaing is quoted as replying, "That it was impossible he could have any objection to what concerned the Lady; but the plate, he had been informed, was obtained in such a way, from the Allies of his King, that he was confident the General could not mean to disgrace himself with keeping possession of it." [5]

THE BOMBARDMENT

Many women and children were removed to Hutchinson Island across the river from the town. Whites and Negroes flocked to James Graham's plantation "from every quarter for safety to the number of some thousands," that gentleman later informed the Lords Commissioners of his Majesty's Treasury, claiming that the refugees had eaten up "a large quantity of Rice & indian corn besides the crop then on the ground." Fifty persons resided together in a single barn in the utmost discomfort, recalled Elizabeth Lichtenstein Johnston.

But there were objections to refugeeing on this delta strand other than personal comfort. The *Truite* with her big 18 pounders was anchored off the eastern end of the island while a short distance downstream were the larger *Bricole* and *Chimère*. American galleys were also nearby. The forces assigned to the defense of the Island were hardly calculated to relieve the minds of the evacuees. In fact they added a new threat, only a little less terrifying than the French and Americans. The garrison stationed on the island was composed of the Cherokee braves and some of the two hundred slaves armed by General Prevost. The arming of the Negroes was an impolitic step thought many, unjustified under any circumstances. The *Georgia Gazette* later found it necessary to defend General Prevost by calling attention to the fact that the French had started it by bringing along colored troops from the West Indies. The Americans were bitter on the subject of the British action, unmindful of the fact that on September 4th the Commissioners of the Navy of South Carolina had sent urgent orders to "Endeavour by Every means in your Power, to Enlist Seamen and able bodied Negroe Men to Serve on board the Rutledge Galley for Six Months." [6] A few months later the editor of the *Gazette* could cite the precedent of General Lincoln's recommendations to Congress on the subject of the formation of a Negro regiment. "In general" the colored soldiers enlisted by Prevost "behaved well," attested that Tory newspaper. But most people in Savannah would breathe easier after they were disarmed.

One day when the French batteries were about to open up, young Elizabeth Lichtenstein was told to go to Hutchinson Island for safety. The future author of *Recollections of a Georgia Loyalist* set out across the town, ducking her comely head with each shot "as if that could save me." Mrs. Lewis Johnston and two of her sons were with Miss Lichtenstein. The youths had been denied permission by their parents to join their older brothers in the British lines. As the little party made its way across Savannah, shells crashing all around, anger got the upper hand of Mrs. Johnston. She suddenly stopped short in the street. "My sons," she said, "I was about to disgrace you; go join your brothers."

In time the populace became more or less accustomed to the bombardment. The cannon balls "gave us far less fear," recalled Elizabeth Lichtenstein Johnston, "than the appalling sound of the small arms." The colored children in the town soon discovered a more profitable pastime than sliding down the steep river bank. Overcoming their initial fears, they would run out in the streets and cover the shells with sand. When the cannon balls cooled off they gathered them up, sixpence each being paid by the English authorities for this somewhat scarce commodity.

The British batteries fired back at the Allied entrenchments, where the cannonade seems to have been received with an aplomb quite equal to that exhibited by the pickaninnies in Savannah. One day a shell burst near Major Thomas Pinckney and Captain D'Oyley while they were superintending the digging of a trench. It covered them with dust and sand. Scarcely turning the handsome head which was later to attract Godoy, Pinckney remarked, "I think, D'Oyley, that must have been very near us." [7]

As the days slipped by the Allies realized more and more that all this was getting them nowhere. In d'Estaing's acid words, "General Lincoln is convinced at last that the English perhaps have the courage to defend themselves." Little or no harm was being done to the British fortifications. The principal French battery was too far away for breaching purposes and too close for demounting and ricochet fire, the observant Johann Hinrichs pointed out. "The Troops may see," said General Prevost in orders issued the day after the bombardment commenced, "by the instance of this morning of how little avail is a Cannonade when the men take care to keep close to their Breast Works." Du Petit-Thouars well described the Allied batteries as having been "erected at great cost of men and time against works of sand which were much more easily repaired than damaged." When the French silenced or demounted a cannon it was only to find, d'Estaing complained, that it was "replaced by another located further to the rear and better protected." The chief damage to the British works seems to have been caused by the little Charlestown battery. William Hasell Gibbes, as the youngest artillery officer, asked and won the right to fire the first American cannon. He claimed that the battery shot away the flag-staff on the English defenses.[8]

The killing of civilians and destruction of homes had not achieved, General Lincoln said, "the desired purpose, that of compelling a surrender." One morning when M. de Tarragon saw a battery fire away into a fog so thick a person could scarcely see fifty paces ahead he observed with the sarcasm that seemed second nature among these Frenchmen, "It was believed that the noise would intimidate the

English, and that they were only waiting for that to surrender." "The artillery and part of the camp blamed Count d'Estaing," he added, "for having entrusted such important batteries to the navy."

A note of doubt and discouragement began to appear in the letters and diaries of the besiegers. "We are hourly expecting that they will strike," wrote Major John Jones on October 7th, careful to warn his wife, however, that "many with myself are of opinion they will not, until we compel them by storm." "We begin to lose confidence upon discovering that all this heavy firing will not render the assault less difficult," said a French officer. "We should not have constructed works," he continued. "In doing so we afforded the English time to strengthen theirs. We regret that we did not attack on the very first day." [9]

The defenders had worked like Trojans since that time. "Moncrieff's cannon rose upon them from day to day like Mushrooms (Champignons)," said the French.[10] The big barracks south of the town disappeared from the view of the Allies in the course of a day and night. The north wall was levelled by the British and the other side reduced to a "good parapet height" from the floor. Filled with sand, it made "a very respectable work in our centre," said General Prevost. The storming of the English lines, which was deemed too costly three weeks before, had now become what the Americans called "the Forlorn Hope."

XI

D'Estaing Decides to Attack

THE French had to do something. Supplies were running short and time shorter. At first they found pigs, turkeys, and geese *"à profusion,"* according to Captain Séguier de Terson, who tells us that marauding was "winked on." Conditions had soon changed. There was no bread—only that bane of the French soldier, rice. The day after the opening of the trenches proved a memorable one for some. In order to protect the sappers the French grenadiers had lain upon their stomachs only two hundred yards from the British works throughout the whole night. As a reward to their officers d'Estaing provided a fine spread. *"Beaucoup de gaieté et de plaisir"* had marked the occasion. The General responded to the toasts with a little talk. It was as though the *"événements fâcheux"* of the morrow were far from everyone's mind, said Séguier de Terson.

A rare stroke of fortune for the French occurred when they captured the *Experiment,* commanded by haughty Sir James Wallace. Demasted in a gale while en route from New York, she was easy prey for the vessels encountered off Hilton Head. Anne, Lady Wallace, "a young lady of great beauty and merit" who had recently become the bride of this forty-eight-year-old English sea captain, was a passenger. She was the daughter of Governor Wright. Also aboard the vessel was General George Garth, "the hero of Fairfield" as the Charlestown press dubbed the destroyer of that New England town, who was on his way to Savannah to relieve Prevost. More important than prisoners was the great quantity of stores on the *Experiment,* including 2,200 barrels of flour, oatmeal, beef and pork, and the payroll of £30,000 sterling. Without the supplies thus obtained the troops "might have died of hunger," said Séguier de Terson, while du Petit-Thouars of the navy could add that "the crews would have died, not only of hunger, but of cold." The customary French confusion seems to have attended the distribution of the stores. There was much dissatisfaction. "The hapless sailors who have such just claims upon these materials have been totally forgotten," complained a *garde de marine* on Bougainville's ship.[1]

It was a strange state of affairs. The besiegers were in want while the besieged had supplies for an extended resistance. There was enough flour on hand at Savannah, according to British commissary records, to supply six thousand men until January 25th; sufficient beef and pork to last until March 25th; and enough rice and oatmeal to supply the town through March 13th.[2] Moreover, hundreds of cattle had been driven into Savannah before the Allies invested the place.

The French were worn out with manning trenches day and night. Violent thunder storms made life miserable for those on duty in the lines. The Georgia climate was "so extraordinary," complained Meyronnet de Saint-Marc, "that during the day we were exposed to the most intense heat and at night to bitter cold." Major John Faucheraud Grimké of Charlestown soon needed his "blue great Coat with a Crimson Cape" which he had misplaced around the camp and for which he was glad to offer a thirty dollar reward.[3] Such articles were in demand. The troops from the Windward Islands had come away with only linen uniforms. They were not so fortunate as some of the Americans. The "very cold weather" had given John Jones a "great cold" and a "small touch of the Gout" but at least the Sunbury officer could write to his wife to ask that Ishmael be sent to him with a pair of "thick Breeches" and "my Blue Coat with 3 ruffle shirts," wishing that his Polly had "tho't to send me a bottle of Ginn." [4] Poor Major Jones! For such things he would have no use in a few days.

It was not the kind of warfare some of the Frenchmen were to see later in the more civilized North, where the Comte de Truguet, d'Estaing's youthful trouble-shooter in Georgia, could do "honor to the French nation" at Boston by his "graceful and easy performance" of the minuet or where the Vicomte de Noailles could fascinate the young gentry of Philadelphia with his violin playing. There were no minuets at Savannah and the only music the French heard there was the strains of the weird pibrochs of the Highlands that drifted across the lines from the camp of the Scotch.

Back on the ships things were in a terrible state. Even the animals refused the two-year-old bread. "Provisions from Charlestown come extremely slow and in small amounts," complained de Borda, d'Estaing's righthand man on the *Languedoc*. They consisted mainly of rice, a resource which "lack of water and of pots for cooking renders almost useless to the fleet," Count d'Estaing informed General Lincoln. There was much sickness and little medicine. Thirty to thirty-five dead were being thrown overboard every day. The sailors cursed the Vice-Admiral in their dying breath.

Beneath the veneer of polite protestations of esteem and attachment which Count d'Estaing's naval officers expressed in the reports they sent him while he was ashore there was bitter talk on the French ships. The feeling against the Admiral is reflected in the Memoirs of du Petit-

Thouars. "Picture to yourself," reminisced that young naval officer, "a squadron of twenty vessels anchored off an open coast, in the stormy season, lacking supplies and anchors; their holds filled with the sick who had almost no hope of fresh provisions while those on land were surfeited." *"Imaginez-vous,"* he continued on the subject of the sailors, "that M. d'Estaing in bringing them to the isles had forbidden them to take along anything more than a canvas coat and two shirts."

As the Siege wore on Bougainville became fit to be tied. "The ambitious vice-admiral," he complained on September 27th, "is advised of the condition of the men and the ships but he seems to have absolutely no regard for them. Of all the scourges which plague the poor human race an ambitious master of its fate is the worst." *"Quelle barbarie!"* he exclaimed, describing himself as *"vox clamantis in deserto."* A hundred times he had protested to de Broves. The reply was always the same—"Write to Count d'Estaing." Near the end Bougainville was recommending that all the captains send a memorial concerning the true situation of the fleet to their "pitiless commander." [5]

Bougainville's sentiments were echoed by one of the cadets on the *Guerrier*. Several soldiers of the Foix Regiment were hospitalized there, suffering from eye trouble. They could see only in the daytime—being the "victims," the young diarist said, "of the boundless ambition of a man who cares nothing whatever about being the cause of so much unhappiness as long as it advances his own ends." "What will be the outcome of it all?" he wondered.

From his ship Bougainville could hear the distant thunder of cannon at Savannah. In his capacity as brigadier general (a rank he still held in the army) d'Estaing might well have given him a command on land. Had not the Count informed General Washington the year before that he had the "greatest confidence" in M. de Bougainville "as

D'ESTAING DECIDES TO ATTACK

regards military science"? When these favored young courtiers of his commander-in-chief were mere children he had been the right arm of the great Montcalm whose sword he now proudly wore!

Perhaps it was just as well, however, that he was not in the field. The usually cheery countenance of the captain of the *Guerrier* was sometimes drawn in pain, his dyspepsia so bad at times that he could partake only of milled chocolate. He was weary of sun and squall and the endless heaving and rolling of an anchored ship. His gay manner was gone. The presence in d'Estaing's fleet of Bougainville's famous frigate, the *Boudeuse,* only served to recall to him his epic days aboard her in the Pacific.

This lonely coast was enough to drive a man crazy. Queer things happened here, things which made a person think he was out of his mind at times. There was the day a large sea fowl lit on a spar of the *Magnifique* and was caught by a seaman. Someone happened to notice a swelling on the bird's neck. They looked closer. A message written in English was hung there. It read, "The brigantine which cruises to the windward of the fleet is the privateer Robuste." "*Ce fait est extraordinaire mais très vrai*" ["Extraordinary but quite true"], wrote M. de Bougainville, glad to have something to record in his Journal besides imprecations against the Vice-Admiral.

Count d'Estaing had informed the Americans upon his arrival in these waters that from the viewpoint of his country's interests in the West Indies he would be a "criminal" if he kept his troops on land longer than eight days. They had already been ashore three weeks. The French had come while summer was in the land—when they left the geese would be honking as they winged southward in the chill night. "*Ce siège éternel,*" they called it in the navy.

If Admiral Byron should follow the French up from the

West Indies d'Estaing's under-manned ships would prove so many lame ducks. Incensed at the requisition of some of the *Guerrier's* best cannoneers and his 18 pounders for use in the Siege, Bougainville swore "before God and men that I will not make myself answerable for her." Worse danger still, a hurricane might destroy the fleet at any moment now. It was the season when the great twisters came howling up in blind fury from their Caribbean lair. As early as September 9th Prevost had predicted to Sir Henry Clinton that "The French cannot, I should think, venture to continue long in their present exposed Situation, on this coast, at this Season of the year." Their ships had now been anchored for over a month where "an English squadron," as the French were informed, "had never dared to remain for eight hours even in the most beautiful weather." The storm which caught the fleet on the way north on September 2nd had crippled many of the vessels. The French were short of cables, tackle, and anchors. Much of the time off Georgia was spent installing temporary rudders. The *Magnifique* was only so in name. She had sprung a bad leak, its nature being such as to make the Vice-Admiral suspect sabotage by an evil-disposed calker. A merchant vessel had to be stayed against her and the pumps kept going night and day. For a time it was feared the big ship could not be saved.

Though by now what d'Estaing called the *"beau moment"* of the usual siege had arrived, that is to say, the point where success was imminent, the situation at Savannah was altogether different. For this was no ordinary siege. Despite all their labors they had "achieved nothing," said the Count who pointed out that "New entrenchments rise while the old are neither abandoned nor taken." If the Allies were to capture a work, their position would be scarcely improved. They would only have new obstacles to

D'ESTAING DECIDES TO ATTACK

face in the way of entrenchments further to the rear. "This strange Siege," said d'Estaing, "is a Penelope's web."

To call everything off and sail away was the part of discretion. But French honour was not to be thus satisfied. A last desperate effort must be made to take the city. The moment was now arrived that Count d'Estaing had described in a letter to the Chevalier Durumain three weeks before. After other resources have failed in war, he said, one must "take sword in hand." "*L'épée à la main.*" How he loved that phrase! A true grenadier of His Majesty the King, that is what he was at heart.

D'Estaing possessed decided ideas as to where the main assault should be launched. Deserters had informed the French that "the right of the enemy works facing the American camp was guarded only by militia."[6] As the Count summed up the situation in his Notes, the area near the Spring Hill redoubt (which he had personally reconnoitered) was "the least fortified, the one where we are least perceived in advance by the enemy and the preferable one for an attack in force."

The British themselves recognized that the weakest point in their line was on the right flank, especially at the salient made by the redoubt atop Spring Hill adjacent to the road to Augusta. Here despite all his military engineers could do the terrain, said Prevost, was "favorable to our enemy." The marshy gorge or hollow west of the high land afforded the Allies an opportunity to approach undetected within a short distance of the works. At the same time the redoubt was far enough away from the marsh, d'Estaing had observed, to permit several columns of troops to pass between them in order to attack further along the British right flank toward the river. "The horses which we saw go out and graze between the entrenchments and the marsh appeared to enter and leave the city without trouble and without having any ditch to cross," wrote the Count who likewise noted that when the enemy came out from their entrenchments and walked along the road they never disappeared from view. It was here M. d'Estaing would strike —at the head of his troops.

Colonel Maitland had been honored with the command of this critical sector. Colonel von Porbeck of the Hessians was field officer on this flank. Among the regular British officers in this portion of the line was Major Beamsley Glasier of the Sixtieth Regiment. Lieutenant Thomas Tawse of the Seventy-first ("to whose sacred Memory, while my Recollection of his unequalled Merit lives," a Britisher was soon to promise, "I'll pay an anniversary Tribute") commanded some Carolina troops assigned to the redoubt. Commanding the King's Rangers was Lieutenant Colonel Thomas Browne, "a Gentleman of family and of liberal and genteel education . . . having considerable patrimony," according to Governor Tonyn of Florida. Because he once expressed his views about the rebellion too freely the liberty-loving citizenry of Augusta had outfitted him with "a genteel and fashionable suit of tar and feathers," to use the words of the *Georgia Gazette*. He had vowed and obtained terrible vengeance upon the Whigs. Ninety North Carolina Volunteers were also assigned to this area. These sharpshooting provincial troops presented a fire power fully equal to the British regulars. They were part of the 1,400 troops a popular and wealthy North Carolina merchant named John Hamilton had raised and equipped at his own expense. This rotund, red-faced Tory Colonel, a veteran of Culloden, was himself stationed elsewhere in the lines.

The decision to attack as well as the point selected introduced the usual dissension in the French camp. The Council of War seems to have been itself a small war. There was a Babel of dissent. "Emphatic remonstrances" were made by Colonel de Noailles against attacking where it was "impracticable."⁷ Colonel Stedingk said that he "confidently predicted" the outcome. He argued that the difficulties of the terrain "quite counter-balanced" the weakness of the works at the point selected for the attack. Instead of leading a column, as d'Estaing ordered, Baron Stedingk "entreated" the General "to let me march with a musket, a volunteer at his side." Colonel de Pondevaux expressed the opinion that *"une Sage retraite"* was the only course, a view in which Dillon and several other French officers concurred. Major Thomas Browne of the Dillon Regiment, who had reconnoitered the British lines, disapproved of the attack, reported Meyronnet de Saint-Marc, maintaining that it was impossible to take Savannah without at least five thousand picked men.

In short, to use the words of a cadet on the *Guerrier*, *"tout le monde s'étoit opposé à cette funeste attaque."* That is to say, everybody was opposed to it except d'Estaing. As usual, the Count cut short those who crossed him. When Colonel de Noailles voiced his objections d'Estaing curtly answered that "his conclusions were those of an old man." "The General would see him go under fire like a young man," replied the Vicomte spiritedly, adding that "from the observations which he had made together with officers whose experience was well known, they all regarded the attack as impracticable, and that they were astonished that the point of attack was not decided by the place where the trenches had been opened."⁸

"Fidelity to the Americans" and "the honor of the King's arms," replied the Count, demanded that he "not raise the siege ignominiously, without striking a vigorous blow." *"Son parti était pris"* ["his decision was made"]. "It was necessary," Meyronnet de Saint-Marc recorded him as saying, "to finish this business with the capture of Savannah." True, confessed d'Estaing, he foresaw "a multitude of obstacles." "But extreme bravery," he added, "can conquer everything, and I thought that the time was ripe to prove to the Americans by a brilliant action, although it might be a bloody one, that the King's troops knew how to dare everything for them." [9]

He was going to make the attempt *"sauter le bâton,"* the French commander told Baron Stedingk—that is to say, as a matter of necessary routine, like a monkey jumps a stick. The Count possessed a strong sense of self-righteousness. The role of martyr to the American cause was one in which he frequently cast himself. Abuse by the Americans, he reported, had "in no way diminished my zeal for the King's allies." "They have greatly mistreated me," said d'Estaing, "without being able to change my way of thinking of them" though 'twas true he had become "a little mistrustful." [10]

It was useless to argue with Monsieur le Comte. "He wishes everyone," said a French naval officer, "to view and think of his plans as he does." Neither in his capacity as admiral nor as general was d'Estaing accustomed to solicit or to accept advice. "His haughty and vain character," continued the author of the *Journal d'un officier de la marine*, "did not admit of advice . . . with his authority always silencing whoever objected. . . . He needs counsel but his prejudices and his headstrong nature prevent his following it or even listening to those capable of guiding him." "In one word," added this officer, d'Estaing "conducted his squadron like a true despot, *by fear;* and succeeded only in causing general revolt and in making himself hated." [11]

General Lincoln acquiesced in the plan of assault. There was not much else one could do. D'Estaing was his superior in rank. Besides, the French army was operating only as a voluntary force. It was the *"pisaller"* ["last resort"], explained French-speaking Major Thomas Pinckney. The plan had been agreed on in principle between the two commanders several days before. The National Archives at Paris contain the original memorandum of their understanding on the subject. It called for an attack "on the night of the 6th or 7th" which was to be centered upon the Spring Hill redoubt, the hour and details to be worked out later. The projected assault was to be made by two columns of French soldiers, consisting of 1,100 and 1,200 men respectively, with 1,000 picked troops constituting the reserve.[12]

If there was disagreement by the Americans as to the locale of attack there is no record of the fact. Possibly Pulaski dissented. On the 6th he presented a written proposal to d'Estaing on the subject of the assault. "The liberty which I take of communicating to you my way of thinking about the attack is authorized," he said, "by the conduct of all great men who, as homage due, receive the advice of others." "Above all else," he said, my "purpose is to please you." In his memorandum General Pulaski proposed three separate points of attack, apologizing for the fact that he "expressed himself with reference to the terrain in terms of the little information I have obtained from the Americans." One assault was to be on the British right flank along the Augusta road; another, on the enemy left wing, was to be made by the Americans under General McIntosh while the main attack would be launched near the right center of the British line. "You will always remember," wrote Pulaski in transmitting these suggestions, "that I wished to be good for something in addition to the dutiful attachment with which I have the honor of being your Excellency's very humble and very obedient servant." [13]

Some of the Americans had a foreboding of disaster. Major John Jones and Lieutenant Robert Carnabie Baillie "staggered" their friends, said James Jackson, by bidding them an affectionate farewell, each certain he would not survive.

General Pulaski possessed a marked tendency toward melancholia. He, too, anticipated death, regarding as an ill-omen the loss of the scapulars that had been blessed by his Church. His last days were not happy. Only the shock of battle seemed to satisfy him. Service with the Americans was irksome. On one occasion during the latter part of the Siege his cavalry had failed to come up promptly on the occasion of an alarm. There had been criticism. Quite sensitive to it, Pulaski sat down and wrote to d'Estaing in French by way of justification. "I desire to measure up to everything," he said, "that is able to please you. Yesterday an American officer commanded the picket. His accustomed laziness caused me the displeasure of learning that, contrary to my orders, he did not occupy his post at the hour . . ." Pulaski had lost one of his cavalrymen to the enemy and apparently had been blamed for it. "I have studied my calling for 18 years and would blush to commit a fault," he wrote, "that would have cost the life of a man. I suffer, however, to hear that several [officers] younger than I am amuse themselves by expressing an unfavorable opinion of me." "I serve in the American army with the view of pleasing France," added the brooding Casimir. "I left my native land expecting to find an asylum in that kingdom. In passing to Turkey I obtained the recommendations of the Duke de Guiton. My prospects were flattering. Change of circumstances has not changed my heart. If your Excellency wishes proof of it, give me the opportunity and I will profit by it, I hope, to merit your approbation. . . ." [14]

Under the plan adopted there were to be two main columns of French troops with a vanguard of 250 grenadiers under Colonel de Béthisy. The vanguard was to seize Spring Hill redoubt while the two columns passed between the marsh and the redoubt in order to assail the entrenchments and battery immediately to its north. The right column, commanded by Colonel Dillon with Major Browne as second officer, was to strike at the entrenchments and battery while the left under Colonel Stedingk was to attack further on the enemy right, marching parallel with the defenses to the end of the abatis before turning. The French reserve was placed under the command of Colonel de Noailles. The American Light Infantry and the Charlestown militia, with Colonel Laurens at the head, were to comprise the first American column, which was to be followed by a second, consisting of the First and Fifth Carolina Regiments under General McIntosh. They were to follow the French left column. The cavalry under Pulaski was to endeavor to reach Yamacraw by penetrating between the battery and the redoubt nearest the river. Feints or false attacks were to be launched by the French at the center and by the Americans on the British left. An amphibious assault was to be made from the Savannah River. At the latest the attack was to begin at four o'clock.

In the Journal of Johann Hinrichs this plan was criticized at some length, the Hessian officer pointing out many things that should have or should not have been done. Hinrichs had not seen the plan of attack when he wrote his critique. Actually it embraced most of his suggestions. On paper at least, the plan was carefully worked out. Success depended on co-ordination, timing, and above all upon surprise. "To take them by surprise was the main point," declared d'Estaing. "In my eyes everything depended on that." [15]

There was to be no surprise. One source informs us that a spy stood outside the tent where these plans were being laid. It is claimed that a member of the Grenadier Company of militia posed as a musket-bearing sentinel at the entrance to the marquee. Later he would disappear in the direction of the British lines. This Charlestown clerk would not, however, disappear entirely from history, for Sergeant Major Curry will be seen again—hanging to a tree after his capture by the Americans at the Battle of Hobkirk. So the story goes, though the past offers little in the way of proof that it was James Curry who betrayed the Allies at Savannah.[16] A furtive, half-mythical figure of the Revolution, he lurks in the deep shadows between tradition and history.

But if it was not Curry, certainly someone else had revealed the Allied plans. D'Estaing himself was less inclined to blame the leak upon "two American deserters" than upon *"des gens de cette nation"* ["American civilians"] who he said kept the British informed of everything. The many Tories among their militia "continually betrayed us," claimed Meyronnet de Saint-Marc, "rendering to the English the most exact account of all our operations." Some of the American militia, he said, even passed the evenings in Savannah, returning by day to the Rebel camp. General Lincoln and his principal officers saw without being able to prevent carryings-on "so dangerous for the common cause." Such was the price, continued this Frenchman, of civil war and divided public opinion.

One may readily sympathize with the French in this respect. Not a few of the American militia seem to have come to Savannah with mental reservations like Sir Patrick Houstoun. Of course, there is no suggestion that this brother of Governor Houstoun betrayed the Americans. But he was hardly the stuff of which patriots are made. Justifying later to the Royal Council his presence among the Rebel militia at Savannah, Patrick contended that he had "received peremptory Orders to go down with the Army." He "carried no Arms, except Pistols, which he generally rode with." In fact, he was so generally looked upon as a Tory that Americans "had been severely questioned and treated for going to dine with him." [17] Soldiers such as

D'ESTAING DECIDES TO ATTACK 99

Sir Patrick Houstoun, Sixth Baronet, were scarcely the materials with which revolutions are won.

Officially the British nowhere admitted any American treachery. But they freely told the French afterward (though Meyronnet de Saint-Marc suspected an effort to create friction among the Allies) that "they knew from one minute to the next all that went on in our camp" and "learned the night before of our principal point of attack and as a result awaited us there with all their forces."

But on the other hand, statements of General Prevost and his aide, Major Moore, imply that although they knew the day the attack was coming they were not sure of its locale. Moore wrote later that when the assault began it was not realized at first where it was centered, while Prevost supposed the French were going to attack on the English left and the Americans on his right.

XII

October Ninth

THERE was little rest for the Allies on the eve of attack. The men were out of their huts and tents at midnight, girding for this battle of nations and races—a struggle in which English Redcoat, Scotch Highlander, Tories from the Carolinas, Georgia, New York and New Jersey, hired Hessian, armed slave, Creek and Cherokee brave, all under a Swiss-born general, were to be pitted against grenadiers of Old France, American patriot, Polish hussar, Irishmen serving under the Bourbon banner, and mulatto and black troops from the French West Indies.

The stakes were high. At this very moment General Clinton's expeditionary force against Charlestown was embarking from New York. The main theatre of British aims and aspirations was being shifted to the South. "Should Georgia be lost I shall have little hope of recovering that Province and also of reducing and Arming South Carolina," Clinton informed Germain when he learned of the arrival of the French fleet off Tybee.[1] The stakes may have been even larger than he supposed. Independence itself was a possibility. For if Savannah fell, Britain's only remaining foothold between Canada and Florida was New York. Her tenancy was a precarious one should the French fleet co-operate in its reduction. Moreover, another setback as disastrous as Saratoga would make the peace party in England more clamorous than ever.

But somewhere above the fog which hung thick and grey across the early morning hours an evil star was shining for the Allies. From the beginning everything went wrong. There was grumbling in the French ranks as the troops formed at the camp. Under decided objections on their part regulars were drafted to fill out militia companies. Numerous changes were made at the last minute. In many instances the men found themselves led by strange officers. It was necessary to yield. "The General said he wished it," declared Captain de Tarragon, implying that that was the way discussions with him usually ended.

D'Estaing seems to have been aware of the treachery before the attack. "Several American soldiers had deserted that very night," wrote Meyronnet de Saint-Marc who asserted that the French commander "was not ignorant of it." They were informed of the fact, he said, "almost at the very time." As his troops marched out of camp, d'Estaing turned towards some officers at his side and remarked that "he had a very poor opinion of this attack" [*"très mauvaise opinion de cette attaque"*]. The men in the ranks seemed well disposed to second this view. But the General was encouraged to go through with the plan by several of his junior officers who, according to Meyronnet de Saint-Marc, "consulted their zeal and the fire of youth rather than prudence." These, to say the least, were hardly favorable auspices for an attack on strongly defended lines.

The French arrived late at the American camp, d'Estaing attributing the delay to having to wait for guides. He says that he had to look around for General Lincoln who could not be found. He had reason to complain of the guides the Americans furnished. "They have assured us of a number of good guides to conduct the columns," says a French memorandum of the preliminary agreement relative to the attack. One of them was a Frenchman in the Continental service named Roman who had helped erect the original defenses of Savannah. He assured the French that he knew the environs. As the troops of the left column emerged from the woods Colonel Stedingk inquired how far his particular point of attack was from the redoubt. Major Roman replied that the fortifications had been altered and that he was unacquainted with the terrain. He proceeded to wash his hands of the matter, refusing to accept further responsibility.[2] Jean-Rémy de Tarragon records a similar experience in connection with the right column. "On arriving at the head of the troops" the American sent to conduct them admitted that he "did not know the road and at the first musket shot disappeared."

"Before the attack," lamented Séguier de Terson, "a thousand men know the road by which the columns are supposed to pass; at the moment when we need to do it, all of them lose their heads and we no longer know who is to conduct us." "Those who said they knew the way for the different Columns to take & who were to be our guides," said Charles C. Pinckney, were not "such masters of the ground as they ought to have been."[3] It was typical of the disorganization and lack of foresight that marked the whole campaign.

There were other causes of delay. French military etiquette of the day gave precedence to regiments in accordance with their seniority. Within regiments themselves positions of honor went to the companies according to the date of commissions of their captains. As the French formed for battle an officer, entitled to a more privileged station than that in which he found his men, insisted on marching his company down the whole line to its rightful place, drums and fifes playing.[4] Off Grenada a few weeks before d'Estaing had experienced the same sort of thing in the fleet. Instead of obeying the Admiral's signals as to combat formation the captains crowded sail, according to the *Journal d'un officier de la marine,* in their race for the particular positions in the line of battle to which rank entitled them. In such a way the Bourbons sometimes waged war in the eighteenth century and in the process lost an empire.

A chill fell across d'Estaing as his troops began to debouch for the attack. The stillness of the pre-dawn was suddenly broken by the eerie skirl of bagpipes. Often during the Siege this music of the "Scotch mountains" ("most sad and most remarkable" as he described it) had drifted across the lines from the camp of the Highlanders. The French now heard the *"lugubre harmonie"* again. It came from a point near the place of attack and well to the right of the usual station of the Seventy-first Regiment. The sound of the bagpipes made "a very great impression" upon the spirit of the French troops, it not only showing, said the Count, that the enemy were aware of his designs but that they "wanted us to know their best troops were awaiting us."

He would have called off the attack then and there "if we had not had the Americans for companions—that is to say," d'Estaing corrected himself, "as masters." But there was no turning back now. Another cogent reason led him on. "My indecision" at that stage, he confessed, "would have made me a laughing-stock" [*"fourni une ample matière à la plaisanterie"*].[5] Better to die than be laughed at by the courtiers of Versailles!

Five o'clock came and the front files had only reached the edge of the wood on the right of the British line. Dawn broke. The troops grew restless. The columns began to form for the attack. The first shots were heard where the false attacks were being launched by the Americans at the extreme left of the British defenses and by the French at the center. They were the signal for the main assault, *l'attaque de vive force.* It was nearly five-thirty.

By this time the presence of the Allies had been discovered by the enemy sentinels. D'Estaing waited no longer for the columns to complete their formation. He would attack with the troops that were ready. The drummers were ordered to beat the charge. The Bourbon battle-cry rang through the ranks. *Vive le roi!* The vanguard "broke pell-mell upon the redoubt," said Captain Séguier de Terson. Under heavy fire the grenadiers of Old France clambered over the abatis. They came on, white shadows that materialized out of the mist and swarmed up the glacis in front of Spring Hill redoubt.

The lines at this point were defended by a few troops of the Sixtieth Regiment, North and South Carolina Loyalists, marines, sailors, and a handful of dismounted provincial cavalry—a total of only 417 men, claimed the English, though the French insisted that the enemy were heavily massed in this sector. Certainly it was significant that on the morning of the attack Lieutenant Tawse and some dragoons had been assigned to the redoubt. In view of the fact that the Allies had been ordered to wear white cockades to distinguish one another during the attack it was also significant that the British would be wearing "large white cockades and shirts over their coats."

Led by Jean-Gaspard Vence and the Chevalier d'Erneville, the storm troops scrambled up the steep sides of the redoubt. Lieutenant Levert de Genville of the Gâtinais Regiment was the first to penetrate the defenses. A French account says that the "defenders astonished at such bravery threw away their arms and ran." The British admitted that "A body of French Grenadiers came on with such a Spirit to attack the old Redoubt upon the Ebenezer Road" that if Tawse and Wickham "had not thrown themselves in very opportunely, it must have been carried." [6]

But no reinforcements arrived to support the vanguard. The two main columns had gone too far to the left, explained d'Estaing. The advance guard was ordered forward too quickly, said others. The initial wave had to fall back, "mown down by the right battery which took them in flank," according to Captain de Tarragon. The French retreated in good order, carrying their wounded, among whom was Colonel de Béthisy.

The French right column now came into action—that is to say, the head of the column did; the rest was in disorder in the swamp. With about eighty grenadiers Colonel Dillon reached the entrenchments. It was a "very brilliant moment" and one that might have been "decisive if he had been supported," said d'Estaing.[7] But he was not. The enemy appeared in force and the French were driven back, the retreat being "infinitely murderous," according to the General. There was desperate fighting along the entrenchments. The lily banners of France were planted on the berm. The valiant Tawse died defending the parapet, his sword in the body of the third man slain by his own hand. An English officer lost his nose, a blow for which a Frenchman paid with his life.

Though wounded in the arm Count d'Estaing continued to direct the assault. Standing on the causeway near the redoubt with his right arm in a sling, he exhibited what a French officer called "perfect self-possession." Three times he rallied his troops and sent them forward. He complained that despite the "exhortations, entreaties, and threats" of the French officers the columns invariably bore to the left and into the marsh. Only the *avant garde* showed real ardor, d'Estaing reported. But who wants to advance, asked a cadet on the *Guerrier*, when soldiers "see and know that they are badly commanded"?

The soil of Savannah ran red with the best blood of Europe. Viscount de Béthisy was severely wounded in three places. Baron von Stedingk sustained a bad contusion on his leg; Chevalier Théobald Dillon a wound which partially crippled him for the rest of his life. The intrepid Major de Browne was killed at the entrance of the redoubt. Viscount de Fontanges went down during the third charge, his thigh ripped open by canister, crying: "We must retire." Casimir Pulaski, representative of a famous Polish house, was mortally wounded.

The loss was terrific in the French ranks and among the under-officers. Of six Lebey brothers who had come with d'Estaing three were killed and another wounded at Spring Hill redoubt while the other two met death elsewhere in the attack. So family tradition goes, at any rate. Chains, nails, bolts, and scrap of all kinds as well as canister fired from cannon at short range and from an English galley at the mouth of Yamacraw Creek cut through the massed troops, making a *"carnage affreuse,"* to use Count d'Estaing's words. In their white uniforms the French were easy targets for riflemen firing deliberately from the banquette of the entrenchments. "Believe me," exulted a Britisher who served a nine pounder in the battery, "I never was happier in my Life than upon this Occasion." [8]

Despite express orders "to take care not to go into the swamp" Stedingk's column made too wide a circuit to the left. The men mired up to their knees. Under heavy fire and without formation they finally reached the causeway to which all the Allied troops seemed to gravitate. There they met the retreating right column which was thrown back upon them. *"Jamais on n'a vu une Confusion pareille,"* wrote Meyronnet de Saint-Marc who added, "The troops, the greater part of whom did not know the officers at their head, paid no heed to anyone."

Colonel Stedingk and a part of his column eventually reached the entrenchments around Spring Hill redoubt. There he had the pleasure of personally planting an American flag. It was another great moment. The day had been won! They had succeeded! "My doubts were all gone," said Stedingk. "I believed the day was our own."

Could this lodgment have been sustained it would have been fatal to the defenders. But the rest of the column was pinned down in the morass. And Maitland's "comprehensive eye" had seen the menace. "Always great," wrote General Henry Lee, he "surpassed upon this occasion his former glory." Major Glasier was ordered to advance with the grenadiers of the old Royal American Regiment and the Marines. There was a savage bayonet charge. The French and Americans had not succeeded in spreading along the parapet and they were driven back. "The moment of retreat, with the cries of our dying comrades piercing my heart," was "the bitterest of my life," declared Stedingk who "wished for death." "Of nine hundred choice troops which I led into action," wrote this officer, "four hundred men and thirty-nine officers were dead or wounded." The Baron had upheld "in a most distinguished manner the honor of the nation of Gustave," reported d'Estaing.

The Americans meanwhile had advanced to the entrenchments around the Spring Hill redoubt but the parapet could not be scaled in the face of the heavy fire. Huddled in the ditch, they were slaughtered by the British. There were heavy losses among American officers. Killed or mortally wounded were Baillie, Berand, Boyce, Bruneau, Bush, DeSaussure, Donnom, Dubois, Farrar, Gaston, Gray, Kinnill, Hume, Jones, Motte, Pulaski, Roux, Sheppard, Vleland, Wickom, Wise.

High praise for the Continental troops came from the French. They "showed the greatest courage, remaining at the foot of the ditch exposed to the enemy's fire without wavering until they received the order of Monsieur le Comte d'Estaing to retire," wrote Meyronnet de Saint-Marc. He was less content with the militia which "at the commencement of the affair took flight in every direction" ["*prirent la fuite de toute part*"]. To the same effect is the *Journal d'un officier de la marine* which speaks of the "astonishing gallantry" of the American regulars. "Although repulsed with severe loss" the Continental troops "return repeatedly to the assault thus furnishing a brilliant illustration of their valor," said another French officer who, with the usual contempt for the American militia, added that "At the first discharge of a gun, two-thirds of the Virginia militia detach themselves." The fact remains that the Virginians suffered the heaviest casualties of any American unit, a return showing 9 men killed and 51 wounded.[9] D'Estaing declared that though Colonel Laurens personally exhibited the "greatest bravery" he was abandoned by his own detachment *"au premier coup de fusil."* But much to the Count's surprise the other American troops, including the Charlestown militia, "advanced with bravery and even order" up to the enemy entrenchments.[10]

Death had a carnival among the Continental standard bearers. Lieutenant James Gray and Lieutenant Alexander Hume were killed while carrying one of the flags which Sergeant McDonald planted on the parapet of the British entrenchments. McDonald later managed to bear it away. Lieutenant Bush, who bore the colors of the Second Regiment, was wounded, whereupon he passed the flag to Sergeant Jasper. The latter handed it back when he himself was struck. The flag fell under Bush in the ditch below the British works, according to the account of Lieutenant Legaré in Garden's *Anecdotes*.

The story that the brave Jasper retrieved the banner which Mrs. Elliott had presented to his Regiment seems to have been the invention of a chronic romancer. A contemporary British Journal of the Siege states that "Two Rebel Standards were once fixed on the Redoubt on the Ebenezer Road; one of them was carried off again, and the other, which belonged to the Second Carolina Regiment, was taken." The famous banner was carried to England as a war trophy. It is still there.

Arriving with General McIntosh's column, Thomas Pinckney saw "such a scene of confusion" as is not "often equalled." Laurens, who found himself separated from part of his command, came up to Major Pinckney and asked *"if we had seen them."* D'Estaing made a somewhat pathetic spectacle. With the help of a drummer he had succeeded in collecting a few men around him. Asked what orders he had for the fresh American units, the Count instructed Pinckney to have them bear further left so as not to interfere with the troops he was rallying.

During the waning moments of the fighting d'Estaing was hit again. A bad wound in the calf of his right leg felled the Count. His had been the role of a *"véritable grenadier dans cette affaire mais un mauvais général"* ["a true grenadier in this affair but a poor general"], wrote Séguier de Terson. "It is not the fault of the troops that Savannah was not taken," he added, "but rather of those who commanded us." The French General owed his life to Laurent de Truguet. Fearful that he might not get an opportunity to participate in the attack, he had implored Count d'Estaing in a letter on September 18th not to forget his promise. *"Mon général,"* he said, "you will put me in despair if you break your word." Count de Truguet was among the first to reach the British entrenchments. Later he found his commander lying among the dead. It was no easy feat to remove him from the field. The first two grenadiers enlisted in that task by d'Estaing's aide were killed.

The circumstances under which Pulaski was mortally wounded have been and remain the occasion of controversy. Some say the brave Pole fell while leading a desperate cavalry charge on the British lines, a story supported by David Ramsay, Thomas Pinckney, and by Major Rogowsky ("two hundred strong. . . . We sped like Knights into the peril"). Such a version was emphatically denied by Captain Paul Bentalou, who was present. The idea of a charge by mounted troops against works which almost required an escalade was fantastic, declared that officer.

According to Bentalou, Pulaski had halted the cavalry at the edge of the wood, awaiting an opportunity to penetrate the works in the event of a breach achieved by the infantry. He saw what was happening at the front. *Mon Dieu,* what a paltry part for the hero of fifty fields! Word came back that the French commander-in-chief was wounded. The attack was flagging. Pulaski spurred his black charger and rode off toward the scene of carnage. A contemporary newspaper account stated that "The bold Pulaski rush'd with his usual ardor upon his horse, a considerable way before his legion, up to the parapet of the enemy" where "a bar shot from one of their cannon . . . gave him a large and mortal wound in his side, just above the hip." [11]

D'Estaing throws some light upon the controversy. The French commander reported that the Polish officer fell "by his own fault in placing himself where he should not have been at the moment," explaining that he had "prematurely advanced in order to avail himself more promptly of the passage we were to open for him." [12] Pulaski's death was described by the Count as "an infinitely great loss to the American cause." The British were something less than sympathetic. "No European power certainly would have employed him," charged the *Royal Georgia Gazette* which scoffed that none but Americans would "have ranked with an assassin as an officer." [13]

An hour after the attack began the order to retreat came. The German Fusilier Company of Charlestown is said to have disregarded the command, continuing to advance until death felled the popular Captain Sheppard, whereupon the outfit retired. Looking around on his fallen men, the despondent Laurens hurled his sword to the ground in wrath, exclaiming, "Poor fellows, I envy you!" Major Thomas Pinckney restored order in his ranks, Garden's *Anecdotes* informs us, by addressing his men in these phrases: "Success, my brave fellows, though richly merited, has not crowned your exertions; yet do not disgrace yourselves by precipitate flight, and, though repulsed, quit the field like Soldiers." [14] Apparently not many French officers resorted to such Thucydidean speeches. "At midday," said Captain de Tarragon, "little groups of men who had lost their way in the swamp were still coming back into the camp." "Not ten soldiers from the same company returned into the camp together," he added.

As soon as the retreat began Maitland ordered a counterattack. The British came out of their works. But the French reserves posted near the old Jewish Burial Ground stood fast. In the language of O'Connor: "The enemy who had advanced to the abatis, seeing the good order and firmness of our rear guard in the face of cannon charged with grape shot, did not dare venture beyond." [15] Colonel de Noailles' maneuver in sending his troops forward to meet the challenge prevented a sortie which might have "caused the destruction of our army," said another French officer. There were some losses among the reserves, including the Adjutant, M. Calignon, who was mortally wounded at de Noailles' side. D'Estaing was a bit critical. "Our corps of reserves by being a little less impetuous would have better received those who were retiring than by going out to look for them," he commented. "His excess of vigor and of courage (respectable fault) have increased the loss," added the Count, who thought that the retreat "should not have cost him a single man."

The false attacks by the Allies were quickly turned back

on all fronts. The British paid not "the slightest attention" to them, reported d'Estaing. The feint by the militia under Generals Williamson and Huger on the eastern side of the lines bogged down in the rice fields where the American losses amounted to 6 killed and 14 wounded. The false attack at the center achieved nothing. Led by M. de Sablière, the volunteers from the West Indies and the French marines advanced from the Allied trenches to the ditch in front of the British works where they discharged their muskets. They were met with a volley that sent them quickly back to the defense of their own works after considerable losses. "The false attack from the trenches," complained d'Estaing, "was not executed as the order specified."

The amphibious assault led by Trolong Durumain never even got started. High hopes were staked on the venture which this young naval officer had enthusiastically pressed upon d'Estaing. It was not his fault that the river attack proved a fiasco. The Count blamed Durumain's misfortune on the "poor will" of the Americans, claiming that one of the two Continental galleys which was to participate dropped her anchor as they got under way and that the other suddenly filled with water. It was easy for him to believe a rumor that an American sailor had been paid four hundred dollars to scuttle his ship.[16] When Durumain saw that the operation was hopeless he ordered the troops assigned to him to debark. Hastening ahead by land with the Comte de Puysegur, he reached the front just as the battle was ending.

Durumain was "accustomed," d'Estaing said, "to play his life as his fortune." He had predicted to M. de Sartine that the Chevalier would become another "Duguay-Trouin" if given a vessel. Lieutenant Durumain got his ship but never lived long enough to play the role of that hero. A few months later he was killed in action at sea.

XIII

Lights and Shadows of a Warm October Morning

"IN MY opinion" General Prevost's troops "have preserved the Empire," wrote the Chief Justice of New York on learning of the victory at Savannah.¹ The news was celebrated in New York by a *feu de joie* participated in by the entire garrison drawn up in review. "A tremendous acclamation proclaimed the heart-felt and universal gladness of the whole city," declared the editor of the *Mercury,* who stated that it was "impossible to describe the joy which sparkled in every countenance." A long poem of exultation appeared in Rivington's *Royal Gazette.*

At London the Park and Tower guns were fired, a rare display reserved for great occasions. In the best vein of English understatement General Prevost had informed Lord Germain that "we got both them [the French] and their American allies off our hands, in a manner which we humbly hope our gracious Sovereign will not think unhandsome." "The siege has rendered famous a sickly hole, which was in the woods, and had only one white man in it at the time General Oglethorpe landed," wrote Anthony Stokes. The outcome was "Providential," thought Governor Wright, who reported to Germain that "the Southern Parts of Nº. America I conceive are now in Your Lordships

Power whereas had the French got Footing here, I fear they wou'd have been Lost." In contemporary British eyes it was "the ever famous 9th of October" or the "Glorious Ninth."

A day of Thanksgiving was decreed by the Governor and Council of Georgia. "The Preservation of this Town, Garrison, and Inhabitants, from the formidable combined Force of French and Rebel Enemies who came against us" was "an Act of divine Providence," declared Sir James Wright. Many skeptics acknowledged, said Chief Justice Stokes, that "our deliverance was miraculous, and arose from the immediate interposition of God in our favor."

Meanwhile the widow of the aide to General McIntosh was reading a letter dated October 5th. "We have the prayers of the Church & I hope from the justness of our cause that God will decide in our favor," Major John Jones had written. Prayer proved equally barren for Polly Jones. "Consider," she had admonished her husband during the Siege, "you have two dear children and a wife whose whole happiness depends on yours. May Heaven guard you, and give me once more a happy sight of you." [2] On the 9th Jones' body would be dumped into a burial pit so shallow a friend is said to have recognized his protruding hand and accorded his shattered remains a decent burial.

For the Americans the defeat was a calamity which left the lower South in a worse way than before the French came. "The most gloomy apprehensions respecting the Southern States took possession of the minds of the people," wrote David Ramsay. That section now lay wide open to expanded British operations to the southward. A new and bloody phase of the American Revolution was about to begin. To the failure of the Allied forces to take Savannah may be traced all the bloodshed and excesses of the civil war that was to be waged in the Carolinas and in Georgia during the next three years. A victory at Savannah, to use the expressive language of Judge William Johnson, would have inflicted "a wound upon royal power from which it would scarcely have recovered in that quarter; and which would have saved oceans of blood, and prevented the exhibition of scenes of barbarous warfare of which the details would shock an Arab." For with General Clinton's springboard for invasion of South Carolina gone it may well be doubted whether the British would have been in position again to attempt a large scale offensive in that direction. A defeat would have upset Clinton's time-table. He himself declared that the loss of Savannah would prevent his proceeding with the projected attack on Charlestown. The arrival in the North of French troops under Rochambeau some months later made a Southern expedition even less feasible. The sum and substance of it was that their victory at Savannah enabled the British to proceed with their new plan of warfare in America, the reduction of the Southern colonies one by one.

The dark wine of youth had been riotously spilled on the 9th. With the fresh breeze that sprang up from the east this warm October morning the fog lifted and the sun shone bright upon a terrible spectacle. "Such a Sight I never saw before," said Prevost's aide, Major Moore, who rode up just as the battle ended—"The ditch was filled with dead" and "Many hung dead and wounded on the Abattis." Several hundred men lay dead "in a space of a few hundred Yards," declared another Britisher to whose "feeling mind" the "cries of many hundred wounded was still more distressing." To one Tory officer, however, the spectacle was more inspiring than horrendous. As he walked about the scene of carnage Captain Roderick McIntosh was heard to exclaim, "A glorious sight—our enemies slain in battle!"[3]

Upon the mind of a young Whig in Colonel William Skirving's militia the bloody spectacle left a deep and abiding impression. The "immediate emotion" aroused in seventeen year old Paul Hamilton by this "slaughter of my countrymen . . . and the loss of some of my particular friends and school fellows" was a thirst for a quick opportunity of "avenging with Interest the stroke we had received at Savannah." From that day on Hamilton possessed an "unconquerable hatred to the cause of Britain." October 9th convinced him once and for all that the "Cause of America was that of Justice." [4] It was the implacable enmity of Americans like this future South Carolina governor that made the British cause utterly hopeless.

Many a Carolina home was left in mourning by the news that came back from Georgia. In the Cheraws District, which suffered heavily, the Reverend Evan Pugh selected a highly appropriate text for the memorial sermon preached by him "for those youths lost at Savannah, 9th October past, from these parts." [5] "Man that is born of a woman is of few days, and full of trouble. He cometh forth like a flower, and is cut down." Job, XIV, 1, 2.

The battle was one of the bloodiest of the American Revolution. Only Bunker Hill exceeded it in casualties sustained by a single side. Scarcity of surgeons and lack of linen prevented wounds from being treated or dressed in many cases. Only the less seriously wounded were saved, declared Captain de Tarragon. Estimates of French losses vary but an official summary signed by M. de Fontanges lists 11 officers killed and 35 wounded and 140 of the rank and file killed and 335 wounded—a total of 521 casualties. The American losses were 231 men including both regulars and militia. For their part the British suffered only 18 killed and 39 wounded on October 9th.[6]

To Prevost's losses should be added 110 Tory troops who capitulated to 6 Americans on October 1st near the Thomas Savage plantation on the Ogeechee River. The detachment, which consisted largely of the convalescents of the Sunbury garrison, had not been able to reach Savannah by water before the blockade became effective. The entire force was captured along with several vessels through an extraordinary ruse by Colonel John White, Captains Elholm and Melvin, and three soldiers who deluded Captain Thomas French into thinking he was confronted by a superior force.[7]

Many anecdotes have been handed down about October 9th. One of the best known and widely publicized turns out to be an unashamed invention by Mason L. Weems, rivaling in every way his fable of young Washington and the cherry tree. In his *Life of Gen. Francis Marion,* Weems told a dramatic story of how Colonel Peter Horry saw the wounded Jasper limp by after the retreat bearing the regimental colors he had saved and of how that night as the immortal Sergeant's life ebbed away Horry listened to his death-bed words, moving phrases that have been repeated by many a historian. If Jasper's highly literate sentiments sound somewhat strange in the mouth of one whose letters, according to General Moultrie, were "ill written and worse spelt," they sound even stranger in the light of Horry's own comment on the subject. Across the margin of his copy of the book where the scene was described he tersely commented, "N.B., I saw Jasper on the Enemies Lines wounded & never Saw him afterwards. M^r. Weems Inventions are Great."[8] Higher than any tribute Weems could pay Sergeant Jasper with make-believe dialogues was a four word eulogy by Isaac Hayne, South Carolina's famous martyr of the Revolution. Colonel Hayne had a sort of hobby of keeping vital statistics. He never recorded more than the bare name and the date of the event. But in his list of those killed at Savannah on October 9th he departed for once from custom. The entry reads: "The Brave Serg^t Jasper."

After the battle Pulaski was carried back to camp where Dr. James Lynah extracted the fatal grapeshot. John Bee Holmes, of Charlestown, and Major Thomas Glascock have each been credited with his rescue. The hero bore the ordeal with what the surgeon called "inconceivable fortitude." He preferred, however, to take his chance of recovery with the French, afraid that if he became a litter case he might be captured and turned over to the Russians, a fate the Polish hero abhorred. Lynah always believed that he might have saved his life had the wounded officer continued under his care.[9] Romantic stories, which time will not quiet, have grown up about the circumstances of Pulaski's death and burial. According to one tale, he died at Greenwich plantation near Thunderbolt and was buried in the dead of night near the house. Many years later a skeleton said to be his was exhumed and reinterred beneath the handsome monument reared at Savannah to the memory of General Pulaski. But the more acceptable version, supported by the newspapers of the day and by Captain Bentalou, is that he died from gangrene aboard a ship en route to Charlestown.

Several of the anecdotes that have come down from October 9th involve the sayings, some no doubt apocryphal, of those who took part in the attack. There is the story of Lieutenant Vleland of the Second Carolina Regiment, who received a severe wound. An amputation became necessary. While the operation was in progress a groan escaped Vleland's lips. Laurens was standing by him. "Pardon, I beseech you, my dear Colonel, this weakness," apologized the wounded officer—"My resolution was overcome by the severity of the agony I suffered. I will no more shrink from the trial ordained me." Death helped Vleland keep his word.

James Jackson watched a similar operation performed on Lieutenant Edward Lloyd whose right arm was almost carried away by a shot. While the stump was being dressed someone commiserated with the wounded officer in regard to the unhappy situation that confronted him so early in life. "As bad a prospect as it presented to so young a man" he would not "change situations," replied Lloyd, with an American officer named Stedman who had not "acted the soldier." [10]

A macaberesque story has been handed down about Samuel Warren, of St. James, Santee. He had formerly been an officer in the British army, but during the Revolution took up arms against the King. Chagrined to hear that her nephew was fighting on the rebel side, an English aunt sent word to him that if the report was true she hoped he would have his leg or arm shot off in his first battle. As a result of a wound received on October 9th Warren's leg had to be amputated. Remembering the wish expressed by his relative, he asked the surgeon to keep the bone. After the War he placed the remnants of the limb in an elegant mahogany case to which was affixed a plate bearing the date of its loss. He sent the box to his aunt with a note. While her wish had been fulfilled he would rather, Warren informed her, be a Rebel with one leg than a Royalist with two.[11]

Count von Stedingk always recalled with satisfaction in later years the sayings of two men who served under him in the attack. During the retreat he came upon a badly wounded French soldier who was stretched beside a number of other men. They blocked the way and Colonel Stedingk stopped short so as not to trample upon their feet. Summoning all his strength, the dying man motioned to him to proceed. *"Passez, mon commandant,"* he said, "thirty men like me have made a road for you."

Another story Stedingk never tired of telling concerned a French soldier who managed to reach an almost impregnable British post during the assault. Asked how he had done it, the hero tersely replied, *"C'est que l'ennemi s'y trouvait"* ["The enemy happened to be there"].[12]

In similar vein was the retort Isidore de Lynch is reputed to have made to General d'Estaing during the attack. Count de Ségur tells the story in his *Memoirs*. The Irish-born officer was dispatched in the heat of the battle with an urgent message to the left column. Instead of passing to the rear of the advancing troops the debonair Lynch proceeded straight across the front, through the cross-fire, ignoring shouts to take a safer path. Having delivered the dispatch, he calmly returned the same way. To the amazement of all he arrived safe and sound. *"Morbleu!"* d'Estaing reprimanded him, "you must have the devil in you. Eh! Why have you selected a route along which you should have died a thousand times?" "Because," replied the happy-go-lucky officer, "it was the shortest."

Count Dillon was anxious for his troops to distinguish themselves in the assault. A story is told that he offered 100 guineas reward to the first man to brave the hail of fire from the British entrenchments and plant a fascine in the ditch below the works. Not a soldier moved. Much mortified, Colonel Dillon began to upbraid them for cowardice. A sergeant-major stepped forward. "Had you not, sir," he protested, "held out a sum of money as a temptation, your grenadiers would, one and all, have presented themselves." [13] With this, the soldiers to a man advanced. Of one hundred and ninety-four only ninety were to return, it is said.

But it was Major d'Erneville of the Volunteers from the Windward Isles who made the most gallant reply credited to these Frenchmen. Severely wounded in the right arm while leading the vanguard, he was taken as a prisoner into Savannah. As the weeks passed his condition did not improve. General Prevost urged the Chevalier to submit to an amputation of his arm which might have saved his life.

The brave Frenchman refused. "With but one hand," protested d'Erneville, "I could not serve my prince in the field; and if so disabled, life is not worth preserving."[14] He died on Christmas day and was buried with full military honors by the British.

XIV

The Count Raises the Siege

AFTER the battle the wounded d'Estaing had ridden on horseback to the French hospital at the waterside settlement called Thunderbolt. There is a story that he shut himself up for three days, refusing to speak to anyone and that the only answer the surgeon could get from him was, "I have a deep wound which is not in your power to cure." [1] Some say that the General pointed to his heart. The wound there was deep indeed and these undoubtedly were moments of bitterness for the Count, bitterness which letters of sympathy from his officers did not assuage. They would have been even more galling had he known what Bougainville was saying about him. The wound in his leg, that sharp-tongued officer was writing, was "rendered dangerous by the state of his blood, and, I think, that of his soul!" [2]

But the story that d'Estaing shut himself up for three days is not supported by the evidence. Captain Séguier de Terson, who was admitted to his presence on the 11th, reported that the Count seemed appreciative of the inquiries about his health. As senior colonel Dillon was ostensibly in command but d'Estaing remained in actual control, making all policy decisions. He himself sent word to General Lincoln on the 9th that the Siege was being immediately raised by the French.

During the remainder of his stay in Georgia the wounded d'Estaing was harassed by requests and demands of all sorts. Besides the details of retreat and embarkation and the complicated problem of the destination of his ships, numerous lesser troubles beset him. The British were demanding the return of two carriages they had lent the French to convey their wounded to Thunderbolt. There were demands from the Americans that they stay on. Dillon and Noailles were nagging him about retreating to Charlestown. There were requests from army officers asking permission to go back to France instead of to the Isles. There were petitions from naval officers for duty on other ships. In short, there was an eternal refrain of *Mon Général* this and *Mon Général* that.

Then there was Mrs. Jourdina Cunningham Baillie. On top of all his other worries this Tory female was now insisting that the Count return "the Chair horse & Saddle & bridle I handed your Excellency the morning after your Arrival at the Orphan House."[3] Horses! It was all these Americans seemed to think about. General Lincoln had even officially complained to him at one point about the French taking horses from the American camp. The Count had had to fall back on the explanation that the blame rested with American civilians.[4] Not only was he being dunned by Mrs. Baillie for the horse but even for a bed borrowed for his personal use after he was wounded. She had also billed him for the cattle, hogs, and poultry the French troops had taken from Bethesda. *Sacrénom!* They belonged to Lady Huntingdon in the first place. Besides the Americans had stripped the plantations around Savannah of everything *they* needed. The only difference was a trifling one—Lincoln had given receipts for what the Americans appropriated.

What a fine contrast between Mrs. Baillie who had tried to fool him by hanging the portrait of "Liberty" in a conspicuous place at Bethesda and the owner of Greenwich! Jane Bowen had "endeavored," she assured the Count, "to furnish everything in my power for the use of the Troops under your Excellency's command." She had provided "Beds & Blankets, fodder for the Cavalry, and Boats and Negroes for obtaining provisions for the Hospital." She had housed naval officers. She had also contributed, she wrote, "all my Horses for the Dragoons." [5] The only thing she asked in return was that her home not be turned into a hospital like the place next door. Despite Mrs. Mulryne's presence the French had pillaged Bonaventure in a way that "would shock you to hear her relate," declared Anthony Stokes.

Such was to be expected in the case of the property of a dyed-in-the-wool Tory like Colonel Mulryne, who had hied himself off to Savannah as soon as the French arrived. But the necessities of war sometimes recognized no distinction between the treatment of foes and friends. General d'Estaing was forced to deny the widow Bowen's request. Her house was badly needed. After all, 12 French officers and 200 men were already hospitalized at Thunderbolt with fever while 377 wounded men had to be accommodated after the attack.

Ironically enough, Monsieur d'Estaing now found himself a patient at Mrs. Bowen's home. He suffered greatly from his wounds and looked "extraordinarily thin," reported a French officer. As he convalesced at "Half Moon Bluff" on the marsh-fringed creek, d'Estaing could reflect bitterly upon the events of the past eighteen months. There was plenty of time for reflection during these long days for we are informed that he slept very little [*"il dort très peu"*].[6] When he left Toulon in April, 1778, a popular song was ringing in his ears:

"*Combattons, vive France, Antoinette et Bourbon.
Vive d'Estaing. Vive tout bon luron.*

F . . . de Keppel, sacrénom.
F . . . de la vieille Angleterre
Et de son pavillon."

There had been those first great moments of expectation when the French fleet arrived in American waters. "I love you tenderly, Monsieur le Comte; you are the man I wish to see at the head of this squadron, and the man who pleases my heart," his kinsman and fellow-Auvergnat, Marquis de Lafayette, had gushed in welcoming him to America.

But some demon of ill-fortune seemed to dog d'Estaing's tracks on this side of the Atlantic. Everywhere he had gone he had been just too late. Nearly everything he attempted seemed to go wrong. In his words, he had encountered an "incredible series of untoward circumstances." "Fortune," he reported to M. de Sartine, had "dealt some hard knocks" and if occasionally she "chucked us under the chin, her caresses were brief and had been sold a little dearly." And now instead of atoning for everything by a brilliant triumph at Savannah he was bringing back, to use the expression of the historian Doniol, the reputation of *"une vaine forfanterie."*

The margin between glory and failure had been so close! How was a general to accomplish anything when he had to contend, said d'Estaing's apologists, "not only against the vagaries of the sea and unforeseen obstacles, but also against disobedience and treachery which dared all because of the uncertainty of punishment"?[7] *Ces Américains!* Their traitors had exposed his plans. They had allowed Maitland to slip into Savannah through the inland waterways. They had misrepresented everything from the state of Savannah's defenses to the size and quality of their army.

But Meyronnet de Saint-Marc tells us that d'Estaing also blamed a fellow-countryman in the American service.

It had been largely upon the proposals of M. de Brétigny that the French came to Georgia. The embittered Count turned on this "old musketeer of the King" during a conference and "accused him of being the cause of the misfortunes that had befallen us." Colonel Brétigny did not take the charge meekly. He "never imagined," he replied warmly, "that he would excite us to come to this country with such large sea forces; besides he had always said that the capture of Savannah could only be by a *coup de main* and if we had attacked the city immediately after landing it would have been taken." The basic error, he had always maintained, was in bringing the American army to Savannah—"It would have been much wiser to persuade General Lincoln to attack Port Royal." The Count cooled off after M. de Brétigny had spoken his mind. "It was better to forget everything," said d'Estaing—"common misfortunes should unite them."

But d'Estaing would find solace of a kind. His very wounds were to be a source of satisfaction. "I even find myself happy in my situation," he wrote Governor Rutledge before he sailed, "since my blood serves to refute bad intentions." The appearance of his fleet on the American coast had resulted in the British evacuation of Rhode Island. The prizes taken off Savannah brought a net $737,955. Furthermore, prior to leaving Georgia he received a communication from John Wereat, President of the Supreme Executive Council of the State, expressing the hope that the French general would "confer on us the happiness of accepting a grant of twenty thousand Acres of Land and the right of Citizenship." [8] The Count later had to remind Georgia of this offer. He received the grant in 1784 at which time the privileges of citizenship were also conferred by the State. The gift of land "gratified him much" and d'Estaing told his friend, Thomas Jefferson, that the title of American citizen was "dear to my heart." It was no more than was his due. After all, was he not, as he later boasted to George Washington, "ye only French general officer who has shed his blood for America"? But we have gotten ahead of the story.

Oblivious to Count d'Estaing's repeated statement that the French could remain only eight days on their coast, the Americans begged him to stay on. "The Repulse seems not to dispirit our men, as they are convinced it was only owing to a mistake of the ground," wrote Charles C. Pinckney to his mother on the day of the assault. "I have not the least doubt but that we shall soon be in possession of Savannah," added Pinckney. In Charlestown the newspapers tried to cushion disappointment over the result of the attack. "The reduction of Savannah is not doubtful," one editor assured his readers, "but suspended only, because not worth so many lives as might be sacrificed by a more rapid progress." [9]

But the French had had enough. The Siege was raised immediately. "No argument could dissuade" d'Estaing, reported General Lincoln, who informed the Continental Congress that he had endeavored to "divert him from his purpose—representing to him, in the strongest terms in my power, the evils, which would attend the measure." "Could he have remained," the American commander told a friend, "I see nothing which could have prevented our success." [10] "What a pity it is," said Charles C. Pinckney, "that Count D'Estaing could not be prevailed on to stay longer, the Enemy I believe are in want both of provisions & ammunition & it is impossible for them to hold out long even if we were only to blockade them." [11]

To the argument that it was a matter of personal honor for him to stay d'Estaing is quoted as replying, "Gentlemen, if my honor is to be lost by not taking the city, it is lost already; but I deem my honor to consist in the honor of my country, and that honor is my country's interest." [12]

Upon learning of the Count's decision Governor Rutledge of South Carolina wrote him in "Astonishment & Concern which I have not Words to express." "Do not then Sir," he entreated, "blast all our Hopes, by withdrawing, in the very Moment of Victory."[13] Rutledge even sent a delegation to see the French General. As an alternative the Count was urged to retreat through South Carolina and to embark his troops from Charlestown. Such a plan was favored by a majority of a Council of War convened by Colonel Dillon.

"*Oh, mon Dieu!*" exploded the impatient Bougainville when he learned such a project was being considered, "*Fais pour nous en miracle*" ["Work some miracle for us"]. For once the great navigator could agree with his Vice-Admiral. D'Estaing's mind was closed on the subject. The embarkation was to be made by way of Thunderbolt and not South Carolina. At his direction Colonel Dillon drew up the plan of retreat though personally opposing it. He argued that if contrary winds should delay the embarkation the whole French army might be destroyed. When he announced the plan, the older officers protested, Dillon reported, "So, at an age at which a man scarcely has his own liberty at his disposal he has the right of exposing troops to the shameful extremity of surrendering without a blow, or reducing them to die of hunger."

Dillon and Noailles took it upon themselves to deliver a strongly worded protest to d'Estaing in which they pressed upon him the advantages of Charlestown as the base of retreat.[14] The matter ended abruptly. "Not moved by so eloquent a document," said Captain de Tarragon, the General sent word that "he wished the retreat to be made by way of the place he had decided upon" and if the two young colonels persisted in their opposition, he intended to "send down M. de Bougainville to command the army." It had been a compliment to them that he had not done so in the first place, explained d'Estaing in his Notes.

THE COUNT RAISES THE SIEGE

Not only did Bougainville's grade entitle him to the command but "he was an excellent officer on both elements."

The Count subsequently relented in his views to the extent of permitting part of the embarkation to be made from Causton's Bluff, a short distance north, but at a more protected place on the same river on which Thunderbolt was located. He had his reasons for resisting what he described in his Notes as "the epidemic of retreat via Charlestown." One of them was that his troops would desert "by the hundreds in order to establish themselves in this country." The Irish were particularly susceptible. "American recruiting officers would have had an abundant harvest in the Dillon Regiment," said the Count. Discipline and desertion had been bad enough as it was since their defeat. "You are aware," Colonel Dillon reminded the French General somewhat curtly, "that personal authority (*moi-même*) is no longer known by your troops." Colonel de Rouvray was complaining during this same period about the "spirit of insubordination" in the Negro corps he commanded.[15] Sentinels had to be placed around the French camp to prevent desertions.

After entering into a formal convention concerning the retreat, the Allies went their separate ways, the Americans leaving twenty-four hours before d'Estaing's troops commenced to retire. The French were unmolested by the British, who seemed content enough with the fact that they were leaving. In Count d'Estaing's words, "the troops returned aboard the vessels not only without leaving anything behind but more than that, without having been attacked, annoyed or even followed." Indeed, there were those who suspected collusion between the French and English. The latter actually proposed, said Dillon, that if they did not accompany Lincoln to Charlestown, their withdrawal would not be impeded. The Americans saw d'Estaing's young officers visit the town daily, a fact that was bound to generate suspicion. In Savannah itself there were puzzled faces. "Very extraordinary," thought one Britisher, that "our Troops never attempted to harass them in their Retreat." [16]

With the raising of the Siege and departure of d'Estaing's troops the Royalist propaganda machine went into full operation. "Mutual Animosities and Revilings have arisen to such a height betwixt the French and Rebels since they were repulsed by us, that they were almost ready to cut one another's Throats," claimed a British sympathizer. "The inhabitants of Carolina declare they never will draw a sword again in the presence of a Frenchman, unless to plunge it into his bosom," reported a New York newspaper which asserted that the Allies had parted company, "mutually execrating each other as unfortunate poltroons." [17]

But on the surface at least cordial relations were preserved. The *Gazette de France* could say that "The greatest union has subsisted between the combined forces." General Lincoln, whose tact had much to do with this show of harmony, informed Congress that d'Estaing "has undoubtedly the interest of America much at heart." "His want of success," added this benign American, "will not lessen our ideas of his merit." Not a word of criticism about the French ever came from Lincoln. "The causes of failure," he said in his Journal, "were such as attend the uncertain events of War and are rather to be lamented than at present investigated." The Journals of the Continental Congress reflect a similar philosophy at Philadelphia. Their defeat was "to be attributed to those incidents which in the hand of Omnipotence determine all human events," President Samuel Huntington told the new French envoy. "Our disappointment is compensated," he added, "by reflecting on the perfect harmony that subsisted between the generals and the troops of the two nations."

THE COUNT RAISES THE SIEGE

Publicly the Americans had nothing but praise for d'Estaing. Every effort was made in the press to smooth things over. A contributor to a Philadelphia newspaper declared that "The wounds which he has received, the blood which he has shed in our service, will be remembered by us. He has displayed a most heroic valour, tempered with prudence, and the troops under his command have acted with the greatest courage." "On all occasions," attested a South Carolinian, "the Count d'Estaing shewed himself a brave man, and acted in every respect consistent with the dignity of his character, as a Nobleman of a distinguished family, and as a gentleman whose best wishes were most ardent for the good and protection of the United States." [18]

In the wake of American criticism of Admiral d'Estaing following the Newport affair John Laurens had deplored the absurd anti-French prejudices "inherited from the British Nation." Association with the Count at Savannah failed to change Colonel Laurens' sentiments. To his father he wrote shortly after the Siege that "We are as much indebted as if his efforts had been attended with the most complete success." [19]

America indeed owed Charles-Henri d'Estaing a great deal. He had responded to her calls at a critical time. Without orders from France he had brought an army to Georgia to co-operate in a campaign which might have turned the whole course of the Revolution. His own blood had been shed in the common cause. He had sacrificed the lives of many brave Frenchmen in the attempt to take Savannah. Mistakes had been made. But the blame for the failure of the expedition should by no means be placed solely at his door. And one should always remember that if M. d'Estaing had been a shade luckier his name would be as familiar in America today as Lafayette's.

XV

The Captains and the Kings Depart

THE French left Georgia in "chaos," said Bougainville. Typical of the confusion was the case of twelve members of the Cambresis Regiment who showed up aboard his *Guerrier*. He sent them to the *Robuste* for orders. De Grasse directed them to the *Languedoc*. From the flagship they were sent back to the *Robuste*. They were thence redirected to the vessel from which they commenced these briny peregrinations. Where the wandering French grenadiers finally landed we are not told for the *Guerrier* changed its destination after starting out for the West Indies.

A severe gale which blew up on October 28th helped disperse the once great armada of Vice-Admiral d'Estaing. At four o'clock that afternoon a cable of the *Languedoc* snapped (one of the seventy lost by the French ships off Savannah). The other cable had to be cut and the big vessel was forced to set sail eastward. In the wake of the flagship M. de Bougainville hurled a parting insult at Count d'Estaing. In his choicest vein of sarcasm he noted in his Journal, "The general has decamped after showing the thoughtfulness of signalling to his squadron the order to remain in perdition on this fatal coast." "When will he re-

THE CAPTAINS AND THE KINGS DEPART

turn and how will all this end up?" wondered Bougainville.

Contrary winds prevented the *Languedoc* from returning to the anchorage. Several of d'Estaing's captains were left on the coast of Georgia without orders. The Vice-Admiral could blame it all on the American pilots. They had assured the French that a storm at this season of the year was "*contre* nature."

De Grasse returned to the West Indies instead of sailing to the Chesapeake as the Vice-Admiral expected. Had he executed his orders as well as the Marquis de Vaudreuil, who took the *Fendant* to Maryland, Charlestown would not have been attacked by General Clinton, d'Estaing told Washington.[1] Fame and glory at Yorktown followed by oblivion and disgrace in France after his disastrous defeat in the West Indies on April 12, 1782, awaited Count de Grasse. Many of these naval officers were to be present that dolorous day. Among them was M. de Bernard de Marigny, who commanded the frigates which transported the troops to Grenada. He was to meet a fiery death in the Battle of the Saintes. Desperately wounded, the Count lay stretched on a bed in his cabin when some sailors burst in and announced that the *César* was about to blow up. "So much the better!" replied the dying de Marigny. "The English will not get her. Close the door, my friends, and try to save yourselves."[2]

But to return to the Savannah expedition, one of the Vice-Admiral's principal worries, judging by the length of his explanations on the subject to the Ministry, seems to have been the fate of Colonel de Noailles. Against his better judgment he had permitted the young nobleman to visit Savannah in company with the English prisoner, Thomas MacKenzie, who persuaded the French that he had business there of a pressing nature for a few hours.[3] Assuring his superiors that M. de Noailles probably got away aboard the *Chimère* which he was certain had remained in the River for several days, d'Estaing sarcastically added that he had told him that the real reason he wanted to go to Savannah was not to see the place, as the Vicomte pretended, but rather to "scold" the enemy for "not having attempted all that he had predicted they could and should do and for not preventing, in accordance with his expectations, the retreat of the Americans and ourselves."[4] How wrong his two young Colonels had been! D'Estaing was not called *"Monsieur la Ressource"* for nothing. He was no fool. "The enemy," the Count would boast to M. de Sartine, "were not able to have and did not have so much as a pistol to show for a trophy."

Just as the French General suspected, Colonel de Noailles did plenty of talking while at Savannah. He was quoted by a British source as saying that "The Panic of the Troops last embarked was such that they would have laid down their Arms had we detached 500 of our Troops to pursue them." He was also represented as declaring that "all the French Land and Sea Officers greatly exclaimed against Comte d'Estaing, and also at the rascally behaviour of the Rebels on the Day of Battle."[5]

As the *Robuste* drew away from the *Languedoc* d'Estaing was honored with a parting *"Vive le roi."* But the sailors did not join in. Captain Séguier de Terson, who was aboard de Grasse's ship, could not help but observe their "great pleasure at getting rid of the vice admiral." On this ever-dominant note of discord and confusion the sojourn of Count d'Estaing's squadron in American waters came to an end.

The crossing proved a terrible one for the *Languedoc*. The first few days were marked by "frightful rolling" in "monstrous seas" which Admiral d'Estaing described as "higher than those I experienced off the Cape of Good Hope." The ship was taking in ten inches of water an hour and the pumps were inadequate. A terrible epidemic of eye trouble developed among the crew. The flagship was without an anchor. To the "inexpressible joy" of everyone aboard her they met up with the *Provence* on the way home and signalled her down. Aboard her were espied two anchors. But the heavy seas did not permit the transfer. "It was the torture of Tantalus," wrote the Count, "to look constantly upon this indispensable equipment and not possess it. Never has an anchor been so greedily eyed. Molière's Miser did not find the eyes of his cash-box so beautiful."

At Brest the Vice-Admiral was coldly received by the French naval authorities. He dispatched a long report to M. de Sartine, the last paragraph of which was written in a hand described by d'Estaing as "still feeble." Apologizing for adding to his lengthy account, he said, "I should prefer, as I had the honor of remarking to you before leaving Martinique, to be thought condemnable rather than to find myself guilty in my own eyes as I would have been had I done anything less." [6] A story is told that d'Estaing asked M. de Sartine to request the King to give him leave to fall at his Majesty's feet in thanks for the confidence that had been reposed in him. "At my feet!" exclaimed Louis XVI. "Oh, no! It is in my arms that I will receive him." [7]

Versailles took its cue from the French people who remembered Grenada and forgot Savannah. A victory-hungry public gave d'Estaing a hero's welcome. Flowers were strewn upon his carriage as it passed through the countryside. "Armed with his glorious crutches," he appeared before the King, who expressed "extreme satisfaction" at his conduct. "An innumerable crowd," it was said, "awaited him at Versailles, and followed him to the house of the Ministers. His procession had the air of a triumph." [8] "I met with a reception infinitely beyond my merits," confessed the Vice-Admiral. Considering what he might have achieved during his fifteen months in American waters as compared to his actual accomplishments, one must concur.

A greater storm than that which scattered the fleet off Georgia would one day overtake these Frenchmen.

Like many of his companions-in-arms d'Estaing was to be caught in the maelstrom of the coming French Revolution. During that epoch he steered a devious course between the liberal principles with which he became imbued and his adherence to the monarchy. He wrote an eloquent letter to the Queen in 1789 warning of the dangers ahead for the royal family. From time to time he transmitted advice to Marie Antoinette which was neither solicited nor heeded. She never forgave or forgot his inexplicable conduct at the head of the National Guard on the terrible days of October 5–6th. He incurred her lasting displeasure. The "whiff of grapeshot" with which he might have ended the Revolution at its very inception was to be postponed for six terror-filled years until a young artillery officer named Bonaparte came upon the scene.

Ambition drew d'Estaing deeper and deeper into the swirling vortex of French politics. When Louis XVI put on the Revolutionary cockade at Paris, the Count exclaimed, "Sire, with that cockade and the Third Estate you will conquer Europe!" Michaud says that he made himself "patriot by calculation without ceasing to be courtier by habit." But he could not forever run with hare and hunt with hound. Called by Fouquier-Tinville as a witness at the trial of Marie Antoinette, he would say nothing to inculpate the widow of Louis XVI, but his testimony proved not only unhelpful to that unfortunate lady but compromising to himself. His quarters were searched. No incriminating papers were found but the search turned up several miniatures of the King, the Queen, and Count d'Artois as well as some medallions of the Festivals of the

Federation—counter-revolutionary propaganda! D'Estaing was brought to trial in 1794, accused of plotting the escape of Louis XVI and of having brought the Flanders Regiment to Paris in '89. "When you cut off my head, send it to the English, they will pay you well for it!" he told his prosecutors at the end of a trial that was not without stains upon his memory. The *ci-devant* darling of the Bourbons was beheaded on April 28, 1794. A grovelling letter of appeal which d'Estaing wrote to the judge went undelivered. He was in his sixty-fourth year.

What of the fate of the other Frenchmen we have met in these pages? It may be interesting to see what became of some of Count d'Estaing's associates of September–October, 1779. Careers that brought fame, turbulence, and tragedy awaited many of these men.

Arthur Dillon had revealed to Colonel Stedingk while in America a premonition that he would die a violent death. It came to him in the French Revolution. Accused of plotting the escape of Danton and Desmoulins, he was guillotined in 1794. The tragic Lucile Desmoulins died the same day. "I have been the cause of your death," she apologized as they awaited the tumbrels that carried them to the scaffold. "You have been the pretext," he corrected her with a smile. He died gallantly. When he reached the scaffold a lady about to be executed asked, "Oh! Monsieur Dillon, do you wish to go first?" Doffing his hat as he ascended the platform ahead of her, the General replied, "What would I not do for a lady!" [9] "*Vive le roi!*" he shouted as he went to his death. One of the Count's daughters was the charming diarist, the Marquise de la Tour du Pin. The other was tall, domineering Fanny Dillon, protégée of Josephine Beauharnais and a favorite of Napoleon, who played the match-maker in her marriage to the celebrated Count Bertrand. She accompanied her husband to St. Helena and remained at the side of the exiled Emperor to the end. General Théobald-Hyacinth Dillon was assassinated in 1792 by his own Jacobin-infected troops when he tried to prevent their panic-stricken flight from the Austrians. His mutilated remains were placed in the Panthéon. In the same year General Joseph O'Moran, who had carried in the summons to surrender at Savannah, went to the guillotine for "inefficiency." Anne-Claude de Tarragon, who had served with his brother in the Armagnac Regiment in Georgia, survived Savannah, Saint Christopher, Tabago, Saint Lucie, and the Battle of the Saintes only to fall a victim to a washer-woman. Informed on by her for corresponding with Bouillé and Lafayette, he was guillotined in 1793.

Louis-Marie de Noailles became the leader of the liberal element among the French nobility, warmly espousing the cause of popular reform in the early stages of the Revolution. It is said that it was he who carried Marie Antoinette to safety when the *canaille* swarmed about the royal carriage on the return from Varennes though others assert that the Queen pointedly spurned his arm on that occasion for that of a member of the "right." Eventually he had to emigrate. He settled in Philadelphia where he added to the fortune he brought with him to America. Within the space of a month in 1794 the guillotine snuffed out the lives of his wife and both of his aged parents.

Re-entering the French military service in 1803, Noailles bravely defended the Môle St. Nicolas for several months. "A French general cannot surrender without shame as long as he has supplies, ammunition and devoted soldiers," he replied to the British demands. Escaping to sea from San Domingo, his ship was hailed down by a British corvette. In perfect English he replied that he too was looking for General de Noailles. That night the French vessel sailed alongside the unsuspecting English ship. At the head of twenty grenadiers he leaped aboard. There was a desperate battle in the dark in which he was wounded. The enemy vessel was captured but General de Noailles died a few days later in Cuba. Jean Gudin has immortalized this outstanding exploit of French naval annals in one of his best marine canvasses.

Though Louis-Antoine de Bougainville believed, as he told Gouverneur Morris, that Louis XVI was "betrayed by the Weakness if not by the Wickedness of his Councillors" he remained unfalteringly faithful to the Bourbons. During the French Revolution the famous explorer nearly realized the fulfillment of a strange prophecy made by him in his Journal years before. "I have read today in the Abbé Vély's History of France," the captain of the *Guerrier* had written, "that Hugues de Bouville, chamberlain of the King and Secretary, was killed in 1315 [1304] in the battle of Mons-en-Puelle while defending the person of King Philip, the Handsome." "It is as the secretary of the cabinet," Bougainville added in a curious strain of mysticism, "that I make a note of this item here." Ready to die for the Bourbons, he stood at the side of Louis XVI when the rabble invaded the Tuileries on the tempestuous nights of June 20th and August 10th, 1792. His presence of mind saved the French monarch's life on the first of those occasions, says Madame Campan in her *Memoirs*. "Put the King in the recess of the window, and place benches before him!" Bougainville shouted as the assassins approached. He escaped the guillotine almost by a miracle. Marked for death, orders were dispatched to bring him to Paris for trial. Robespierre's sudden fall resulted in his release. The fascinated Napoleon, who teasingly called him "*M. le Royaliste*," made Admiral de Bougainville a Count of the Empire.

A number of the noblemen who served under d'Estaing at Savannah left France in the Revolution. The list of *émigrés*, in addition to Noailles, included the names of

Prévalaye, d'Hervilly, Vaudreuil, Puysegur, Rouvray, Bruyères, Colbert, Béthisy, and Albert de Rions. The last commanded the naval base at Toulon during the violent days there in 1790. When the mob demanded that he deliver up an officer serving under him, he stepped forward and said, "If you want another victim here am I but if you want one of my officers you must first pass over me." Clubbed, kicked and insulted, de Rions was dragged to prison through the streets amid cries of "Hang him! Cut off his head!" He later emigrated and served in the army of Condé.

Outstanding among the counter-revolutionists was Admiral Jean-Honoré, Comte de Trogoff. As a young *lieutenant de vaisseau* he had carried Captain Séguier de Terson's men on a September evening in 1779 to the rendezvous near the *Languedoc* off Tybee. In the French Revolution Admiral de Trogoff delivered his squadron over to the British at Toulon and helped them capture that port from the Revolutionists.

Few strove harder to secure the safety of the Bourbons than Count d'Hervilly, who had taken over Fontanges' duties when the latter became a casualty at Savannah. He was commended by d'Estaing for his services. During the French Revolution d'Hervilly suggested to the King that he be allowed to expel the Assembly forcibly, arguing that it would be "a mighty day for the royal cause." When the mob stormed the Tuileries it was he who regretfully delivered the King's order to the faithful Swiss Guard to hold their fire. In 1795 he led an unsuccessful *émigré* descent on the French coast. Mortally wounded, he died in London.

Despite his aristocratic background, Guy-Pierre, Comte de Kersaint, who commanded the *Iphigénie* at Savannah, entertained Republican sentiments. Author of a well-known pamphlet attacking feudal privileges, M. de Kersaint for a time possessed great influence in the Assembly.

But as a Girondin he denounced the September massacres. "It is time that gibbets were erected for the murderers," he declared, insisting amid the boos of the Jacobin galleries upon a fair trial for the deposed ruler. After the King's execution he resigned, unable to undergo, Kersaint informed the Assembly, "the shame of sitting there among men of blood." On trumped-up charges that he had insulted the Republic by resigning and conspired to restore the monarchy he was guillotined after a mock trial.

In the States-General, in which a number of the veterans of Savannah served, the Marquis de Vaudreuil proved a strong member of the "right." On the night of October 5-6, 1789, the old naval hero forced his way with some other officers into the royal palace. Reaching the side of the King, they helped keep the mob at bay. De Vaudreuil later emigrated to England, returning to France, as did many of his former associates, after Bonaparte's rise to power.

Many of the Frenchmen who were present at the Siege of Savannah survived the Reign of Terror and won prominence in the time of the Directory, the Consulate, and the Empire.

Imprisoned for a spell during the Revolution, Laurent de Truguet attained a position of considerable influence in the Directory, holding the portfolio of Minister of Marine and later the post of ambassador to Spain. He lost favor with Bonaparte after facing him down before the Council of Five Hundred. "Of what pamphlets do you speak?" exclaimed the angry First Consul as he advanced on Truguet when the latter charged that pamphleteering was corrupting the public spirit. D'Estaing's aide had not faltered twenty years before in the face of British cannon at the Spring Hill redoubt. He did not flinch now. "You know as well as I do," he replied, standing his ground firmly.

Another former naval lieutenant of d'Estaing who became Minister of Marine of France was Georges-René Pléville Le Peley. He had been badly hurt in the anti-French riots at Boston while the squadron was there following the Newport affair. Yet it was Le Peley, we are told, who won the Count over to the idea of the expedition to Georgia. As a result of being wounded at sea, he had a wooden leg which itself had been shot off twice in subsequent naval engagements. "The bullet has fooled itself; it has only given work to a carpenter," joked the salty veteran on one such occasion. Despite his disability he managed to distinguish himself on October 9th by re-forming a company in the swamp while under fire. Le Peley adopted the principles of the French Revolution and in 1798 became Minister of Marine.

Several of d'Estaing's young soldiers later rose to be generals. Among them was Isidore de Lynch, who refused to follow his aristocratic friends into exile during the French Revolution. He signalized himself in the Battle of Valmy and filled posts of responsibility under Napoleon. Jean-Baptiste Jourdan quickly jumped to the rank of general in the French Revolution. He led the Republican troops to the great victory at Wattignies and went on to become a Marshal under the Emperor. Claude Dallemagne, who also served in the ranks in Georgia, became one of France's bravest generals. He commanded Bonaparte's best storm troops in Italy, was highly commended for his services at Lodi and Austerlitz, and was made a Baron of the Empire. In the casualty lists at Savannah one finds the name of Lieutenant Labarre of the Dragoons of Condé, who was wounded in the chest during the attack. In the French Revolution Labarre adopted the popular cause, became a general, and died a hero's death in the defense of the Pyrenees against the Spanish. His name and deeds were inscribed on a column in the Panthéon. Gaultier de Kervé-

THE CAPTAINS AND THE KINGS DEPART 143

guen had ranked high on d'Estaing's board of strategy at Savannah. Captain de Tarragon mentioned his name among d'Estaing's staff officers who supposed that the mere noise of cannon was going to intimidate the British into surrender. Napoleon thought little of the military capabilities of Gaultier, whom he described as "good for office work." But it was a talent that was put to excellent use in various military and civil posts during the days of the Directory, the Consulate, and the Empire.

Many of the young officers in Count d'Estaing's fleet at Savannah were also to be heard from in later years.

Maurice-Julien Émeriau, then a mere boy of eighteen, had been one of the first to reach the British entrenchments on October 9th. For his gallant services as chief of squadron in the Battle of the Nile he was promoted to rear admiral. That and a warm letter of sympathy from General Bonaparte was consolation for a shattered arm. Later Émeriau was given high naval commands by the Emperor. Édouard de Missiessy, an officer aboard the *Vaillant* at Savannah, fled France during the Terror. Missiessy became friendly with Bonaparte on his return and rose to great prominence in the navy under the Emperor, who made him a Count. Pierre-Raymond de Brisson, who served on the *César*, attained a degree of fame by a book describing his shipwreck on the African coast and his life as a Moorish slave.

Among the *gardes du pavillon* in d'Estaing's fleet at Savannah was a sixteen-year-old nobleman, Pierre-Charles de Villeneuve. His was a name destined to become one of doleful memory for France. Sympathizing with the Revolutionary principles, Villeneuve rose rapidly in rank. It was he who led the French and Spanish fleets into the awful catastrophe of Trafalgar. Fearful of the Emperor's wrath, the melancholic Admiral later took his own life, thankful, he wrote, that "I have no child to receive my horrible inheritance, and live under the weight of my name!"

Henri Gantheaume, who served in the fleet at Savannah, survived the terrible holocaust of Casabianca's ship at Aboukir Bay. "If you have come out alive," Bonaparte wrote at the time, "it is clear that you are destined by fate to avenge our navy and our friends." It was Gantheaume's frigate that carried the future emperor back to France. Gantheaume later held important naval commands under him. "You hold in your hands the destinies of the world," Napoleon told him in 1804. But this veteran of Savannah was never destined to measure up to these hopes. In the retrospect of St. Helena the former Emperor would complain: "The instant I put forward any new idea, immediately Gantheaume and the whole of the naval section were on my back.—Sire, you can't do that.—"

Perhaps in Aristide-Aubert du Petit-Thouars the Emperor might have found an answer to his prayer for a successful admiral. In the early stages of the French Revolution he headed an expedition that was sent to search for the missing La Pérouse who was accompanied on his ill-fated voyage to the Pacific by the Marquis de Pierrevert, another veteran of Savannah. The mission came to grief when du Petit-Thouars was arrested in Brazil as a result of developments in France. After a sojourn in America he returned to France at the end of the Reign of Terror to reclaim the rank of which he had been stripped because of his noble birth. As captain of the ancient *Tonnant* he was to know a night of greater conflagration than the one at Savannah when he steered a boat "under the walls of a city ablaze." His death in the Battle of Aboukir was an epic of valor. Both of his legs were shot off. What was left of his body he ordered propped up in a barrel of bran on the quarter-deck. From that position he directed the firing as long as a gun was serviceable. Then an arm was carried away. "Never surrender!" du Petit-Thouars murmured as he died. "Crew of the *Tonnant, n'amène jamais ton pavillon!*" ["Never lower your flag!"] When the victors boarded the ship they found only corpses on the demasted deck. But the tricolor was still flying.

XVI

And What of Colonel Maitland?

THE story of the subsequent careers of the Americans who fought at Savannah is drab reading beside the turbulent, often tragic chronicle of the French. Many of them were to make their bright mark in public life in the days to come.

Thomas Pinckney was Governor of South Carolina, Congressman, Minister to Great Britain and the head of an important mission to Madrid. Charles Cotesworth Pinckney also became a diplomat, winning fame for his role in the "XYZ Affair." He was twice the unsuccessful Federalist candidate for the Presidency. William Few, Pierce Butler, and James Jackson were to be United States Senators. Jackson also served as Governor of Georgia and in Congress. Four veterans of the Siege—Charles Cotesworth Pinckney, Pierce Butler, John F. Grimké, and William Few—became members of the Federal Constitutional Convention. Joseph Habersham was Postmaster-General under Presidents Washington, John Adams, and Jefferson. The catalogue of disasters of Benjamin Lincoln during the Revolution in no way diminished Washington's esteem for him. The New England General was accorded the honor of receiving Lord Cornwallis' sword at Yorktown. He was Secretary of War for a time during the Confederation. Lincoln quelled Shays' Rebellion in 1787. David Meriwether and Samuel Hammond represented Georgia in Congress, Hammond

AND WHAT OF COLONEL MAITLAND? 147

later serving as President of the Territorial Council which governed Missouri. Hugh Rutledge, Grimké, and William Hasell Gibbes distinguished themselves in the judicial field. Paul Hamilton became Governor of South Carolina and Secretary of the Navy under Madison.

Many a county bears the names of men who fought on the American side at Savannah. The memory of Jasper was so honored in Georgia, South Carolina, Mississippi, Texas, Missouri, Indiana, Illinois, and Iowa. Marion is close behind in such honors. Such was the influence of Weems' book upon Americans of his day that Georgia even named a county for a veteran of the Siege whom General Horry called "a Thief & a Villain." John Newton took part in a guerrilla exploit near Savannah in company with Sergeant Jasper, an incident which Weems dramatized in his *Life of Gen. Francis Marion*. On the margin of the book Horry wrote the terse commentary, "Jasper was an honest Man; but Newton was a Thief & a Villain—"

One of the first Frenchmen to come to the aid of America during the Revolution had been Pierre-Charles L'Enfant. The day before the attack on the lines at Savannah the Major led five men through a brisk fire in a futile attempt to ignite the abatis in front of the British works. Severely wounded during the assault, he was left for dead on the field. It was months before he could walk. No map-books of America bear his name. But L'Enfant has left a greater memorial, for it was he who laid out Washington, D. C., "the city of magnificent distances."

To Governor James Wright and Lieutenant Governor John Graham the decision to abandon Georgia in 1782 was a bitter disappointment which left propertied Tories the "Melancholy Alternative," they complained, "either of leaving the Province, in a destitute Condition, to pine under Want in a Strange Country or else stay behind & fall into the hands of their inexorable enemies." Sir James lived out the rest of his days in England struggling to obtain compensation from the British Government for his extensive property losses. He lies in Westminster Abbey, a tribute to his role in the defense of Savannah. Lord Germain informed him after the Siege that, "His Majesty commands me to express to you His particular satisfaction in your firm and spirited Conduct, and to assure you that He imputes much of the successful Resistance made to the Enemy to that Ardour and Resolution of which you gave the Example." [1] His son, Major Wright, who was an officer in the Georgia volunteers, commanded a British redoubt during the Siege of Savannah. He, too, retired to the mother country, his exile embittered by recollections of his family's great prestige in America.

Augustin Prevost took home with him from Georgia a testimonial of his officers to his "polite, disinterested and impartial behaviour." According to General Henry Lee, he had gained "distinguished applause" for the "wisdom, vigilance, and courage" displayed by him in the Siege of Savannah. General Prevost died in 1786, awaiting a promotion that never came.

A few weeks after the Allies departed, gazing at the sand defenses that had turned them back, Captain Johann Hinrichs observed that "There is no more fascinating sight for a soldier than that of the demolished works of the truly great Moncrieff." Another officer who went out the same day and took what he called "a Peep at the Works on the Ebenezer Road" was not as impressed as this Hessian officer. "The Ditch of the Lines [is] easily to be leapt over," observed Captain Peter Russell—"the Abbatis trifling and the right of the Works may be doubled without Difficulty." "Astonish^g.," he exclaimed, "how they were defended!" [2] Moncrief won equal laurels at Charlestown in 1780, General Clinton's gratitude to him for his services there being "greater" than he was "able to express." Moncrief died in 1793 as a result of wounds received in a French sortie at Dunkirk. "When such an officer as Colonel Moncrieffe falls," declared the English press, "and at such a moment as he unfortunately fell, the misfortune may be great indeed, because, it may be irreparable."

Several of the British officers who participated in the Siege later became governors of Crown possessions on this side of the Atlantic, among them John Skinner, whom we met at Savannah as a lieutenant in the Sixteenth Regiment. General Skinner is credited with saving Jamaica from the fate of San Domingo and commanding the expeditions that captured Guadeloupe and Surinam.

When the French left Georgia, Sir James Wallace and his wife were taken to France aboard the *Sagittaire*.[3] He reaped satisfying revenge on his captors during the Battle of the Saintes in which he commanded the *Warrior*. Wallace later served as Governor of Newfoundland.

Stephen De Lancey became Chief Justice of the Bahamas and Governor of Tabago. Lord Wellington has touchingly described the death of his son, Sir W. H. De Lancey, who was mortally wounded at the side of the Iron Duke during the Battle of Waterloo. John Harris Cruger, who married a De Lancey, commanded the redoubt which was attacked by General Williamson's troops at Savannah. The brilliant and successful defense of Ninety-six by this former Mayor of New York ranks him with the greatest British heroes of the War.

And what of Colonel Maitland, who had "heroically reestablished," said Colvill, "the declining glory of the British arms, in one of those most important and critical moments which decide the fall or the rise of nations"? "Like the gallant Wolfe," wrote another Britisher, he had the satisfaction of seeing "the most brilliant success accompany his exertions in behalf of his country."[4] And like that hero

Maitland did not survive his day of glory. "Though the vigor of his mind was unabated" he had been "feeble" during the Siege, according to reports that came back to England. When it was all over he retired to his quarters, not to leave. Colonel Maitland died on October 26th, 1779.

Contemporary accounts attributed his death to the fever he had contracted in Carolina and to his over-exertions. He had remained almost constantly in the trenches throughout the Siege. But there is another version. In his *History of Georgia,* Hugh McCall asserted that Colonel Maitland "had long been in the habit of indulging himself freely with his glass" which had become "constitutionally necessary for the preservation of health." He abstained during the Siege, only to return "to his former habits" when the enemy left, gratifying them "to such an extent," asserted McCall, "as to produce convulsions, of which he died suddenly." [5] To the same effect was the earlier statement in Weems' *Life of Gen. Francis Marion* that Maitland became "so elated" by the victory that he "took to hard drinking, and killed himself in *a single week.*"

The origin of the story cannot be tracked. One suspects that its source was a letter appearing in an issue of Mrs. Crouch's Charlestown *Gazette* during January, 1780, which is no longer extant. It was described by the *Royal Georgia Gazette* as a "scurrilous" one about a "late honourable Colonel" who had fought at Savannah on October 9th, its authorship being attributed to a "Renegade and impudent Rebel." One can only surmise that the communication in question was a slander of Colonel Maitland. To this dead end of uncertainty comes the search for the source of the tale Weems and McCall repeated.

But one may well ask how such a man would have been given or could have discharged so well the large responsibilities confided to Lieutenant Colonel Maitland. How could such an individual as these American writers de-

AND WHAT OF COLONEL MAITLAND? 151

scribe have been so universally respected in life or so widely lamented in death? It is true that General Prevost in his official report to Lord Germain failed to mention the services of the Scotch officer, though he generously meted out praise to others. In his poem "Savannah" the Reverend Robert Colvill refers to the "vengeful fangs" of "Envy's insidious harpies," exclaiming, "Felon! to reap where OTHERS sow!" Could he have been alluding to Prevost who might well have resented Maitland's strong comments to his superiors about surrender? The Colonel had used equally vigorous language at Charlestown the previous May. However, one finds it hard to believe that the General's oversight was attributable in any way to Maitland's conduct. Spite was not one of his failings. While he did not mention Colonel Maitland in his official report, Prevost informed Clinton on November 6th that he was "extremely sorry" to announce his passing, a fact "very much, and very justly regretted by all who knew him, both as a Gentleman, and as an Officer." He went on to say that his death could be described as "literally to have happened on Actual Service," the "fatigues" of which left him in "a very declining way." [6]

In fact, nothing but praise and no shred of anything derogatory to Maitland's character or personal habits came from those who served with him at Savannah. "What a providential thing was it that he lived so long," wrote a grateful Scotch merchant of the town. English officers acknowledged on their return to London that they owed everything to his "bringing 800 men across the swamps, deemed almost impassable, and forcing his way through the enemy's troops to join Gen. Prevost; who without them, could hardly have made any resistance." [7] In Charlestown the defeat was attributed in large part by the press to the fact that the British possessed the "advantage of the presence, skill, and activity of so able and indefatigable an officer as the Hon. Col. Maitland." His memory, said the historian Stedman, "will be dear to Britons so long as manly fortitude, unstained honour, and highly-improved military talents, are held in estimation."

No British soldier of the Revolution received higher contemporary accolade. At least five poems, including Colvill's lengthy "Savannah," were inspired by his death. In "Lines written by a Young Gentleman on hearing of the death of Colonel MAITLAND" a Savannahian poeticized,

"If Britain's love to Patriot Zeal be true,
And Steady Courage what her Troops revere;
To thee, Good Spirit, shall be paid as due,
A Nation's sorrow, and a Soldier's tear." [8]

The "Brave and Free" would "yearly pilgrims come," predicted Colvill, "To weep at MAITLAND'S hallow'd tomb"—

"The Realm you sav'd with loss of life,
Each spring shall flow'ry wreaths bestow:
Her village maids, with pious strife,
Fresh garlands on thy marble throw."

In similar vein, Mrs. De Lancey in some lines entitled "On the Death of Colonel Maitland," wrote,

"Yet while a grateful King and Country sighs,
O'er the lov'd Ashes, Marbles proud, shall rise."

Another admirer of the Colonel answered Mrs. De Lancey's poem with some stanzas in which Maitland's shade suggested that though Caesar's "haughty tomb" had

"Fall'n beneath the ruthless Hand of Age!
Yet Caesar lives in Maro's sacred Page!
So when in Ruin Lies the laurel'd Bust,
And Tombs and Statues moulder in the Dust,

AND WHAT OF COLONEL MAITLAND? 153

*Thy Verse, D—y, shall transmit to Fame
Immortal as your own, your Maitland's Name."* [9]

Mrs. De Lancey's lines fell somewhat short of immortalizing her Maitland. His fame was soon forgot. His has been the fate of most British heroes of the American Revolution—unrecognized in this country, forgotten at home. No marble tomb commemorates his memory, not even a tablet. No stone marks his burial place.

"Last Monday," reported the *Royal Georgia Gazette* at the time, "died here, greatly lamented by the whole army and inhabitants, the Hon. Lieut. Co. MAITLAND, of the 71st Regiment, brother to the Right Hon. the Earl of Lauderdale: and the next evening his remains were deposited with all the honours of war in the family vault of the Hon. John Graham, Esq.—; We must leave to some able pen the drawing the character of this truly brave and valuable officer." [10] Several years later the body of Nathanael Greene was interred in the same vault. That fact was forgotten after a few decades and a long speculation began as to the burial place of the New England General. During the course of a search for his ashes the Graham vault was opened in 1901. The bones of the American hero were found and identified by means of a coffin plate. But the official report of the Committee negatives the fact that the remains of the Scotch officer were within the vault. There is no record of Colonel Maitland's burial elsewhere. Somewhere in a nameless grave this great but forgotten soldier of the Empire sleeps the long and dreamless sleep.

So, too, dust of our dust, sleep many a brave Frenchman and American who fell at Savannah for the cause of America on a foggy October morning long, long ago.

This page intentionally left blank

Appendix

CHRONOLOGICAL SUMMARY OF ALLIED OPERATIONS AGAINST SAVANNAH IN 1779

August 16, 1779. Vice-Admiral Charles-Henri d'Estaing sails from Cap François in San Domingo in command of a large fleet with four thousand land troops aboard. The French plan of operation was to touch at Charlestown or some point to its south in order to render military assistance to the Americans in that quarter in response to their many appeals. The Toulon squadron, which d'Estaing had brought to America the year before, was to sail on to France via Halifax and Newfoundland at the completion of a brief campaign.

August 21. Conference of officers is held on the flagship *Languedoc*. Sealed landing orders are delivered to commanders of troops.

August 22. Merchant convoy departs from fleet bound for France, leaving 22 ships of the line, 10 frigates, a cutter, and several transports in d'Estaing's expedition.

September 1. Several faster vessels are dispatched to Charlestown to apprise the Americans of the arrival of French land and naval forces and of Count d'Estaing's willingness to co-operate with them against the British army in the South.

September 2. A gale encountered by the fleet off the coast of Georgia cripples a number of the French ships, preventing the expedition from proceeding further northward for the time.

September 3. English discover the French vessels en route to Charlestown off Tybee Island. D'Estaing's emissary, the Vicomte de Fontanges, arrives at Charlestown late at night.

September 4. Council of War is held at Charlestown between French and American officers and officials and a plan is agreed on for joint operations against British-held Savannah. General Lincoln promises, barring unforeseen contingencies, to have 1,000 troops in

Georgia by September 11th. South Carolina militia is called up by Governor Rutledge. General Prevost sends dispatch to Lieutenant Colonel Maitland in command of the British garrison at Beaufort ordering him to evacuate that port and proceed to Hilton Head Island and thence to Savannah. French fleet is reunited off Georgia after storm.

September 5. Orders sent to Colonel Maitland are intercepted by Americans in Skull Creek. Another dispatch is sent this day by General Prevost to Beaufort, directing troops to remain there but to be ready to move at a moment's notice if Maitland should learn from any source that Savannah is real objective of the French.

September 6. Contingent of American troops leaves Charlestown for Combahee. Governor and Council at Savannah order slave owners to furnish slaves and tools for work on defenses around the town. Captain James Moncrief with a hundred British troops is sent to Tybee Island to strengthen the post at the mouth of the Savannah. Vessels which were dispatched to Charlestown rejoin the French fleet, bringing back pilots and American guides.

September 7. D'Estaing directs Count Albert de Rions to block Port Royal and anchor a vessel at the mouth of the Broad River in order to cut off the British troops at Beaufort, a mission which that officer is unable to accomplish when his American pilot refuses to carry the *Sagittaire* into Port Royal Sound. Main body of French fleet appears off Tybee Island where 42 sail are counted by the British.

September 8. General Benjamin Lincoln leaves Charlestown to join his army. Expresses are sent by Prevost ordering evacuation of outlying British posts. At sunset four French frigates cross the bar and anchor before Tybee. British warships retire up the Savannah River.

September 9. D'Estaing makes a descent with a few soldiers on Tybee Island and finds fort at mouth of Savannah River abandoned and burned by English. Prevost sends dispatches to General Clinton and to Admiral Byron advising them of the presence of French fleet off Savannah. British troops are assigned to posts around the town. Count d'Estaing returns to the flagship *Languedoc* and reviews the French troops assembled in long boats preparatory to their embarking on the *Diadème, Annibal, Sphinx, Provence,* and *Fantasque* in order to move southward for projected landing along Vernon River.

September 10. Effectives of Sunbury garrison under command of Colonel John H. Cruger reach Savannah. Cannon are landed from British ships for use on defenses.

September 11. A few of Pulaski's cavalry cross the Savannah River ahead of the American army in order to reconnoiter the vicinity of Ebenezer, twenty-three miles west of Savannah. English sloop *Ariel* of twenty guns captured by M. de La Pérouse, commanding the frig-

APPENDIX

ate *Amazone*. French landing craft enter Ossabaw Sound. D'Estaing orders the *Truite, Chimère,* and *Bricole* to proceed up the Savannah River as close to the city as possible.

September 12. Handicapped by the lack of boats, Americans begin passage of Savannah River at Purysburg. Lincoln sends message to d'Estaing from Zubly's Ferry. Colonel Maitland sails in evening from Beaufort via inland water passage with 800 troops comprising the British garrison at that place. Count d'Estaing at the head of the initial contingent of French troops lands at night at Beaulieu, fourteen miles south of Savannah.

September 13. French vanguard advances to a road crossing three miles from Beaulieu. General Lachlan McIntosh's units effect junction with main force under Lincoln, making a total of approximately 1,500 American troops. General Prevost issues message of encouragement to his men. Heavy squall at night leaves tentless French soldiers in bad state.

September 14. French continue to debark at Beaulieu. British put hundreds of slaves to work under direction of Captain James Moncrief on the ring of defenses around Savannah. The four original redoubts become thirteen. English sailors and marines are ordered ashore where they are incorporated with the land forces.

September 15. French troops move up on Savannah in force, led by Count d'Estaing. General Lincoln learns that d'Estaing's army is ashore and accelerates his march on Savannah. Americans march from Ebenezer to Cherokee Hill, ten miles from town. British complete landing of cannon from the vessels.

September 16. Count d'Estaing sends Captain O'Moran into Savannah with a summons to surrender. British drag out the negotiations by asking for terms and for further time to consider question of capitulation. At noon Maitland's troops arrive at Savannah by water after finding a way into the Savannah River through the creeks behind Dawfuskie Island. British hold a Council of War in afternoon at which it is determined to defend the city. American army arrives before Savannah and encamps at Millen's plantation. General Lincoln remonstrates with French for calling on British to surrender to the arms of the King of France. D'Estaing grants Prevost's request for a truce which was to terminate at the firing of the evening gun next day.

September 17. Count d'Estaing writes to General Lincoln informing him of the granting of a suspension of arms. Allied commanders go to Brewton Hill where they watch last of Colonel Maitland's troops enter Savannah. The addition of the Beaufort garrison raised the total British strength to about 2,350 regulars, provincials, sailors, and militia. There were also 200 armed Negroes and 80 Creek and Cherokee Indians among the defending forces.

September 19. D'Estaing and Lincoln reconnoiter British defenses. American galleys exchange fire with English vessels in the Savannah River.

September 20–21. More troops are debarked at Beaulieu, bringing total French strength at Savannah to around 3,500. *Rose* and other English vessels are sunk in Savannah River in order to block the channel. British burn houses and barns near flanks of lines to prevent their affording protection to Allies.

September 22. French army in three divisions (d'Estaing's, Dillon's and de Noailles') encamps in new location, east of the Ogeechee Road. Americans, now 2,000 strong, pitch camp to the left of the French, their posts extending to McGillivray's Plantation on the Savannah River. Savannah becomes completely invested. French begin to land heavy cannon and mortars at the new base established by them at Thunderbolt on St. Augustine Creek, five miles from city. Skirmish takes place at night between French troops and an advanced English post.

September 23. Allies entrench themselves during night only three hundred yards from center of Prevost's works.

September 24. British Light Infantry under Major Colin Graham makes a morning sortie against French works and briefly takes possession of advanced trench. Heavy losses among French troops (12 officers and 85 men, killed and wounded) result when they pursue the enemy too close to English lines. Count d'Albert de Rions commanding the *Sagittaire* captures H.M.S. *Experiment* off Hilton Head with General George Garth, army pay-roll, and large amount of supplies aboard. A merchant ship under convoy of *Experiment* is captured on same day by the *Cérès*.

September 25. Allies continue erection of batteries and extend their entrenchments closer. Savannah is shelled by American galleys in river and by a French land battery. British battery at Trustees' Garden repels American galleys.

September 26. Major de Browne, commanding French trenches, causes an alarm in Allied camp when his troops fire at night on what d'Estaing called an imaginary enemy. He is reprimanded by his General for drinking on duty and promises to reform.

September 27. British begin the demolishment of the big barracks at center of their lines and in next two days convert lower portion of it into a strong breastwork. A number of casualties among French result when a working party is mistaken by them at night for an enemy patrol.

September 28. French flute *Truite* anchors in Black River nearly opposite the city. Situation of fleet and dissatisfaction there are indicated by attacks on Count d'Estaing in the journals of M. de Bougainville and other French naval officers during this period.

September 29. British decline request on behalf of General McIn-

APPENDIX

tosh that his family, as well as other women and children in Savannah, be permitted safe conduct from the besieged town.

September 30. Erection of three French batteries and one American battery progresses.

October 1. Savannah is cannonaded by the *Truite* and the American galleys with little effect. By a ruse Colonel John White and Captains Elholm and Melvin with four American soldiers capture over a hundred troops of the Sunbury garrison on the north bank of the Ogeechee under command of Captain Thomas French. Five vessels are also taken by White.

October 2. Cannonade of city by the *Truite*.

October 3. Bombardment of town is commenced late at night by French batteries. Many shells are thrown into Savannah by 37 cannon and mortars.

October 4. Governor Wright and Lieutenant Governor Graham move their quarters to a tent in British lines near Spring Hill. Ensign Pollard is killed by a shell in a house on the Bay. Four Negroes are killed in the cellar of Graham's residence. Seven more lose lives in a fire started by a shot that struck a house near the Church.

October 5. Bombardment continues, causing considerable loss of life and damage to property in Savannah. Two women and two children are killed in the cellar of the Laurie house on Broughton Street. Shell which struck the provost kills two men and wounds nine more. Little damage is done by Allied batteries to the British fortifications. Allied generals consider plans for an attack on the lines.

October 6. General Prevost's request that women and children be allowed to go aboard vessels down Savannah River under French protection until end of the Siege is declined. Pulaski sends suggestions to General d'Estaing respecting his ideas as to plan of attack. Carcasses are thrown into Savannah and a house is set on fire.

October 7. Shelling of Savannah continues. House in which Chief Justice Anthony Stokes resided is destroyed by fire, and as a result he loses several slaves and most of his papers. Over a thousand shells fall on city during five days of bombardment.

October 8. Decision is reached by Allies to attack British lines on following day. Plan is agreed upon, over considerable objection by some French officers, for principal assault to be made on the Spring Hill redoubt and the works to its north along the British right flank where Colonel Maitland commanded. False attacks were to be launched by the French at the center, by the Americans on the left, and by the Chevalier Durumain from the Savannah River itself. Major L'Enfant makes gallant but futile attempt to ignite the abatis in front of British works. Day passes in preparation for attack. Deserters or spies warn British of plans.

October 9. Allied troops take arms at midnight. D'Estaing reviews his troops at 2 A.M. before marching out of camp. Shortly after daybreak two columns of French soldiers, led by a vanguard, with a column of Americans and a corps of reserve (approximately 3,000 troops in all) make an assault on British lines at Spring Hill. Allies are repulsed with heavy losses after fifty-five minutes of fighting. False attacks at other points are quickly turned back. Count d'Estaing, who was wounded twice during the assault, turns command over to Colonel Dillon and rides to Thunderbolt. Truce is agreed on for burial of dead. Casualties among French total 11 officers killed and 35 wounded with 140 rank and file killed and 335 wounded. Total losses among American regulars and militia is 231 of whom 21 officers were killed or mortally wounded and 16 officers wounded. British losses on October 9th totalled 3 officers and 15 men killed and 1 officer, 3 subalterns, and 35 of the rank and file wounded. Count d'Estaing informs Americans of his intention to raise the Siege immediately.

October 10. Dismantlement of the French batteries is commenced.

October 11. French Council of War is held at which a majority of officers express opinion in favor of a retreat by way of Charlestown. The wounded Casimir Pulaski dies at sea en route to Charlestown.

October 12. Vicomte de Noailles dictates a letter to d'Estaing, which is signed by Count Dillon, protesting the General's decision to retreat by way of Thunderbolt. Governor Rutledge writes to Count d'Estaing urging that Siege not be abandoned.

October 13. D'Estaing adheres to his plan of retreat but directs departure from Causton's Bluff near Thunderbolt. French enter into formal convention with Americans as to details of retreat.

October 15. American militia depart. M. de Brétigny arrives from Charlestown and proposes that French send 900 troops there. D'Estaing refuses. Heavy desertions among the French.

October 18. American regulars break camp and retreat on Zubly's Ferry, the sick and the artillery having been previously evacuated. French depart later and encamp that night at cross-roads leading to Brewton Hill. Count d'Estaing returns during day aboard the *Languedoc*.

October 19–21. French troops embark unmolested at Causton's Bluff and return to the ships on the coast.

October 22. General Lincoln, who had reached Charlestown the previous evening, sends report of Siege to Continental Congress.

October 24. Colonel de Noailles and Lieutenant Trolong Durumain visit Savannah in connection with exchange of prisoners.

October 25. M. de La Motte-Piquet's squadron, including the *Magnifique*, departs for Leeward Islands. D'Estaing completes draft of his Observations or Notes on Captain O'Connor's Journal of the Siege of Savannah.

October 26. Lieutenant Colonel John Maitland dies at Savannah.

APPENDIX

M. de Vaudreuil sails with *Fendant* and *Diadème* for Chesapeake Bay.

October 28. Gale forces *Languedoc* to set sail eastward and *Tonnant* and *Provence* are shortly forced to follow. Several French naval captains are left behind without sailing orders.

October 29. Governor Wright issues a proclamation for a day of public Thanksgiving for the victory.

October 31. French vessels in Savannah River reach Cockspur Island. Count de Broves convenes naval Captains and it is determined to set sail.

November 1. Frigates under command of Comte de Marigny depart for Grenada.

November 2. Last French ship clears bar and departs from coast of Georgia.

December 5. Count d'Estaing having arrived at Brest after difficult passage sends report of the expedition to Georgia to M. de Sartine, Minister of Marine.

Notes

I. IMPERILED CITY

1. "The Siege of Charleston; Journal of Captain Peter Russell, December 25, 1779, to May 2, 1780." Edited by James Bain, Jr. *The American Historical Review* (1889), IV, 482.
2. Letter of Hessian officer identified as "S.D.H_____n" written from Savannah on January 16, 1779. *Letters from America, 1776–1779, Being Letters of Brunswick, Hessian, and Waldeck Officers with the British Armies During the Revolution.* Translated by Ray W. Pettengill (Boston and New York, 1924), 202. The letters there translated were originally printed in Schlözer, *Briefwechsel, meist Historischen und politischen inhalts* (Göttingen, 1776–1782).
3. John Richardson to John Porteous, "Savannah River in Georgia On Board the Vengeance," March 15, 1779. *The American Historical Review* (1902), VII, 294.
4. Letter dated May 1, 1849, written by Francis T. Brooke of Virginia entitled "A Narrative of My Life for My Family." Louise Pecquet du Bellet, *Some Prominent Virginia Families* (Lynchburg, Va., 1907), II, 354–355. Brooke served at Savannah during the closing days of the Revolution. Watson's description of Savannah society in 1778 is in *Men and Times of the Revolution; or Memoirs of Elkhannah Watson* (New York, 1861, 2nd ed.), 62.
5. Letter of Anthony Stokes to his wife, November 9, 1779. Frank Moore, *Diary of the American Revolution. From Newspapers and Original Documents* (New York, 1863), II, 228. When Chief Justice Stokes is quoted hereafter throughout this book the source, unless otherwise indicated, is this letter.
6. Elizabeth Lichtenstein Johnston, *Recollections of a Georgia Loyalist* (New York and London, 1901), 45.
7. Sir James Wright to Lord George Germain, November 5, 1779. *Collections of the Georgia Historical Society* (Savannah, 1873), III, 260. The source of the quotation in the text immediately preceding the one

taken from this letter is a journal of the Siege of Savannah written by Governor Wright. *Ibid.*, 262.
8. General Augustin Prevost to Admiral Byron, September 9, 1779. Public Record Office of Great Britain, London. Colonial Office Papers, Class 5, Vol. 131, pp. 17-20.
9. General Augustin Prevost to Sir Henry Clinton, September 6, 1779. A copy of this communication is among the British Headquarters Papers of Sir Henry Clinton in possession of Colonial Williamsburg, Inc., (No. 2258).

II. THE POMP AND GLORY

1. General Prevost to Governor Tonyn of Florida, September 11, 1779. Public Record Office, London. Colonial Office Papers, 5/98.
2. D'Estaing to M. de Sartine, Minister of Marine (sometimes spelled Sartines), December 5, 1779. Archives Nationales, Paris. (Marine), Series B⁴ 142, p. 137. This 70 page report of the Savannah campaign was sent by d'Estaing from Brest on his return to France. The voluminous French naval archives connected with the War of American Independence were photostated for the Library of Congress and are available at Washington. D'Estaing usually signed his name "Estaing" but French custom in his case authorizes the style "d'Estaing" when the name is used by others.
3. *The Siege of Savannah, in 1779, as Described in Two Contemporaneous Journals of French Officers in the Fleet of Count d'Estaing* (Albany, N. Y., 1874), 70. These journals were translated under the editorship of Charles C. Jones, Jr. For the sake of convenience this work is hereafter cited as *French Officers' Journals.*
4. Henry Lee, *Memoirs of the War in the Southern Department of the United States* (New York, 1870, revised edition), 136.
5. Quoted by Jean Joseph Calmon-Maison in *L'Amiral d'Estaing (1729-1794)*, (Paris, 1910), 274. D'Estaing's letter to Maréchal de Mouchy is quoted in *Gentilshommes Démocrates* by the Marquis de Castellane (Paris, 1890), 6. The statement made by d'Estaing to M. de Sartine concerning Colonel de Noailles is from the Vice-Admiral's report dated December 5, 1779. Archives Nationales (Marines), B⁴ 142, p. 138.
6. Compare *Henri Christophe dans L'Histoire D'Haiti* by Vergniaud Leconte (Paris, 1931), 2, and *Black Majesty, The Life of Christophe King of Haiti* by John W. Vandercook (New York, 1928), 11-17. The statement in Leconte's work that Christophe was wounded at Savannah appears also in *The Order of the Cincinnati in France* by Asa Bird Gardiner (Newport, 1905), 190, and in *The French in America During the War of Independence of the United States 1777-1783* by Thomas Balch, translated by E. S. and E. W. Balch (Philadelphia, 1895), II, 82. The fact that Henri Christophe was but twelve years old in 1779 lends support to the theory that he came to Georgia as valet rather than soldier.
7. *French Officers' Journals*, 62.

III. THE AMERICANS

1. This account was reprinted in the *Pennsylvania Gazette and Weekly Advertiser* (Philadelphia), September 29, 1779. The previously mentioned item in the *Gazette of the State of South-Carolina* appeared in the issue of that paper on September 8, 1779.
2. *Faites et motifs Préliminaires* (Facts and Preliminary Motives) written by Count d'Estaing in connection with the Savannah campaign, 4. A copy of this manuscript is in the Library of the Service Hydrographique de la Marine in Paris. It is inserted as a preface to d'Estaing's observations on O'Connor's Journal of the Siege of Savannah. See note 9 of this Chapter.
3. M. de Brétigny to d'Estaing, undated. Archives Nationales (Marine), B⁴ 168, p. 255.
4. General Lincoln to President of the Continental Congress, September 5, 1779. Papers of the Continental Congress in the Library of Congress.
5. From a copy among the Benjamin Lincoln Papers in the New York Public Library of the answers furnished to the French at Charlestown by the Americans relative to the co-operation of the two armies. The document is in the Thomas Addis Emmet Collection.
6. General Moultrie to General Lincoln, September 26, 1779. William Moultrie, *Memoirs of the American Revolution, So Far as It Related to the States of North and South-Carolina, and Georgia* (New York, 1802), II, 35, 33.
7. Pulaski to General d'Estaing, September 12, 1779. Written from "Lomel at 5 o'clock in the evening." Archives Nationales (Marine), B⁴ 168, p. 205.
8. Benjamin Lincoln's Order Book (Vol. 2) under date of September 14, 1779. MS in De Renne Collection, Library of the University of Georgia, Athens.
9. Observations of Count d'Estaing on O'Connor's *Journal Du Siège de Savannah. Septembre et Octobre 1779*, 73. MS. Antoine-François-Térance O'Connor, a twenty-nine-year-old military engineer who had been educated at the School of Engineers in France, wrote a journal of the Siege which d'Estaing supplemented at some length with his own commentaries.

IV. IN WHICH COLONEL MAITLAND STARTS SOUTH

1. Sir Robert Douglas, *The Peerage of Scotland*, revised by John Philip Wood (Edinburgh, 1813, 2nd. ed.), II, 73.
2. The Memorial of Captain John Maitland of the Marines to His Grace the Duke of Newcastle (1761). Add. MS. 32930, fo. 406. The British Museum, London. Maitland requested that the rank of Major or Lieutenant Colonel be conferred upon him.

3. From a letter dated November 8, 1779, written by a Scotch merchant who was posted in a redoubt at Savannah, *The Scots Magazine* (Edinburgh, December, 1779), 715.
4. John S. Keltie, *A History of the Scottish Highlands, Highland Clans and Highland Regiments* (Edinburgh, 1885), 470 n.
5. *The Gazette of the State of South-Carolina*, July 9, 1779.
6. Sir Henry Clinton to Maj. Gen. Augustin Prevost, New York, September 9, 1779. Public Record Office (London), America and West Indies, Colonial Office Papers, Vol. 15, fo. 214. The immediately preceding quotation is from *The Gazette of the State of South-Carolina*, July 30, 1779, which quoted *The Royal Georgia Gazette* of July 15, 1779.
7. *The South-Carolina and American General Gazette*, September 10, 1779. A similar account appeared in *The Gazette of the State of South-Carolina* on September 15, 1779.
8. This journal which was kept by an unidentified English naval officer appeared in *The Royal Gazette* (New York) on December 15th, 1779. It is printed in *The Siege of Savannah, by the Combined American and French Forces, under the Command of Gen. Lincoln, and the Count d'Estaing, in the Autumn of 1779* (Albany, N. Y., 1866), 57–79. Edited by Franklin B. Hough. This work contains letters, accounts, etc., of the Siege of Savannah which appeared in *The Royal Gazette*, published in New York by the Tory editor, James Rivington. Hough's work is hereafter cited under the title of *Siege of Savannah*.
9. *The Siege of Charleston With an Account of the Province of South Carolina: Diaries and Letters of Hessian Officers From the von Jungkenn Papers in the William L. Clements Library*. Translated and edited by Bernhard A. Uhlendorf (Ann Arbor, 1938), 137. The quotation is from the Journal of Captain (later Lieutenant General) Johann Hinrichs. *Ibid.*, pp. 161–173.
10. General Augustin Prevost to Sir Henry Clinton, July 14, 1779. This letter, which is among the Colonial Office Papers at the Public Record Office at London, was printed in *Report on American Manuscripts in the Royal Institution of Great Britain* (London, 1904), I, 472–474. The Montpelier mentioned by Prevost is a city in southern France noted for its healthy climate.

V. PREVOST GETS A SUMMONS

1. The report made by Minis concerning suitable landing places near Savannah is found in B. F. Stevens' "Facsimiles of Manuscripts in European Archives Relating to America 1773–1783," a copy of which is in the Library of Congress (No. 2013). Depositions were also furnished by Levi Sheftall and Chief Justice John Glen. After the landing Sheftall and Minis served as guides for d'Estaing while Glen and a Mr. Lloyd were assigned to conduct the detachment of Colonel de Rouvray. Archives Nationales (Marine), B⁴ 167, p. 386.
2. *Journal de la Campagne de Savannah En 1779*. B. F. Stevens, "Facsimiles of Manuscripts in European Archives Relating to America 1773–1783" (No. 2010). A convenient English translation accompanies

this as well as the other French documents relating to the Siege of Savannah in Stevens' Facsimiles. The author of the Journal is given as "Pechot," a name probably used for purpose of anonymity. The real author was the Chevalier Jean-Rémy de Tarragon, a captain in the Armagnac Regiment at Savannah. See *Extrait du Journal de Campagne du Chevalier Jean-Rémy de Tarragon Capitaine commandant les chasseurs du régiment d'Armagnac et major de la division de Dillon au siège de Savannah 1779* (Moulins, 1935).
3. Count d'Estaing's Notes on O'Connor's Journal of the Siege of Savannah, 13.
4. A. de Cazenove, *Le Siège de Savannah. Extrait de la Revue de Midi* (Nîmes, 1903), p. 30. This work is based upon the journal of Philippe Séguier de Terson, who entered the French army in 1756. He was a captain in the Agénois Regiment at the time of the Siege of Savannah. The translations of the journal are mine.
5. Von Stedingk to King Gustave III of Sweden, January 18, 1780, as translated in "Count Stedingk," *Putnam's Monthly*, October, 1854, p. 352. The original letter is printed in *Mémoires Posthumes de Feld-Maréchal Comte de Stedingk* by Le Général Comte de Bjornstjerna (Paris, 1844), I, 36–44.
6. *Comte rendu des opérations faites par l'armée française, commandée par Mr. d'Estaing devant Savannah (Amérique)*, 3. This journal of the Siege of Savannah was written by Meyronnet de Saint-Marc, a young lieutenant on the *Marseillais*. A manuscript copy, which is not in his handwriting, is in the New-York Historical Society. The original was located in the Bibliothèque Municipale of Avignon, France. No. 2750, pp. 139–146 (folio pages). That institution also possesses the day by day journal or log of the *Marseillais* which was kept by the Chevalier Meyronnet de Saint-Marc during his 21 months of service aboard her in 1778–1779. At one point during the Siege of Savannah he was in charge of the French landing boats at Thunderbolt. His account of the happenings on land during the Siege was apparently second-hand.
7. D'Estaing to Pulaski, September 13, 1779. Archives Nationales (Marine), B⁴ 168, p. 232. Pulaski's letter is *ibid.*, p. 205. Years later Captain Paul Bentalou stated that the Dragoons stopped a horseman, wearing a red coat, while riding through the woods. The messenger bore a dispatch from d'Estaing to General Lincoln and the letter to Pulaski mentioned above. Bentalou accurately recalled that in d'Estaing's communication the French commander informed Pulaski that he "was very sure he would be the first to join him." See *A Reply to Judge Johnson's Remarks on an Article in the North American Review, Relating to Count Pulaski* (Baltimore, 1826), 33.
8. Pulaski to Lincoln, 6 A.M., September 14, 1779. Quoted in *American Historical and Literary Autographs*, Catalogue No. 159, p. 27. Carnegie Book Shop, 140 East 59th Street, New York City. Curiously, a note was appended by J. Washington asking General Lincoln to permit d'Estaing to land 1,000 men on the White Bluff Road if "proper." Lincoln states in his Journal under date of September 14th that he received a message from a Captain Washington who had "seen the Count." On the 15th the American commander noted that he heard directly that day from d'Estaing to the effect that he would camp nine miles from Savannah

that night and "next day reconnoitre it in person." There is in existence another dispatch from General Pulaski to Lincoln dated September 14th. It was written at 3 A.M. from the "widow Gibbon's house, on the way to Ogeeche's ferry" and recounts Pulaski's operations in the vicinity. It mentions the necessity of keeping a "free Communication with Count d'Estaing" but refers to no meeting. The original is in the Archives and Museum of the Polish Roman Catholic Union in Chicago.

9. Count d'Estaing's Notes on O'Connor's Journal of the Siege of Savannah, 14f. The portrait of Lady Huntingdon which the French saw at Bethesda now hangs in Hodgson Hall, home of the Georgia Historical Society.

10. From a statement summarizing what the "Madame Widow Morel" had "furnished" to the French army. The bill, which is written in French, is dated September 17, 1779. It is found in Archives Nationales (Marine), B⁴ 167, p. 202. Mrs. Jourdina Cungm [Cunningham] Baillie sent an itemized statement of what was taken from Bethesda. Archives Nationales (Marine), B⁴ 168, p. 326.

11. The Prevost-d'Estaing correspondence is in the Archives Nationales (Marine), B⁴ 168, pp. 182–191 and 194–202 and in the Public Record Office (London), America and West Indies, Colonial Office Papers, Vol. 155.

12. The Journal of Séguier de Terson (p. 32) states that "Captain Moran" carried in the message. A roster of the officers of the battalion of the Dillon Regiment, which served at Savannah, in the Benjamin Lincoln Papers in the Thomas Addis Emmet Collection carries the name of Captain O'Moran but not that of "Moran." There is a recommendation by Colonel Dillon in the French Archives regarding promotions among the officers of his Regiment at Savannah which cites O'Moran but mentions no "Moran." O'Moran was badly wounded during the English sortie on the morning of September 24th.

VI. THE BRITISH DIG IN

1. Alexander Garden, *Anecdotes of the American Revolution* (Charleston, 1828), 108f.
2. Prevost to L. V. Fuser, September 11, 1779. Clinton Papers in the William L. Clements Library, Ann Arbor, Michigan. General Prevost must have written to Colonel Fuser in German as the dispatch quoted from is described as a translation by the latter.
3. From a British Regimental Order Book, July 2–October 2, 1779, the original of which is in the Library of Congress. The quotations are respectively taken from orders that were issued by Prevost on September 12th and 13th. According to Colonel Cruger, of New York, the British had decided to defend the town regardless of whether Maitland ever arrived. "Weak as we were," he wrote, "we were determined to have fought Monsieur had he thought proper to come on, tho' the odds were against us." "The Siege of Savannah, 1779, as Related by Colonel John Harris Cruger." *Magazine of American History*, II (August, 1878), 489–492.

NOTES   169

4. Prevost to Clinton, September 9, 1779. *The Colonial Records of the State of Georgia* (Atlanta, 1937), XXXIX, 254. Typewritten copy of unpublished British records as compiled by Allen D. Candler. General Prevost's letter of September 8th to General Clinton on similar lines is in the British Headquarters Papers of Sir Henry Clinton in possession of Colonial Williamsburg, Inc. (No. 2262).
5. Minutes of the Governor and Council of Georgia, July 11, 1780. MSS in the Georgia Historical Society. These papers have been edited by Lilla M. Hawes and published in *The Georgia Historical Quarterly* under the title of "The Proceedings and Minutes of the Governor and Council of Georgia, October 4, 1774 through November 7, 1775 and September 6, 1779 through September 20, 1780." For McLean's statement see *ibid., XXXV* (September, 1951), 205.
6. Affidavit of John Murray of Christ Church Parish, dated June 6, 1780, filed in the case of The King *vs.* Glen. A copy of the original was furnished to me by the late Telamon C. Cuyler of Wayside, Georgia.
7. Lieutenant Colonel Archibald Campbell to William Eden, January 19, 1779. B. F. Stevens, "Facsimiles of Manuscripts in European Archives Relating to America 1773–1783" (No. 1252).
8. Lewis Butler, *The Annals of the King's Royal Rifle Corps* (London, 1913–1932), I, 324. Butler evidently quoted from a private letter. There are letters in the Public Record Office at London dated July 14th and 30th, 1779, in which General Prevost complains to Clinton of illhealth and expresses the wish that the command were in younger hands. See abstracts in *Report of American Manuscripts in the Royal Institution of Great Britain* (London, 1904), I, 474, 483.
9. From an account bearing the date-line, Charlestown, September 22, 1779, printed in *The Boston Gazette and the Country Journal* on November 15, 1779. Apparently this was a reprint of an item in a Charlestown newspaper.
10. Governor Wright to Lord Germain, April 6, 1780. *Collections of the Georgia Historical Society* (Savannah, 1873), III, 288. For the statement that Wright cast the deciding vote in the Council of War at Savannah see Lorenzo Sabine, *Biographical Sketches of Loyalists of the American Revolution* (Boston, 1864), II, 458.
11. From General Prevost's official report to Lord Germain dated November 2, 1779, in which an official journal of the Siege of Savannah was included. Public Record Office (London), America and West Indies, Colonial Office Papers, Vol. 307, fo. 207. A copy is in Stevens' "Facsimiles of Manuscripts in European Archives Relating to America 1773–1783" (No. 2020). Prevost's report was contemporaneously published, among other places, in *The Gentleman's Magazine*, XLIX, 633ff. (London, 1779) and *The Westminster Magazine*, pp. 683–687 (London, 1779).
12. Minutes of the Governor and Council of Georgia, September 6th, 1779. *The Georgia Historical Quarterly*, XXXV (March, 1951), 32. The preceding reference in the text to the burning of the Tattnall house is based on manuscript British records in the Department of Archives and History of the State of Georgia in Atlanta. See "Bonds, Bills of Sale, Deeds of Gift, Powers of Attorney," 1778–1782, Part 1, 75; also 1779–1789, pp. 267–269.
13. Captain (later Admiral) John Henry was at Savannah during the Siege.

His report concerning the naval aspects of that episode is reprinted in Hough's *Siege of Savannah*, 134–146.

14. Anthony Stokes, *A Narrative of the Official Conduct of Anthony Stokes of the Inner Temple, London, Barrister at Law; His Majesty's Chief Justice, and one of his Council of Georgia; and of the Dangers and Distresses He underwent in the Cause of Government* (London, 1784), 73.
15. *The Royal Georgia Gazette* (Savannah), December 16, 1779.

VII. MAITLAND FINDS A WAY

1. From a Charlestown, South Carolina, account dated September 22, 1779, which appeared in *The Boston Gazette and the Country Journal* on November 15th, 1779. A similar report was printed in *The South-Carolina and American General Gazette* on September 17th, 1779.
2. Rutledge and Lincoln to d'Estaing, September 5, 1779. Archives Nationales (Marine), B⁴ 168, p. 220. The translation into French is on page 223.
3. D'Estaing to M. de Sartine, December 5, 1779. Archives Nationales (Marine), B⁴ 142, p. 148. The order to d'Albert de Rions, *capitaine de vaisseau*, dated September 7, 1779, is found in B⁴ 166, 05.
4. Fontanges stated that d'Estaing attributed the failure to cut off the Beaufort troops "to my negligence and to the little care I took in getting a response to this important point during the 8 hours I was at Charlestown." The French Consul's reply is dated September 23rd. Copies of General de Fontanges' letter and Plombard's answer are in the Archives Nationales (Marine), B⁴ 167, 113ff. and 109ff., respectively. Some of the Frenchmen blamed their own commander. "This unfortunate junction would not have taken place," said Captain de Tarragon, "if our general had marched direct to Savannah on landing or if he had sent a fifty-gun vessel into the river at Port Royal as the council of war held by the Americans at Charlestown had requested."
5. Joseph Clay to John Lewis Gervais, September 22, 1779. *Letters of Joseph Clay, Merchant of Savannah, 1776–1793. Collections of The Georgia Historical Society* (Savannah, 1913), VIII, 142.
6. "Epitaph on the Hon. Col. Maitland" by "Dr. C_____r" in *The Scots Magazine*, 1779, p. 684.
7. *The Boston Gazette and the Country Journal*, November 15, 1779, quoting a Charlestown writer.
8. The order given to Durumain, Costebelle, and de Puysegur to ascend the Savannah is in Archives Nationales (Marine), B⁴ 166, p. 278. Among the French maps pertaining to the Siege of Savannah in the William L. Clements Library at the University of Michigan is a chart of the Savannah River which was prepared in October 1779 by the Comte de Chastenet de Puysegur. It shows the depths of the stream from Tybee bar to a point in Back River opposite Yamacraw. It was prepared with evident care by this skilled hydrographer. D'Estaing called M. de Puysegur's navigation and soundings of the Savannah River *"un chef-d'oeuvre."* Family papers of Bernard-Jacques-Hubert, Comte de Puysegur of Paris, France.

NOTES 171

9. Report of General Prevost to Lord Germain, November 2, 1779. Governor Wright's statement is from his journal of the Siege published in *The Royal Georgia Gazette* on November 18, 1779, and reprinted in *Collections of The Georgia Historical Society* (Savannah, 1901) V, Part I, pp. 129–139. The Journal of the naval officer referred to in the text appeared in Rivington's *Royal Gazette* on December 15th, 1779. See Hough's *Siege of Savannah, op. cit.,* 57ff.
10. Charles Stedman, *The History of the Origin, Progress, and Termination of the American War* (London, 1794), II, 126.
11. Fontanges to d'Estaing, September 16, 1779. Archives Nationales (Marine), B^4 167, p. 112.
12. Count d'Estaing's Notes on O'Connor's Journal of the Siege of Savannah, p. 19. The Count's statement about his mortification at seeing the Beaufort troops pass is from his letter to the Chevalier Durumain, dated September 20, 1779. Archives Nationales (Marine), B^4 166, p. 287. D'Estaing also remarked that the "impossibilities" encountered by the *Truite* in ascending the Savannah would "cost the lives of many men." I have adopted Durumain's own mode of signing his name rather than the more generally used "du Rumain."
13. Journal of Captain Séguier de Terson, *op. cit.,* 33. The circumstances of the capture of M. de Cambis are found in the Journal of Meyronnet de Saint-Marc. The line from *Les Fourberies de Scapin* as misquoted by Séguier de Terson in his journal reads, *"Mais que diable alliez-vous faire dans cette galere?"*

VIII. THE ALLIES RESORT TO THE SPADE

1. Letter written by Major T. W. Moore, dated November 4, 1779, published in Rivington's *Royal Gazette,* December 29, 1779. See Hough's *Siege of Savannah,* 83.
2. The French strength at Savannah as stated in the text is taken from a document in the Archives Nationales (Marine), B^4 167, p. 247. The summary of the British forces is from a "List of the English Troops, Militia, etc. within the town on the 9th October 1779 according to Statements of Deserters." B. F. Stevens' Facsimiles (No. 2016). Another document in the Archives Nationales (Marine), B^4 167, p. 250, shows an estimated strength of 2,935 English troops. An official return of the British forces in Georgia by General Prevost, dated November 15, 1779, is among the Clinton Papers in the William L. Clements Library at Ann Arbor, Michigan. It indicates that on that date 3,050 officers and men were present and fit for duty.
3. *The Royal Gazette* (New York), December 15, 1779.
4. *Comte rendu des opérations faites par l'armée française, commandée par Mr. d'Estaing devant Savannah (Amérique), op. cit.,* p. 7.
5. Johnston, *Recollections of a Georgia Loyalist, op. cit.,* 62. Mrs. Johnston stated that her husband conducted Viscount de Noailles to General Prevost's headquarters where the summons was delivered by the French officer in "an elegant style."
6. "Burlesque Letter, Attributed to a French Officer" published in Riving-

ton's *Royal Gazette,* January 12, 1780. See Hough's *Siege of Savannah,* 96. The letter purports to have been written by a French officer off Tybee to a friend in Charlestown but is quite possibly a satire by some Englishman. Choiseul's characterization of d'Estaing is taken from Maurice Besson, *Le Comte D'Estaing* (Paris, 1931), 57.

7. Archives Nationales (Marine), B⁴ 168, p. 220. The translation of the American communication into French is found on page 223.
8. D'Estaing to Lincoln, September 17, 1779. Archives Nationales (Marine), B⁴ 168, p. 242. The original is among the Lincoln Papers in the Thomas Addis Emmet Collection, New York Public Library.
9. M. L. Weems, *The Life of Gen. Francis Marion* (Philadelphia, edition of 1839), 60. Use of material in Weems' work must be accompanied by a strong monition. The Parson borrowed General Horry's unpublished account of Marion's Brigade, taking such liberties with the manuscript in his "Life" of General Marion that Horry was to complain to him, "Most certainly 'tis not my history, but your romance." General Horry's name was not carried as a co-author until after his death. See A. S. Salley's introduction to *A Sketch of the Life of Brig. Gen. Francis Marion* by William Dobein James (1821) in reprint by Continental Book Company, Marietta, Ga., 1948. The Horry manuscript unfortunately is not extant. However, his own volume of Weems' *Life of Gen. Francis Marion* containing his (Horry's) marginal notes or commentaries is in existence, a photostat being in possession of Mr. Salley. Horry did not deny or comment upon the remarks attributed by Weems to Marion in connection with the granting of the truce. Following that incident there appears in Weems' book a burlesque dialogue between d'Estaing, using broken English, and Colonel Laurens. As to this passage Horry commented, "All this of Count De Stangue is the fruitful Invention of the Brain of Mr. Weems—"
10. Count d'Estaing's "Facts and Preliminary Motives," p. 5. Library of the Service Hydrographique de la Marine, Paris.
11. D'Estaing to M. de Sartine, Minister of Marine, December 5, 1779. Archives Nationales (Marine), B⁴ 142, p. 145.
12. *Letters of Joseph Clay, Merchant of Savannah, 1776-1793, op. cit.,* 144, 147, 149.

IX. SEEDS OF FAILURE

1. From *Extrait du Journal d'un officier de la marine de L'Escadre de M. le comte d'Estaing* (Paris, 1782) as translated in Balch, *The French in America During the War of Independence of the United States 1777-1783, op. cit.,* II, p. 119. The charge of insubordination of this type was vigorously denied by Édouard Chevalier in his *Histoire de la Marine Française Pendant la Guerre de L'Indépendance Américaine* (Paris, 1877), 2, 109f., 152, 154.
2. *French Officers' Journals,* 58. The immediately preceding reference in the text as to Count d'Estaing's statement to General Washington is from the former's letter of December 25, 1783. See Gardiner, *The Order of the Cincinnati in France, op. cit.,* 12.

3. These excerpts are from d'Estaing's report to M. de Sartine, December 5, 1779, in Archives Nationales (Marine), B⁴ 142, p. 126 and from Count d'Estaing's Notes on O'Connor's Journal of the Siege of Savannah, p. 21.
4. *French Officers' Journals*, 63.
5. Allan Maclean Skinner, *Sketch of the Military Services of Lieutenant-General Skinner and his Sons* (Stafford, 1863), p. 19. Skinner's friend was evidently Lieutenant Henry McPherson of the 1st Battalion of the Seventy-first Regiment as McPherson was the only British officer killed in the sortie of September 24th.
6. Count d'Estaing's Notes on O'Connor's Journal of the Siege of Savannah, 36. The next night (September 27th) something very similar occurred, complained d'Estaing, despite "all I have said, my reproaches, my reprimands." The French left flank and the right flank started shooting at each other by mistake and several lives were lost. "But for the firmness and good conduct of M. de Sigoier, captain of the grenadiers of the Foix regiment, the damage would have been very great," reported Count d'Estaing, *ibid.*, 37. The official journal of General Prevost recorded that a brief sortie was made on the night in question by a body of troops under Major McArthur of the Seventy-first. The occasion mentioned by the Count apparently occurred later the same night. See *French Officers' Journals*, 23f.
7. Account of the Siege of Savannah by General Thomas Pinckney in *Garden's Anecdotes of the American Revolution, op. cit.*, 21.
8. "Journal of Major Gen. Lincoln from September 3rd to October 19th, 1779." MS. Papers of the Continental Congress. The Library of Congress.
9. D'Estaing's letter to Colonel John Laurence [sic], dated September 6, 1779, is among the Lincoln Papers in the Thomas Addis Emmet Collection in the New York Public Library. Laurens' letter to Count d'Estaing is translated from the version found in Chevalier's *Histoire de la Marine Française Pendant la Guerre de L'Indépendance Américaine, op. cit.*, 146. The date of the communication is not indicated by Chevalier.
10. "The Siege of Savannah, 1779, as Related by Colonel John Harris Cruger." *Magazine of American History*, II (August, 1878), 489–492.
11. *Ibid.*, 41. The translation is mine.
12. Stedingk to King Gustave III of Sweden, January 18, 1780, as translated in "Count Stedingk," *Putnam's Monthly*, October, 1854, 352.
13. Vicomte de Noailles, *Marins et Soldats Français En Amérique Pendant la Guerre de L'Indépendance des États-Unis (1778–1783)*, (Paris, 1903 ed.), 102n.

X. THE BOMBARDMENT

1. *French Officers' Journals*, pp. 24f.
2. John Jones to his wife, October 7, 1779. Seaborn Jones Papers in Duke University Library. The letters written by Major Jones during the Siege to his wife who had refugeed to Jacksonborough in South Caro-

174   STORM OVER SAVANNAH

    lina are in George White, *Historical Collections of Georgia* (New York, 1854), 535–536.
3. *Mémoires et voyages du Chevalier Aristide-Aubert du Petit-Thouars, capitaine de vaisseau* (Paris, 1822). "Expédition de Savannah," 239–242. See also, Admiral Bergasse du Petit Thouars, *Aristide Aubert du Petit Thouars. Héros d' Aboukir, 1760–1798. Lettres et documents inédits* (Paris, 1937), 24–29.
4. *A Narrative of the Official Conduct of Anthony Stokes, op. cit.,* 50.
5. *The Virginia Gazette* (Williamsburg), October 23, 1779.
6. A. S. Salley, Jr., ed., *Journal of the Commissioners of the Navy of South Carolina July 22, 1779—March 23, 1780* (Columbia, S. C., 1913), 16. The *Rutledge* was captured by the British off Tybee on November 4th and renamed *Viper*. The command of the galley was given to John Steele, master's mate of the *Rose*, in recognition of his gallant conduct on October 9th in the British battery north of Spring Hill redoubt.
7. Alexander Garden, *Anecdotes of the Revolutionary War in America* (Charleston, 1822), 111f.
8. "William Hasell Gibbes' Story of his Life." *The South Carolina Historical and Genealogical Magazine,* L (April, 1949), 65.
9. *French Officers' Journals,* 26.
10. Extract of a letter from Savannah dated October 22, 1779, which was quoted by Governor Tonyn in a dispatch sent by him to General Henry Clinton. Public Record Office, London. Colonial Office Papers, 5/98.

XI. D'ESTAING DECIDES TO ATTACK

1. From the journal of a cadet on the *Guerrier*. Entry for October 14–15, 1779. MS. Records in the Library of the Service Hydrographique de la Marine, Paris, 721. This terse but expressive diary was kept by an unidentified *garde de marine* on Bougainville's ship.
2. "Provisions remaining in His Majesty's Magazines at Savannah 24th Octr 1779." Clinton Papers in the William L. Clements Library at Ann Arbor, Michigan.
3. "Order Book of Maj. John Faucheraud Grimké, August 1778 to May 1780." *The South Carolina Historical and Genealogical Magazine,* XVII (April, 1916), 84.
4. Letters of John Jones to his wife, Polly, October 5 and 7, 1779. MSS. Seaborn Jones Papers in Duke University Library.
5. The quotations from Bougainville's journal are from R. de Kerallain, *Bougainville à L'Escadre du Cte D'Estaing Guerre d'Amérique 1778–1779* (Paris, 1927).
6. *Relation du Siège de Savannah capitale de la nouvelle Géorgie, province du Sud de l'Amérique Septentrionale.* Archives Nationales (Marine), B⁴ 142, p. 199. This thirteen page account was prepared by an unidentified French officer. Pulaski had pointed out the same thing about the Spring Hill sector in a memorandum to d'Estaing proposing

a plan of attack. "According to the report of one of the deserters who has passed by the same place, it is presumed that the right wing of the enemy is more accessible than one imagines and the number of soldiers on that side is very feeble." *"Le plan d'attaque au Camp retranché des Anglais auprès de la ville de Savanna 6 Octobre, 1779."* Archives Nationales (Marine), B⁴ 168, p. 207.

7. *French Officers' Journals*, 38. The Spring Hill redoubt was located approximately where the Central of Georgia Depot now stands on West Broad Street. In *Historic and Picturesque Savannah* Adelaide Wilson has commented eloquently upon the obliviousness of the "hurrying throngs of humanity, each absorbed in his tiny circle of cares or pleasures" to the great memories associated with the spot. *Ibid.*, 60. The Railroad's excavations at the site failed to turn up much in the way of relics. A former officer of the Company reminisced that when the depot grounds were enlarged "30 skeletons" were found about three feet underground near the foot of Liberty Street "buried in a Row with what was decided to be the Hessian uniform." The principal relic unearthed was a "large solid gold Buckle." Reminiscences of George W. Shaffer, ex-Treasurer of the Central Rail Road, transmitted to General Henry R. Jackson, President of the Georgia Historical Society, in a letter dated "May, 1893." MS.

8. Captain de Tarragon's Journal of the Siege of Savannah as translated in B. F. Stevens' "Facsimiles of Manuscripts in European Archives Relating to America 1773–1783." The approximate location of the Allied trenches in present-day Savannah was in the general area between Taylor and Gaston streets on the north and south and Drayton and Price streets on the west and east. The barracks near the center of the lines was located where the DeSoto Hotel stands.

9. D'Estaing to M. Gérard, October 26, 1779. Archives Nationales (Marine), B⁴ 168, p. 59. I have used the translation of this passage in Joachim Merlant, *Soldiers and Sailors of France in the American War for Independence (1776–1783)* as translated from the French by Mary Bushnell Coleman (New York, 1920), 89f.

10. "Facts and Preliminary Motives," 7. Library of the Service Hydrographique de la Marine, Paris.

11. *Extrait du Journal d'un officier de la marine de l'Escadre de M. le comte d'Estaing, op. cit.*, 4–5. The translation is mine. Compare the following character sketch of Count d'Estaing by a member of the Chamber of Agriculture of San Domingo: "Wide-awake mind, full of activity; less judgment. The heart of an Auvergnat, good and honest. Subject to violent spells of anger; impenetrable secrecy." Quoted in Merlant, *Soldiers and Sailors of France in the American War for Independence (1776–1783), op. cit.*, 59.

12. Archives Nationales (Marine), B⁴ 167, p. 396.

13. Pulaski to d'Estaing, October 6, 1779. Archives Nationales (Marine), B⁴ 168, pp. 207f., 209.

14. Pulaski to d'Estaing, apparently dated October 2, 1779. Archives Nationales (Marine), B⁴ 168, p. 206.

15. Count d'Estaing's Notes on O'Connor's Journal of the Siege of Savannah, 63.

16. Weems, *The Life of Gen. Francis Marion, op. cit.*, 71. The statement of that author that the deserter was later captured and hanged cannot be confirmed. However, it was not challenged by General Horry in his comments on the margin of the book. The first historian to identify James Curry as the deserter was William Gordon in *The History of the Rise, Progress, and Establishment, of the Independence of the United States of America* (New York, 1789), III, 33. Research in Charleston failed to identify Curry.
17. Minutes of the Governor and Council of Georgia, July 11, 1780. *The Georgia Historical Quarterly*, XXXV (September, 1951), 204f.

XII. OCTOBER NINTH

1. General Clinton to Lord Germain, New York, November 10, 1779. MS. Clinton Papers in the William L. Clements Library, University of Michigan, Ann Arbor. The same thought was expressed by Clinton in a letter that day to William Eden. He indicated in it, however, that if Savannah should fall the expedition might be shifted to Virginia. See B. F. Stevens' "Facsimiles of Manuscripts in European Archives Relating to America 1773–1783" (No. 1032).
2. *French Officers' Journals*, 29f. The guide was evidently Major Roman de Lisle of the Georgia Continental Line.
3. Charles Cotesworth Pinckney to his mother, October 9, 1779. MS. C. C. Pinckney Papers in the Library of Duke University. This letter is published in Charles C. Jones, Jr., *History of Savannah, Ga.* (Syracuse, 1890), 289 n.
4. Joseph Johnson, *Traditions and Reminiscences Chiefly of the American Revolution in the South* (Charleston, 1851), 239. An eye-witness informed Johnson of this incident.
5. Count d'Estaing's Notes on O'Connor's Journal of the Siege of Savannah, 74–75. Captain O'Connor stated that "The fire of the Scotch regiment which held the redoubt was very lively." An English map shows the 2nd Battalion of the Seventy-first Regiment stationed at a point east of Spring Hill. Three companies of the Highlanders constituted a reserve on October 9th. Apparently they did not participate to any real extent in the fighting. They were ordered to support the charge of the Sixtieth and though they came up rapidly the Allies had been driven from the works by the time the Seventy-first arrived.
6. L. V. Fuser to General Clinton, October 30, 1779. Public Record Office, London, Colonial Office Papers, 5/98. The French account referred to in the text immediately before this reference is from a history of the Gâtinais Regiment in the American Revolution found in *Les Combattants Français de la Guerre Américaine 1778–1783* by the "Ministère des Affaires Étrangères." 58th Congress, 2d. Session. Document No. 77 (Washington, 1905), p. 305.
7. Count d'Estaing's Notes on O'Connor's Journal of the Siege of Savannah, 67.
8. From a letter written to a friend in New York by a "Gentleman of the

General Hospital at Savannah," November 24, 1779. Hough's *Siege of Savannah*, 81.
9. The return is among the Benjamin Lincoln Papers in the Thomas Addis Emmet Collection, New York Public Library. The statement concerning the conduct of the Virginia militia is from *French Officers' Journals*, 32.
10. Count d'Estaing's Notes on O'Connor's Journal of the Siege of Savannah, 73.
11. *Connecticut Journal* (New Haven), December 29, 1779, quoting an account in a Boston paper by a "gentleman from the southward recently in town."
12. Count d'Estaing's Notes on O'Connor's Journal of the Siege of Savannah, 73. The part of the quotation that Pulaski died by "his own fault in placing himself where he should not have been at the moment" is from d'Estaing's report to M. de Sartine dated December 5, 1779. Archives Nationales (Marine), B^4 142, p. 125. Additional evidence as to the circumstances of Pulaski's death (though hardly reliable) comes from Thomas Garrett, a 105-year-old veteran of the Revolution, who told a reporter for a Charleston newspaper in 1836 that while he was assisting a wounded soldier General Pulaski rode up and remarked, "My brave fellow, take care, you are in a dangerous position." To this remark Garrett claimed that he replied: "General, if you intend to be in a place of safety I'll keep near you." He said that the famous cavalry officer fell just after riding away from him. *The Charleston Courier*, August 30, 1836. Clipping in Thomas Gamble Scrap Books in the Savannah Public Library.
13. *The Royal Georgia Gazette*, December 2, 1779.
14. Alexander Garden, *Anecdotes of the Revolutionary War*, op. cit., 112. The language attributed to Colonel Laurens is also of questionable authenticity since it is taken from M. L. Weems' *Life of Gen. Francis Marion*, op. cit., 64f. In the marginal notes which Horry wrote in his own volume of that work he did not challenge Weems' allusion to the incident, a fact considered in using the quotation here.
15. O'Connor's Journal of the Siege of Savannah, 62; Count d'Estaing's Notes, 70. A manuscript journal entitled "Journal de M. Le Comte D'Estaing" in the records of the Historical Society of Pennsylvania repeats the quoted statement of Captain O'Connor word for word. In *French Officers' Journals* (36f.) there is a fuller account of the conduct of the reserves. Based on a statement once made by Rev. T. G. Steward, Haitian sources sometimes credit the saving of the Franco-American army to the bravery of the Negro volunteers who it is said comprised the corps of reserve. See for example, J. N. Léger, *Haiti, Her History and Her Detractors* (New York and Washington, 1907), 42 n. A table showing the composition of the French troops during the attack which is incorporated in Captain de Tarragon's Journal would indicate that the reserve was not composed of any Negro soldiers. However, General Thomas Pinckney's account of the Siege refers to a corps of West Indian troops in the reserve.
16. Count d'Estaing's Notes on O'Connor's Journal of the Siege of Savannah, 69.

XIII. LIGHTS AND SHADOWS OF A WARM OCTOBER MORNING

1. William Smith to Lord Carlisle, New York, December 10, 1779. *The Manuscripts of the Earl of Carlisle, Preserved at Castle Howard* (1897), 435.
2. White, *Historical Collections of Georgia, op. cit.*, 537.
3. White, *Historical Collections of Georgia, op. cit.*, 473, quoting "Reminiscences of Captain Roderick McIntosh" by John Couper, April 16, 1842.
4. "Extracts from a Private Manuscript written by Governor Paul Hamilton, Sr., During the Period of the Revolutionary War, from 1776–1800." *Year Book—1898. City of Charleston, So. Ca.*, 304f.
5. Alexander Gregg, *History of the Old Cheraws* (Columbia, S. C., 1925 ed.), 296. The quotation is from an entry in Pugh's Journal for November 21, 1779.
6. The American losses of both regulars and militia on October 9th are shown according to units in "A Return of the killed and wounded in the action at Savannah Oct. 9th, 1779." Lincoln Papers, The Siege of Savannah. Thomas Addis Emmet Collection, the New York Public Library. In his report to Congress, dated October 22, 1779, General Lincoln stated that 170 Continental troops were killed or wounded in the attack. The statement of French casualties is based on an official return found in the Archives Nationales (Marine), B⁴ 167, p. 375. The British losses are taken from General Prevost's report. Their casualties during the entire Siege amounted to only 38 killed, 58 wounded, and 48 deserted, according to an official return signed by Prevost. See the Clinton Papers in the William L. Clements Library, Ann Arbor, Michigan.
7. General Prevost's report of the Siege gives a somewhat different version of the reason for the surrender. Colonel White's accomplishment is confirmed by the Journal of General Lincoln and also by a letter from Charlestown, dated October 6, 1779, which was printed in *The Virginia Gazette* (Williamsburg), on November 6, 1779. The original report by White of the episode was mentioned by Francis Bowen who saw it among the papers of Benjamin Lincoln while preparing his biographical sketch of the New England general. The manuscript was acquired in 1924 by Colonel Preston Davie of New York City. The only letter of White found in the Thomas Addis Emmet Collection of Lincoln Papers is dated January 29, 1780. In it he asked permission of General Lincoln, despite his ill-health, to take the field again in view of the projected British attack on Charlestown. Colonel White died a few months later as a result of the exposures he underwent during the Siege of Savannah.
8. It is interesting to compare Weems' imaginary version of Jasper's dying comments and the dramatic death-bed discourse of Pulaski in Louvet de Couvrai's novel, *Amours du Chevalier de Faublaf*. A portion of this work was translated and published in America under the title of *The Interesting History of the Baron De Lovzinski. Written by Himself. With a Relation of the Most Remarkable Occurrences in the Life of*

the Celebrated Count Pulaski (Hartford, 1800). Americans of the day recognized this book as fiction, something most of them failed to do in the case of portions of Weems' *Life of Gen. Francis Marion*.
9. From a letter written on January 7, 1854, by James Lynah, a grandson of Dr. Lynah, to the *Philadelphia Herald* which was reprinted in *Historical Magazine*, 1866, 286. The fatal grapeshot extracted from Pulaski's groin by the Charlestown surgeon is in Hodgson Hall, home of the Georgia Historical Society, where it was deposited by J. H. Lynah of Savannah. Another grim memento of the past possessed by the Society is "Splinters from the bone of the arm of Colonel Maitland" which was shattered by a cannon ball in the battle of Lagos Bay, Spain, between the British and French in 1759. The fragments which are identified as such in eighteenth century handwriting were presented by the Right Honorable Ian Colin Maitland, Fifteenth Earl of Lauderdale, who resides at Thirlestane Castle, Lauder, Scotland.
10. Notes written by James Jackson on David Ramsay, *The History of the Revolution of South-Carolina, From a British Province to an Independent State* (Trenton, 1785). Stedman was evidently Captain James Stedman of the Georgia Continental Line.
11. William B. Stevens Papers in the Georgia Historical Society. The story is given as it is recorded in Stevens' hand. Different versions are found elsewhere; for example, in *The Romance of Lower Carolina* by C. Irvine Walker (Charleston, S. C., 1915), 109.
12. *Mémoires Posthumes du feld-maréchal Comte de Stedingk, op. cit.,* I, 52.
13. T. S. Arthur and W. H. Carpenter, *The History of Georgia, from its Earliest Settlement to the Present Time* (Philadelphia, 1852), 185f.
14. Hugh McCall, *The History of Georgia, Containing Brief Sketches of the Most Remarkable Events up to the Present Day* (Savannah, Ga., 1811, 1816), II, 269 n. I have changed the remark attributed to Major d'Erneville from the third to first person and the tense to the present. McCall spells the name "d'Ernonville" but the French casualty lists show it as given here.

XIV. THE COUNT RAISES THE SIEGE

1. Merlant, *Soldiers and Sailors of France in the American War for Independence (1776–1783) op. cit.,* 91. Merlant does not give the source of the quotation.
2. From Bougainville's journal, October 14, 1779. Kerallain, *Bougainville à L'Escadre du Cte D'Estaing Guerre d'Amérique, 1778–1779, op. cit.,* 44.
3. Mrs. Jourdina Cungm [Cunningham] Baillie to Count d'Estaing, Bethesda, October 14, 1779. Archives Nationales (Marine), B^4 168, p. 327.
4. D'Estaing to Lincoln, *"Au Camp Devant Savannah,"* September 23, 1779. Lincoln Papers, The Siege of Savannah. Thomas Addis Emmet Collection, New York Public Library.

5. Jane Bowen to Count d'Estaing, Greenwich, October 7, 1779. Archives Nationales (Marine), B⁴ 168, p. 321. The basis of my statement that d'Estaing was hospitalized at the Bowen house is the paper of William P. Bowen, Sr., printed in Henry Williams, *An Address Delivered on Laying the Corner Stone of a Monument to Pulaski, in the City of Savannah, October 11, 1853* (Savannah, 1855), 33. See also Adelaide Wilson, *Historic and Picturesque Savannah, op. cit.*, 77. In *French Officers' Journals* (p. 66) it is said that d'Estaing "rode on horseback to the village of Thunderbolt." The orders signed by the French General during the period in question are headed "Thunderbolt Bluff."
6. From *Journal de la campagne du vaisseau le Marseillais de 74 canons portant 36 ... 18 et ... 8. Commandé par monsieur de la Poïpe de Vertrieux, Capitaine des vaisseaux du Roy*. Manuscript in the Bibliothèque Municipale of Avignon, Vol. 2750, pp. 73, 73vo. The name of the author of this Journal, who was an officer on the *Marseillais*, does not appear on the manuscript but it was evidently written by Lieutenant Meyronnet de Saint-Marc. It is an entirely different manuscript from the Journal of that officer which has been previously mentioned and quoted from throughout this work.
7. *Campagne de M. le Comte d'Estaing en Amérique ou Mémoire pour servir de réfutation au Libelle contre ce Vice-Amiral* (Brussels, 1782), 71. This pamphlet is a defense of d'Estaing against the critical *Extrait du Journal d'un officier de la marine*, the author of which is disparagingly referred to as "*l'Anonyme*" by a writer who chose to remain equally so.
8. John Wereat to Count d'Estaing. Archives Nationales (Marine), B⁴ 168, p. 212.
9. *The Gazette of the State of South-Carolina*, October 13, 1779.
10. General Lincoln to Major Everard Meade, Charlestown, November 1, 1779. Lincoln Papers, The Siege of Savannah. Thomas Addis Emmet Collection, New York Public Library. The source of the immediately preceding quotation in the text is the letter from General Lincoln to Samuel Huntington, President of the Continental Congress, dated October 22, 1779. Papers of the Continental Congress. No. 158, pp. 279–282. The Library of Congress.
11. Charles Cotesworth Pinckney to his mother, October 15, 1779. C. C. Pinckney Papers in the Library of Congress.
12. *Annals of Congress, 7th Congress, 2nd. Sess.*, 149. From a speech by Hon. James Jackson in the United States Senate.
13. Rutledge to d'Estaing, October 12, 1779. Archives Nationales (Marine), B⁴ 168, p. 172. Count d'Estaing later ordered the *Chimère*, the *Bricole*, and the *Truite* to Charlestown to assist the Americans in the event of an attack on that place. The two latter vessels were sunk there to block the channel.
14. The protest which is dated October 13, 1779, is found in Archives Nationales (Marine), B⁴ 167, pp. 39–41 (folio pages). The letter of Dillon from which the preceding quotation in the text was taken is dated October 12, 1779. It is in Archives Nationales (Marine), B⁴ 167, pp. 35–36. A manuscript copy is in the Thomas Addis Emmet Collection in the New York Public Library among the Lincoln Papers. Copies of these

letters are found in the Journal of Jean-Rémy de Tarragon. On the margin of his copy of the protest is a notation that it was sent "under M. de Dillon's name but dictated by the Viscount de Noailles." Captain de Tarragon's younger brother, Anne-Claude, served as assistant adjutant general of Dillon's Division at Savannah.

15. De Rouvray to General d'Estaing, October 12, 1779. Archives Nationales (Marine), B⁴ 167, p. 233. Dillon's observations concerning lack of discipline is from the letter dated October 13, 1779, referred to in note 14 of this Chapter.
16. L. V. Fuser to General Clinton, October 30, 1779. Public Record Office, London, Colonial Office Papers, 5/98. Colonel de Noailles' statement that the English "send us word that they would not disturb us in our retreat unaccompanied by the Americans" is found in the letter to d'Estaing dated October 13th referred to in note 14 of this Chapter.
17. *The New-York Mercury, or, General Advertiser*, December 10, 1779.
18. From a letter dated October 23, 1779, in *The Pennsylvania Gazette and Weekly Advertiser* (Philadelphia), November 17, 1779. The preceding quotation in the text concerning Count d'Estaing is from the December 1st, 1779, issue of the same newspaper.
19. John Laurens to Henry Laurens, Charlestown, October 23, 1779. Lincoln Papers, The Siege of Savannah. Thomas Addis Emmet Collection, New York Public Library.

XV. THE CAPTAINS AND THE KINGS DEPART

1. Count d'Estaing to General George Washington, December 25, 1783. Gardiner, *The Order of the Cincinnati in France, op. cit.*, p. 12. The order given to de Grasse to proceed with his squadron to the Chesapeake for provisioning is in the Archives Nationales (Marine), B⁴ 166, p. 188. However, a French naval officer states that orders were also received from the Admiral "not to depart until they had been furnished with his final instructions." See *French Officers' Journals*, 49.
2. Chevalier, *Histoire de la Marine Française Pendant la Guerre de L'Indépendance Américaine, op. cit.*, p. 307. Comte de Marigny is not to be confused with his brother, Charles-René, Vicomte de Bernard de Marigny—another well-known French naval officer.
3. Thomas MacKenzie to Monsieur _____, aboard the *Amazonne*, October 17, 1779. Archives Nationales (Marine), B⁴ 166, p. 242. After the capture of the *Ariel* Count de La Pérouse courteously offered his services to Captain MacKenzie who requested of him, "Commit me to the care of Thomas Pinckney. He will not forget an old friend and school-fellow, even in a captive enemy." It was a coincidence that MacKenzie's brother later saved the life of Major Pinckney when the latter was wounded during the Battle of Camden. Rev. Charles Cotesworth Pinckney, *Life of General Thomas Pinckney* (Boston and New York, 1895), 60.
4. D'Estaing to M. de Sartine, December 5, 1779. Archives Nationales (Marine), B⁴ 142, p. 137.
5. Hough's *Siege of Savannah*, 54f. From a journal of the Siege printed in *The Royal Gazette* (New York), November 18, 1779.

6. D'Estaing to M. de Sartine, December 5, 1779. Archives Nationales (Marine), B⁴ 142, p. 154.
7. Edwin Martin Stone, *Our French Allies* (Providence, 1884), 128. The source of the anecdote is a contemporary French letter. In d'Estaing's report to M. de Sartine he says that he desired to pay his respects to the Minister and to let him know that he counted more than ever on justice and the good will of the King which the friendly offices of de Sartine could secure for him.
8. *Campagne de M. le Comte d'Estaing en Amérique ou Mémoire pour servir de réfutation au Libelle contre ce Vice-Amiral, op. cit.*, 75.
9. From family records in possession of Comte Dillon of Auch, France, who kindly furnished the author with biographical information as to the Dillons who participated in the American War of Independence.

XVI. AND WHAT OF COLONEL MAITLAND?

1. Letter to Governor Wright from Lord Germain, January 19, 1780. *The Colonial Records of the State of Georgia* (Atlanta, 1937), XXXVIII (Part II), 247. Typewritten copy of unpublished British records compiled by Allen D. Candler.
2. "The Siege of Charleston; Journal of Captain Peter Russell, December 25, 1779, to May 2, 1780." Edited by James Bain, Jr. *The American Historical Review*, IV (1899), 482.
3. Passenger lists of the vessels bound for France from Georgia. B. F. Stevens, "Facsimiles of Manuscripts in European Archives Relating to America 1773–1783" (No. 2019). These lists are revealing in places. For example, Count Arthur Dillon appears to have carried a retinue of six servants back to Europe.
4. Letter from London dated December 22, 1779. *The Scots Magazine*, 1779, p. 685.
5. II, p. 279.
6. General Augustin Prevost to Sir Henry Clinton, Savannah, November 6, 1779. British Headquarters Papers of General Clinton in possession of Colonial Williamsburg, Inc., Williamsburg, Virginia (No. 9848).
7. Letter from London dated December 22, 1779, in *The Scots Magazine*, 1779, p. 684f.
8. *The Royal Gazette* (New York), December 15, 1779, under the date line, Savannah, November 18, 1779.
9. These and Mrs. De Lancey's lines which appeared in Rivington's *Royal Gazette* on April 26, 1780, are printed in Hough's *Siege of Savannah*, 112–114. The Mrs. De Lancey to whom the authorship of the poem was attributed could have been either Mrs. Stephen De Lancey, wife of Lieutenant Colonel De Lancey, or Mrs. Oliver De Lancey, each of whom had married into the distinguished Tory family of that name in New York.
10. This death notice appeared originally in *The Royal Georgia Gazette* and was reprinted in *The New-York Gazette and The Weekly Mercury* on December 13, 1779.

Bibliography

MANUSCRIPT SOURCES

French:

Archives Nationales (Marine), Paris, France. The portions relating to the Siege of Savannah are mainly filed in volumes 142, 166, 167, and 168 of Series B⁴. However, materials are also scattered through several other volumes. The army reports and headquarters papers relating to the Savannah campaign are in the Archives Marine though some such material is found in the Archives Guerre. The Archives consist of a mass of military and naval dispatches, reports, letters, orders, and miscellaneous documents. They are not arranged in accordance with any particular method. Each of these cartons contains between 350 and 500 pages of manuscript material. The author has translated or examined only certain significant portions of the Archives pertaining to the Siege of Savannah, a mere fraction of the whole. A considerable part consists of purely routine reports or orders. In many instances the almost illegible handwriting makes translation very difficult. Photostats of the portions of the French National Archives connected with the War of American Independence are in the Library of Congress. They have been catalogued.

Count d'Estaing. There are hundreds of letters, reports, and orders of General d'Estaing relating to the Savannah expedition in the Archives Nationales. In the words of Édouard Chevalier, author of a French naval history of the period, M. d'Estaing *"écrivait beaucoup."* His writings in his fine, small hand take up a larger portion of the French National Archives than that of any other commander, according to Lacour-Gayet.

Among the more significant d'Estaing items (including some not in the Archives Nationales) are the following:

(a) *Faites et Motifs Préliminaires* (Facts and Preliminary Motives).

This document which was written by d'Estaing was added as a preface to his "Observations on O'Connor's Journal." This manuscript, which is in the Library of the Service Hydrographique de la Marine in Paris, is a summary of Count d'Estaing's reasons for undertaking the Savannah campaign. It is eleven pages in length.

(b) "Observations of Count d'Estaing on O'Connor's Journal of the Siege of Savannah." Library of the Service Hydrographique de la Marine in Paris. These notes or observations consist of d'Estaing's commentaries written in parallel column to the entries for the same date in Captain O'Connor's Journal. They appear under the respective head of "E" and "O." The observations of d'Estaing were written aboard the *Languedoc* while that vessel was still off the Georgia coast, being dated October 25, 1779. The Journal of O'Connor and d'Estaing's comments upon it cover pages 12–79 of a manuscript entitled *Journal du Siège de Savannah. Septembre, et Octobre, 1779*. Another copy is in the Archives Guerre, A^4, pp. 150ff. A third copy is in the hands of an English manuscripts dealer and has been offered for sale in America. The rough draft of the observations of Count d'Estaing and of his report to M. de Sartine is in the Archives Nationales (Marine), B^4 166, pp. 343–404 (folio pages). It is fortunate that this original draft was transcribed in readable form as it is almost indecipherable. The translations in this book of the O'Connor-d'Estaing manuscript are mine.

(c) *Journal de M. Le Comte D'Estaing. Avril 1788* [sic]—*Octobre 1779*. MS in the Historical Society of Pennsylvania, Philadelphia. The part relating to the Savannah campaign covers seven pages. This journal was acquired by the Society in 1904. In so far as the Siege of Savannah is concerned it is more or less a digest of O'Connor's Journal. The manuscript refers to d'Estaing in the third person.

(d) D'Estaing's report on the Savannah campaign sent from Brest to M. de Sartine, Minister of Marine, December 5, 1779. Archives Nationales (Marine), B^4 142, pp. 119–154. These are folio numbered pages, the report being actually 70 pages long.

(e) The Orderly Book of General d'Estaing's Headquarters from the day of the landing at Beaulieu until the embarkation some five weeks later. Archives Nationales (Marine), B^4 167, pp. 266–310 (folio pages).

Journal of a *garde de marine* on the *Guerrier*. This diary was kept by a young cadet on Bougainville's ship while the vessel was in American waters. The original is in the Library of the Service Hydrographique de la Marine in Paris. The portion relating to the period spent off Georgia covers pages 635–722 of the records. I have tried without success to identify the author of this journal.

Journal de ma Campagne, faite sous les ordres de M^r le Cte d'Estaing Vice-amiral de France, commandant l'Escadre du Roy partie *de Toulon le 13 Avril 1778*. This journal of an unidentified naval officer is in reality a log-book of the *Languedoc*. It is not of much value to a study of the Siege of Savannah. A facsimile (with an English translation) is in B. F. Stevens' "Facsimiles of Manuscripts in European Archives Relating to America 1773–1783." (No. 2011).

Journal of an unidentified French officer entitled *Siège de Savannah par le Comte d'Estaing 1779*. A manuscript copy of this journal, written in a clear, beautiful hand, is in the De Renne Collection in the Library of the University of Georgia. It is not apparent whether the author was a naval or an army officer. This Journal is one of the two journals translated by Charles C. Jones, Jr. (or rather by his daughter as we are informed in the Catalogue of the De Renne Collection) and published in *The Siege of Savannah, in 1779, as Described in Two Contemporaneous Journals of French Officers in the Fleet of Count d'Estaing* (Albany, N. Y., 1874), 1–52.

Miscellaneous French letters among the Benjamin Lincoln Papers in the New York Public Library include two communications from d'Estaing to General Lincoln and one from the French commander to Colonel Laurens. They are in the Thomas Addis Emmet Collection. For a complete list of these papers see *Calendar of the Emmet Collection of Manuscripts, etc., Relating to American History* (New York, 1900), 365–370.

Meyronnet de Saint-Marc, *Comte rendu des opérations faites par l'armée française, commandée par M^r. d'Estaing devant Savannah (Amérique)*. This twenty-two page manuscript journal of Chevalier Meyronnet de Saint-Marc, a young *lieutenant de vaisseau* on the *Marsellais*, is now owned by the New-York Historical Society. It is not in Meyronnet's hand but there is a note appended by him at the end identifying the journal as his. The original of this Journal was located in the Bibliothèque Municipale of Avignon, France. Vol. 2750, pp. 139–146 (folio pages). A reproduction of the manuscript is in the Library of Congress. It is entitled *Détail des opérations faites par l'armée française de M. le Cte. d'Estaing devant Savannah*. The name of Meyronnet de Saint-Marc does not appear on the original.

Journal de la campagne du vaisseau le Marseillais de 74 canons portant 36 . . . 18 et . . . 8. Commandé par monsieur de la Poïpe de Vertrieux, Capitaine des vaisseaux du Roy. Commandant la compagnie des Gardes de la Marine à toulon armé le 6 fevrier 1778 dans le port de toulon. MS in the Bibliothèque Municipale of Avignon, Vol. 2750, pages 2–84 (folio pages). The name of the author is not shown on the journal but the similarity in handwriting to the journal mentioned above, the fact that it was written by an officer aboard the *Marseillais*, and other circumstances indicate strongly that it was written by Lieutenant Meyronnet de Saint-Marc. Pages 61–84 cover the period of d'Estaing's expedition to Georgia and the return to France. The journal is a faithful, day-by-day factual account of the voyage of the *Marseillais* from the time she left Toulon in April, 1778, until December 31, 1779, when the author debarked in France. However, it is of an impersonal nature, and is to a large extent merely a log of the vessel during the American campaign.

Antoine-François-Térance O'Connor, *Journal Du Siège de Savannah*. A copy of the journal is in the Library of the Service Hydrographique de la Marine in Paris. Captain O'Connor was a French engineer of Irish descent. The *Journal* is a transcript of the original with d'Estaing's commentaries and observations copied in parallel column. A rough copy of O'Connor's *Journal* is found in the Archives Nationales (Marine), B⁴ 167.

Orders for the attack by the Allied forces on October 9th, 1779. A manuscript copy of d'Estaing's orders is in Archives Nationales (Marine), B⁴ 167, pp. 298–300 (folio pages). A signed copy is found among the Benjamin Lincoln Papers in the Thomas Addis Emmet Collection. A reproduction of the orders of the French General in connection with the false attack upon the British center is in B. F. Stevens, "Facsimiles of Manuscripts in European Archives Relating to America 1773–1783." The American and French orders are published in *Magazine of American History*, II (September, 1878), 548–551.

Puysegur MSS in possession of Bernard-Jacques-Hubert, Comte de Puysegur of Paris, a direct descendant of Antoine-Hyacinthe-Anne de Puysegur de Chastenet who commanded the *Truite* at Savannah. These miscellaneous papers include a short summary of M. de Puysegur's services at Savannah written by Count d'Estaing.

Relation du Siège de Savannah capitale de la nouvelle Géorgie, province de Sud de L'Amérique Septentrionale. This matter-of-fact account of the Siege was written by an unidentified French officer. It is in the Archives Nationales (Marine), B⁴ 142, pp. 197–200 (folio pages).

Jean-Rémy de Tarragon, *Journal de la Campagne de Savannah En 1779*. A copy is in Stevens' "Facsimiles of Manuscripts in European Archives Relating to America." (No. 2010). A convenient English translation accompanies it. The place in the French archives where this 28 page manuscript is deposited is not revealed. The signature "Pechot" which appears at the end of the manuscript was evidently a pen name used by Captain de Tarragon for the sake of anonymity. The Journal is printed in a brochure, edited by Lieutenant Colonel Adrien de Tarragon, entitled *Extrait du Journal de Campagne du Chevalier Jean-Rémy de Tarragon Capitaine commandant les chasseurs du régiment d'Armagnac et major de la division de Dillon au siège de Savannah 1779* (Moulins, 1935). There are a few minor differences between the printed version and the manuscript copy of the

Journal which is found in Stevens' Facsimiles. M. Rèmy de Tarragon of Limoges, France, a descendant of the author of the Journal, kindly furnished me with a copy of this little work.

American:

Peter Horry. General Horry's copy of M. L. Weems' *Life of Gen. Francis Marion* (Philadelphia, 1809) with his marginal comments thereon is in possession of his descendants. A. S. Salley, of Columbia, kindly made extracts for me from a photostat in his possession. Horry's Notes are of great value in exposing some of Weems' inventions.

The James Jackson MSS in the Georgia Historical Society contain a transcript of the notes Jackson wrote on Ramsay's *History of the Revolution of South-Carolina,* 2 vols. (Trenton, 1785). They were copied by William Bacon Stevens from the original or possibly from a copy which, according to a survey made in 1825 by Joseph V. Bevan, was in the Archives of the State of Georgia. A manuscript obituary or autobiographical sketch among the Jackson papers contains only a brief allusion to his part in the Siege of Savannah.

The Seaborn Jones Papers in the Duke University Library include three letters written during the Siege by Major John Jones to his wife who was refugeeing at Jacksonborough, South Carolina. The original of a letter sent from Zubly's Ferry on September 14, 1779, which was presented by Charles C. Jones, Jr., to Dr. Thomas Addis Emmet is in the Emmet Collection in the New York Public Library. The four letters are published in George White, *Historical Collections of Georgia* (New York, 1854), 535–536.

Benjamin Lincoln. The Lincoln Papers in the Thomas Addis Emmet Collection in the New York Public Library (under the head of "Siege of Savannah") include American casualty lists and returns, letters of various French officers (including d'Estaing), maps, and many documents not connected in any way with the Siege. It is notable for the number of prints of French, British and American officers. The particular Collection is carefully bound and arranged with Hough's *Siege of Savannah* and Jones' *French Officers' Journals.* The main Lincoln items are his letter to Major Everard Meade dated November 1, 1779, and two letters to him from Count d'Estaing. A journal of the Siege of Savannah by General Lincoln is in the Library of Congress among the Papers of the Continental Congress. His account is not very revealing. It is styled "Journal of Major Gen. Lincoln from September 3rd to October 19th, 1779." The last page of the original is missing but a contemporaneous rough draft thereof is in the Library of Congress. Lincoln's official report dated October 22, 1779, is also among the Papers of the Continental Congress in that institution. No. 158, pp. 279–282. It is printed in Franklin B. Hough, ed., *The Siege of Savannah* (Albany, N. Y., 1866), 149–156. Several other communications from Lincoln to the Congress during the period of the Savannah Campaign are also in the Library of Congress. General Lincoln's Order Books of this period are in the De Renne Collection at the University of Georgia.

Miscellaneous manuscripts in the Georgia Historical Society which relate to the Siege include the following:

(a) A manuscript history of Georgia by Joseph Vallance Bevan written about 1825 contains a chapter on the Siege of Savannah. The account is based on the limited sources available at the time. The following curious, unexpanded statement appears about Pulaski: "In fact, none of the vulgar stories commonly repeated about himself, or his conduct during the siege, appear to be entitled to the least degree of credit."

(b) A letter from Ensign Moses Buffington of Captain Parr's South Carolina Royalists to his "ever honoured" parents, dated December 8, 1779, contains a poorly spelled account of the Siege of Savannah. With corrected spelling it appeared in *The Magnolia, or Southern Appalachian* (Charleston, 1842–1843), II (1843), 378.

(c) Lynah Papers. These manuscripts consist of several letters written to James Lynah who in 1854 wrote to the *Philadelphia Herald* on the subject of the operation performed by his grandfather at Savannah upon General Pulaski. Included among them is a letter giving recollections of the reminiscences of Dr. Nicholas Belleville about Pulaski. ("He seemed to fight as if enjoying a banquet.") There is also among these papers a certificate as to the authenticity of the fatal grapeshot.

(d) Letter from General Lachlan McIntosh to General Moultrie, August 10, 1779, describing low morale of the Virginia militia. The only McIntosh paper relating to the period of the Siege is in the Benjamin Lincoln Papers, Thomas Addis Emmet Collection, in the New York Public Library. It is dated October 16, 1779.

(e) The William Bacon Stevens papers in the Georgia Historical Society include a memorandum in Stevens' hand of the story about Samuel Warren of South Carolina and his English aunt. I have not been able to verify this anecdote. Captain Warren was officially listed among the American wounded on October 9th.

Pinckney Papers. The C. C. Pinckney Collection in the Library of Duke University contains the original of the letter written by Charles Cotesworth Pinckney, Jr., to his mother on October 9, 1779, and printed in Charles C. Jones, Jr., *History of Savannah, Ga.* (Syracuse, 1890), 289. Among the C. C. Pinckney MSS in the Library of Congress is a letter to his mother dated October 15, 1779, in which he reproves her for her attitude toward his brother who apparently had been guilty of writing to his new wife more frequently while in camp before Savannah than to his parent.

A photostat of the only Thomas Pinckney manuscript relating to the Siege which was located is in the South Carolina Historical Society in Charleston. The original was not found. The document in question which is entitled "Account of the Siege of Savannah" was prepared by General Pinckney at the request of Alexander Garden and appeared in *Anecdotes of the American Revolution* (Charleston, 1828), 20–27. The only other Thomas Pinckney manuscript known to have been written in connection with the Siege appears to be no longer extant. It was a letter from General Pinckney to William Johnson in 1822 in which he took the Judge to task for several statements in his Life of General Greene, including the one that "even at the last moment the attack might have succeeded" had, among other things, "all the corps of the American army fought with equal bravery." In a letter to his son enclosing the communication Pinckney stated that old age had "blunted those feelings which would have dictated a more indignant refutation of the calumny." See Thomas J. Kirkland and Robert M. Kennedy, *Historic Camden* (Columbia, S. C., 1905), 196f.

The Casimir Pulaski manuscripts in the Archives and Museum of the Polish Roman Catholic Union at Chicago include a dispatch sent by that officer to General Lincoln on September 14, 1779. The Archives Nationales contain several communications written by Pulaski to d'Estaing in French during the Savannah campaign. The letters are dated September 12th, October 2nd and 6th, 1779. See Archives Nationales (Marine), B⁴ 168, pp. 205–209.

British:

British Regimental Order Book, July 2–October 2, 1779. MS in the Library of Congress. Apparently it is the same manuscript to which William B. Stevens had access and which was described by him as an orderly book of General Prevost. It was then in the Tefft Collection. Stevens quoted from it in his *History of Georgia*, 2 vols. (New York, Philadelphia, 1847, 1859), II, 203f.

Sir Henry Clinton Headquarters Papers.

(a) The Clinton Collection in the William L. Clements Library at the University of Michigan contains various records including intelligence reports, letters, maps, casualty lists, and commissary returns during the period of the Siege of Savannah.

(b) British Headquarters Papers of General Henry Clinton in possession of Colonial Williamsburg, Inc. They include the originals of the dispatches from General Prevost to Lord Clinton reporting the presence of the French fleet off Georgia. This Collection is in microfilm form in the New York Public Library.

Miscellaneous British MSS in the Department of Archives and History of the State of Georgia in Atlanta. These papers include a number of documents connected with the Siege of Savannah. Among them are two letters signed by Captain Mowbray of the *Germain* relating to the service of his Majesty in the Savannah River. They are dated September 17th and 26th, 1779. They also number several official documents in respect to the burning by the British of the residence of Josiah Tattnall in the environs of Savannah. See "Bonds, Bills of Sale, Deeds of Gift, Powers of Attorney," for 1778–1782 and for 1779–1789.

John Maitland. No letters of Lieutenant Colonel Maitland were located at Thirlestane Castle in Lauder, Scotland. The Duke of Newcastle Papers in the British Museum contain the memorial sent by Captain Maitland in 1761 requesting promotion and recounting the loss of his right hand in the battle in Lagos Bay, Spain. Maitland stated that he had been an officer for sixteen years. He must therefore have entered the army at a very youthful age. This is the only Maitland manuscript catalogued in the British Museum. Apparently no papers of Colonel Maitland during the time of the Siege are in existence. A letter written by him to General Moultrie belonging to a slightly earlier period is published in the latter's *Memoirs*.

Minutes of the Governor and Council, Savannah, September 6, 1779—September 20, 1780. These manuscript records in the Georgia Historical Society were edited by Lilla M. Hawes and published in *The Georgia Historical Quarterly*, XXXV (March, 1951), 31–59; (June, 1951), 126–151; and (September, 1951), 196–221.

Public Record Office Papers (America and West Indies), Colonial Office. London. Class 5, Vols. 98 and 131. This massive collection contains a number of letters connected with the Siege of Savannah, including General Prevost's report of his victory and the dispatches sent by him before the blockade became effective to General Clinton, Colonel Fuser, and Admiral Byron. The papers in the Public Record Office relating to the American Revolution are catalogued and abstracted in *Report on American Manuscripts in the Royal Institution of Great Britain* (I, London, 1904; II, Dublin, 1906). A number of these manuscripts are found in facsimile form in Stevens' "Facsimiles of Manuscripts in European Archives Relating to America 1773–1783." The Headquarters Papers of Sir Henry Clinton, in possession of Colonial Williamsburg, Inc., contain the originals of some of the Public Record Office manuscripts which in certain instances are found only in abstract form in Great Britain. The old and new style designations of the British Public Record Office papers are confusing. Mr. Kenneth Coleman of Atlanta, a student of Georgia's Revolutionary history, kindly made available to me his microfilm of certain of the above records.

BIBLIOGRAPHY

PRINTED JOURNALS, MEMOIRS, AND CONTEMPORARY ACCOUNTS OF THE SIEGE OF SAVANNAH

French:

Bougainville à L'Escadre du Cte D'Estaing Guerre d'Amérique 1778-1779 (Paris, 1927) by René de Kerallain. This interesting little work quotes copiously from the journal kept by M. de Bougainville while his ship was off the Georgia coast. The author was a descendant of the famous navigator.

Campagne de M. le Comte d'Estaing en Amérique ou Mémoire pour servir de réfutation au libelle Contre ce Vice-Amiral (Brussels, 1782). Pages 64-75 of this pamphlet contain a defense of the Count's actions in respect to the Siege and attack to the criticisms in Extrait du Journal d'un officier de la marine de l'Escadre de M. le Comte d'Estaing, op. cit. The author of this defense was anonymous. A copy is in the John Carter Brown Library, Providence, Rhode Island.

Extrait du Journal d'un officier de la marine de l'Escadre de M. le comte d'Estaing (Paris, 1782). Copies of this journal which was written by an unidentified French naval officer are in the Library of Congress and in the De Renne Collection in the University of Georgia Library. The portion of this journal pertaining to the Savannah campaign (i.e., pp. 101-126) was translated by or under the direction of Charles C. Jones, Jr. and published in The Siege of Savannah, in 1779, as Described in Two Contemporaneous Journals of French Officers in the Fleet of Count d'Estaing (Albany, N. Y., 1874), 57-70. The journal itself offers no clue to the identity of the author. It appears too critical to have been written by d'Estaing's trusted assistant, M. de Borda, a suggestion once made by Thomas Balch. For example, on September 28, 1779, Chevalier de Borda says at the end of a report, "I close, *mon cher général*, by offering a thousand prayers for you. My heart and my head desire that you succeed." Archives Nationales (Marine), B⁴ 166, p. 32.

Mémoires et voyages du Chevalier Aristide-Aubert du Petit-Thouars, capitaine de Vaisseau (Paris, 1822). The description of du Petit-Thouars' experiences at Savannah were set forth in a letter written by him to his friend, Deodat de Dolomieu, in 1785.

Relation De L'Attaque de Savanach [sic]. A copy of this two page account is in the John Carter Brown Library in Providence.

Mémoires Posthumes du Feld-Maréchal Comte de Stedingk by Le Général Comte de Bjornstjerna, 3 vols. (Paris, 1844). Stedingk wrote in French. His letter to the King of Sweden dated January 18, 1780, furnishes a good description of the Savannah campaign. Mémoires, I,

36-44. The letter to King Gustave III is translated in "Count Stedingk," *Putnam's Monthly*, October, 1854, 352-353.

Journal of Philippe Séguier de Terson, a captain in the Agénois Regiment. This journal is printed, with commentaries and notes by A. de Cazenove, in *Le Siège de Savannah. Extrait de la Revue de Midi* (Nîmes, 1903). A copy is found in the De Renne Collection at the University of Georgia.

Journal of Captain Jean-Rémy de Tarragon. See French Manuscripts, *supra*.

American:

Paul Bentalou, *A Reply to Judge Johnson's Remarks on an Article in the North American Review, Relating to Count Pulaski* (Baltimore 1826). He wrote another pamphlet in 1824 entitled *Pulaski Vindicated from an unsupported Charge, Inconsiderately or Malignantly Introduced in Judge Johnson's Sketches of the Life and Correspondence of Major General Nathaniel [sic] Greene*. Both pamphlets allude to the Siege of Savannah in which Captain Bentalou served with Pulaski's Legion.

Letters of Joseph Clay, Merchant of Savannah, 1776-1793. Collections of the Georgia Historical Society (Savannah, 1913), VIII. The original letter-books are in possession of the Georgia Historical Society. Colonel Clay, who was present at the Siege of Savannah, wrote several letters during that period.

"William Hasell Gibbes Story of his Life." Edited by Arney R. Childs. *The South Carolina Historical and Genealogical Magazine* (Charleston, 1900–   ), L (April, 1949), pp. 59-67. Gibbes' autobiographical sketch is unfortunately meagre in regard to his experiences during the Siege of Savannah.

"Order book of Maj. John Faucheraud Grimké, August 1778 to May, 1780." *The South Carolina Historical and Genealogical Magazine*, XVII (January, April, and July, 1916). The order book covers the period of the Siege.

Joseph Habersham. A letter written by Colonel Joseph Habersham on September 28th, 1779, from "Col Wylly's Tent," was in existence some years ago. In it Habersham related that Samuel Elbert was a prisoner at the time within the British lines at Savannah. I was not able to find the original. Charles C. Jones, Jr. mentioned the fact that he had seen this letter. See *The Life and Services of the Honorable Maj. Gen. Samuel Elbert of Georgia* (Cambridge, Mass., 1887), 35 n.

Paul Hamilton, Sr., "Extracts from a Private Manuscript written by Governor Paul Hamilton, Sr., During the Period of the Revolutionary War, from 1776-1800." *Year Book—1898. City of Charleston, So. Ca.*, 299-327. Governor Hamilton served at Savannah at a very youthful age. These reminiscences graphically describe his reactions to the

BIBLIOGRAPHY

Allied losses on October 9th but are devoid of details of his experiences during the Siege.

"Account of the Siege of Savannah" by General Thomas Pinckney in Garden's *Anecdotes of the American Revolution*, 20–27. See American manuscript sources, *supra*.

David Ramsay, *The History of the Revolution of South-Carolina, from a British Province to an Independent State*, 2 vols. (Trenton, 1785). Dr. Ramsay was present during the Siege of Savannah and his history is for that reason listed among original sources though there is nothing in his account in the way of personal reminiscence or anecdote.

Major Rogowski's memoirs of Casimir Pulaski's part in the attack on October 9th. Rogowski's dramatic and imaginative account of the circumstances under which the Polish hero was mortally wounded is quoted by Charles C. Jones, Jr., in his *History of Georgia*, II, 402 n.

British:

Robert Colvill, *Savannah, a Poem in Two Cantos to the Memory of the Honourable Colonel John Maitland* (London, 1780). Twenty pages, including a preface. There were several editions. Copies are in the Library of the University of Georgia, the Library of Congress, the New York Public Library and the Georgia State Library. The Reverend Mr. Colvill of Dysart, Scotland, is described in *The Lives of Eminent Scotsmen* (1822) as "an assiduous but unsuccessful wooer of the muses; he was for a time, one of the most constant of Ruddiman's weekly contributors."

"The Siege of Savannah, 1779, as Related by Colonel John Harris Cruger." *Magazine of American History*, II (August, 1878) 489–492. Colonel Cruger's account of the Siege was sent with a letter, dated November 8, 1779, to his father and brother in New York.

Journal of Captain Johann Hinrichs. This inquisitive-minded Hessian officer was not present at the Siege of Savannah but visited the town a few weeks later. His journal describes the country and its economy and reviews at some length the military aspects of the Siege of Savannah. The journal with an excellent translation is printed in *The Siege of Charleston With an Account of the Province of South Carolina: Diaries and Letters of Hessian Officers From the von Jungkenn Papers in the William L. Clements Library*. Translated and edited by Bernard A. Uhlendorf (Ann Arbor, 1938).

Journals in Hough's *Siege of Savannah* reprinted from *The Royal Gazette* of New York. There are three such "journals." They are: (1) a report made by Captain John Henry of the English navy (*ibid.*, 134–146); (2) a journal by an unidentified British naval officer (*ibid.*, 57–79) which also appeared in *The Historical Magazine* (Boston, 1857–1875), VIII, January, 1864; and (3) a journal (Hough, pp. 25–

52) which appeared in *The Royal Gazette* (New York) on December 11, 1779. The latter journal was printed in *The Royal Georgia Gazette* at Savannah on November 18, 1779. As reprinted in a Charlestown paper the following month this journal was published in *Collections of the Georgia Historical Society*, V, Part 1 (Savannah, 1901), 129–139. In two or three places the language of the journal in question is identical to that of Governor Wright's account of the Siege hereinafter mentioned. Possibly the journal as published in the newspapers was a composite affair.

Elizabeth Lichtenstein Johnston, *Recollections of a Georgia Loyalist* (New York and London, 1901). Miss Lichtenstein was in Savannah during the Siege. She later married Captain William Martin Johnston. Her recollections were written in 1836 when she was seventy-two.

T. W. Moore, letter written by concerning Siege, November 4, 1779. This account by an aide-de-camp of General Prevost appeared in Rivington's *Royal Gazette* on December 29th of the same year. See Hough's *Siege of Savannah*, 82–88.

Augustin Prevost. General Prevost's report to Lord Germain dated November 2, 1779, embodied a journal of the Siege of Savannah. See British manuscripts, *supra*. Prevost's official dispatch was contemporaneously printed at London in *The Gentleman's Magazine* and in *The Westminster Magazine* in December, 1779. Two years later while visiting at Valenciennes, General Prevost, who spoke French, wrote a journal of the Siege of Savannah in that tongue. In the main he followed his original account. This journal was translated by Charles Edgeworth Jones and published in *Publications of the Southern History Association* (Atlanta, 1895–1907), I (October, 1897), 259–268.

The Annual Register, or a View of the History, Politics, and Literature, for the year 1779 (London, 1780), 207–214.

Anthony Stokes. Chief Justice Stokes' letter to his wife dated November 9, 1779, contains a good account of the Siege. See Frank Moore, ed., *Diary of the American Revolution. From Newspapers and Original Documents*, 2 vols. (New York, 1863), II, 223–231. Stokes' *View of the Constitution of the British Colonies, in North America and the West Indies, at the time the Civil War broke out on the Continent of America* (London, 1783) mentions the loss of his papers by fire during the bombardment of Savannah. There are several references to the Siege of Savannah in *A Narrative of the Official Conduct of Anthony Stokes of the Inner Temple, London, Barrister at Law; His Majesty's Chief Justice, and one of his Council of Georgia; and of the Dangers and Distresses He underwent in the Cause of Government* (London, 1784). A copy of Stokes' narrative is in the Library of Congress.

James Wright. Governor Wright wrote a journal of the Siege of Savannah which is published in *Collections of the Georgia Historical*

BIBLIOGRAPHY 195

Society (Savannah, 1873), III, 262-268. Letters from Sir James to Lord Germain in reference to the Siege are found *ibid.,* 260f., 270f. Wright's Journal and his accompanying letter of November 5th are in *The Colonial Records of the State of Georgia* (Atlanta, 1937), XXXVIII (Part II). Typewritten copy of unpublished British records compiled by Allen D. Candler.

CONTEMPORARY NEWSPAPERS AND MAGAZINES

The Boston Gazette and the Country Journal, October-December, 1779. The Library of Congress.

The Charlestown Gazette, published by Mrs. Crouch, 1779. Files of the three Charleston papers mentioned in this bibliography are in the Charleston Library Society in that city.

Connecticut Journal (New Haven), November-December, 1779. The Library of Congress.

The Gentleman's Magazine (London, 1779), Vol. XLIX.

Johnston, James. A pamphlet published in 1780, entitled *Account of the Siege of Savannah; Chiefly Extracted from the Royal Georgia Gazette* (Savannah, 1780). De Renne Collection, Library of the University of Georgia. The pamphlet consists principally of the journal of the Siege which appeared in that newspaper on November 18, 1779.

New Jersey Archives—Newspaper Extracts, 1778-1780, Vols. III, IV. Contains extracts from newspapers describing exploits of Major Maitland in New Jersey in 1778.

The New-York Gazette and The Weekly Mercury, 1779-1780. Photostats of this newspaper for these years are in the Library of Congress.

The New-York Mercury, or, General Advertiser, December 10, 1779. The Historical Society of Pennsylvania.

The Pennsylvania Gazette and Weekly Advertiser (Philadelphia) September-October-November, 1779. The Library of Congress.

The Royal Gazette (New York), a Loyalist newspaper published by James Rivington. Much of the material that appeared in its columns relating to the Siege was reprinted later in Hough's *Siege of Savannah.* Files of *The Royal Gazette* are in the Library of Congress and in the New-York Historical Society. The Right Honorable Ian Colin Maitland, Fifteenth Earl of Lauderdale, kindly made available a contemporary reprint of the eulogy to Colonel Maitland which was published in Rivington's *Gazette* on December 15, 1779.

The Royal Georgia Gazette (Savannah). Publication of this Tory newspaper was suspended when the French appeared before Savannah. A series of articles concerning the Siege was printed in its columns during November and December, 1779. The most complete file of the *Gazette* during the period is in the Library of the University of Georgia at Athens.

The Scots Magazine (Edinburgh), December, 1779.

The South-Carolina and American General Gazette (Charlestown), 1779.

The Gazette of the State of South-Carolina (Charlestown), 1779.

The Virginia Gazette (Williamsburg), 1779. Photostats of the *Gazette* for that year are in the Library of Congress.

The Westminster Magazine (London), December, 1779.

SECONDARY WORKS AND MATERIAL

The following list represents the secondary sources cited in the footnotes and others that have proven useful in this study of the Siege of Savannah and of its participants. It is by no means exhaustive of the secondary and background works consulted. In some instances books mentioned among the primary sources have been relisted here. Works in the French language (or translations) have been classified under the head of "French" and those by Americans or Englishmen under that head, translations of German writings being included among them.

French:

Balch, Thomas (translation by E. S. and E. W. Balch), *The French in America During the War of Independence of the United States 1777-1783*, 2 vols. (Philadelphia, 1895). The second volume contains brief biographical sketches of French officers.

Bellessort, André, *La Pérouse* (Paris, 1926).

Besson, Maurice, *Le Comte D'Estaing* (Paris, 1931). This work is based to a large extent on Calmon-Maison's biography of Admiral d'Estaing.

Biographie Générale, 46 vols. (Paris, 1854-1856). The first eight volumes of this work were styled *Nouvelle Biographie Universelle*.

Biographie Universelle, edited by Joseph-François Michaud, 45 vols. (Paris, 1854-1865).

Bjornstjerna, Count de, *Mémoires Posthumes du Feld-Maréchal Comte de Stedingk*, 3 vols. (Paris, 1844).

Calmon-Maison, Jean Joseph, *L'Amiral d'Estaing (1729-1794)* (Paris, 1910). This is the best existing study of Count d'Estaing.

Campan, Jeanne Louise Henriette, *Memoirs of the Private Life of Marie Antoinette*, 2 vols. (New York, 1917).

Castellane, Marquis de, *Gentilshommes Démocrates* (Paris, 1890). Contains chapter on Louis-Marie, Vicomte de Noailles.

Chevalier, Édouard, *Histoire de la Marine Française Pendant la Guerre de L'Indépendance Américaine* (Paris, 1877). This work presents a comprehensive account of French naval operations during the American Revolution, including those off Savannah.

Colomb, Pierre, "Memoirs of a Revolutionary Soldier." Translated and published in *The Collector* (New York), Mary A. Benjamin, ed. See issues of October and November, 1950, and January, 1951. Colomb was a Frenchman who enlisted in the American service. He was captured when Savannah fell in 1778.

Combattants Français de la guerre Américaine 1777–1783 by the "Ministère des Affaires Étrangères." 58th Congress, 2d. Session, Document No. 77. (Washington, 1905). Contains rosters of crews of the French ships and of the French regiments that fought in America.

Couvrai, Louvet de, *Amours du Chevalier de Faublaf*, a portion of which was published in America under the title of *The Interesting History of the Baron De Lovzinski. Written by Himself. With a Relation of the Most Remarkable Occurrences in the Life of the Celebrated Count Pulaski* (Hartford, 1800). Imaginative account of Pulaski's last moments.

Cunat, M., *Histoire du bailli de Suffren* (Paris, 1852).

Doniol, Henri, *Histoire de la Participation de la France à l'Établissement des États-Unis d'Amérique* (Paris, 1889).

Du Petit Thouars, Admiral Bergasse, *Aristide Aubert du Petit Thouars. Héros d'Aboukir, 1760–1798. Lettres et documents inédits* (Paris, 1937).

Guizot, M. and Madame Guizot de Witt, *The History of France from the Earliest Times to 1848*. 8 vols. Translated by Robert Black (New York, 1869–1898).

Kerallain, René de, *Bougainville à L'Escadre du Cte D'Estaing Guerre d'Amérique 1778–1779* (Paris, 1927).

Lacour-Gayet, "Old France and Young America; Campaign of Vice-Admiral D'Estaing, in 1778." Translated from the French. *The United Service* (L. B. Hamersly, Jr., ed.) Vol. 8 (New York), October, 1905, pp. 301–321.

La Rochefoucauld-Liancourt, Duke de, *Voyage dans les États-Unis d'Amérique, fait en 1795, 1796 et 1797*, 8 vols. (Paris, 1799). M. de La Rochefoucauld discussed the Siege of Savannah with residents of the city while he was there.

Lasseray, André, *Les Français sous les treize étoiles* (Paris, 1935).

La Varende, Jean de, *Suffren et Ses Ennemis* (Paris, 1948).

Leconte, Vergniaud, *Henri Christophe dans L'Histoire D'Haiti* (Paris, 1931). Contains a brief reference to Christophe's military services at Savannah.

Merlant, Joachim, *Soldiers and Sailors of France in the American War for Independence (1776–1783)* as translated from the French by Mary Bushnell (New York, 1920).

Noailles, Amblard Marie Raymond Amédée, Vicomte de, *Marins et Soldats Français En Amérique Pendant la Guerre d' L'Indépendance des États-Unis (1778–1783)*, (Paris, 1903 ed.).

Pluyette, Colonel, "*Étude critique des opérations de L'amiral d'Estaing aux États-Unis et aux Antilles (1778–1779)*." *Bulletin Historique et Scientifique de L'Auvergne*. *L'Académie des Sciences, Belles-Lettres et Arts de Clermont-Ferrand*. Second Series, 1921 and 1922, *passim*. The Savannah Campaign (briefly treated only) is *ibid.*, 1922, pp. 121–128. A copy of this publication is in the New York Public Library.

Pontgibaud, de, *A French Volunteer of the War of Independence (the Chevalier de Pontgibaud)*. Translated and edited by Robert B. Douglas (New York, 1898). De Pontgibaud was not at Savannah during the Siege but his journal contains glimpses of some of the Frenchmen who were.

Ségur, Comte Louis-Philippe de, *Mémoires du comte de Ségur*, 7 vols. (Paris, 1842).

Soulés, François, *Histoire Des Troubles de L'Amérique Anglaise*, 7 vols. (Paris, 1787).

Thiers, M. A., *The History of the French Revolution*, 5 vols. Translated by Frederick Shoberl (London, 1838).

Thiéry, Maurice, *Bougainville, Soldier and Sailor* (London, 1932). Translation by Anne Agnew. There is little about the Savannah episode in this interesting biography.

British and American:

Annals of Congress, 7th Congress, 2nd Sess. (1803), p. 172. Speech of Hon. James Jackson in United States Senate in which he quoted d'Estaing's reputed reply to the Americans concerning his perseverance in the attempt to take Savannah.

Appleton's Cyclopaedia of American Biography (New York, 1888–1889), 6 vols.

Arthur, T. S., and W. H. Carpenter, *The History of Georgia, from its Earliest Settlement to the Present Time* (Philadelphia, 1852). Contains the anecdote about Count Dillon and the reward he offered to his troops.

Bartram, John, *Diary of a Journey through the Carolinas, Georgia, and Florida from July 1, 1765, to April 10, 1766* (London, 1766).

Beatson, Robert, *Naval and Military Memoirs of Great Britain from 1727 to 1783* (London, 1804), 6 vols.

Bellet, Louise Pecquet du, *Some Prominent Virginia Families* (Lynchburg, 1907). 2 vols. Volume two contains "A Narrative of My Life For My Family" written in 1842 by Francis T. Brooke who served at Savannah during the closing stages of the Revolution.

Bonsal, Stephen, *When the French Were Here* (New York, 1945). Contains brief mention of the Siege of Savannah, being principally

BIBLIOGRAPHY

"A Narrative of the Sojourn of the French Forces in America, and their Contribution to the Yorktown Campaign." Mr. Bonsal's researches carried him into the Archives Nationales in Paris.

British Martial Register, The (London, 1806), III, 59-66. Account of Siege of Savannah.

Butler, Lewis, *The Annals of the King's Royal Rifle Corps* (London, 1913-1932), 5 vols. A photograph of the colors of the Second Regiment of South Carolina is in volume one. The flag borne by Jasper is not a trophy of the King's Royal Rifle Corps at London as some have asserted. My efforts to locate the colors in England were not successful.

Carrington, Henry B., *Battles of the American Revolution 1775-1781* (New York, 1876).

Chappell, J. Harris, *Georgia History in Stories* (Atlanta, 1905). The author quoted a remark to General Lincoln attributed to Count d'Estaing that Savannah was surrounded and that "the city will be ours before sunset without the firing of a gun!" I have never been able to locate the source of this undocumented quotation and am completely at a loss to know where it came from.

Chronological History of Savannah, A. E. Sholes, Compiler (Savannah, 1900). Contains photograph of the house (now destroyed) used by Prevost as his headquarters. It was located on the north side of Broughton between Bull and Drayton Streets. There is also a picture of the old Sheftall house (later Kent) on St. James or Telfair Square showing the hole made by a French cannon ball during the Siege.

Collections of the Massachusetts Historical Society (1904), Seventh Series, IV, 259-260. Letter of Samuel Barrett, August 23, 1778, criticizing the abandonment by the French of the Siege of Newport.

Crawford, Mary MacDermot, *The Sailor Whom England Feared* (New York, 1913). John Paul Jones' statement concerning the preference shown the nobility in the French navy in 1778, quoted on page 9f., *supra,* was taken from this work.

Davis, John, *Travels of Four Years and a Half in the United States of America; during 1798, 1799, 1800, 1801, and 1802* (London, 1803). Davis compared the city to a village on the Cliffs of Dover.

de Koven, Mrs. Reginald, *The Life and Letters of John Paul Jones,* 2 vols. (New York, 1913). Jones' comment about d'Estaing's loyalty to the king, quoted on page 15, *supra,* is taken from this work.

DeSaussure, Wilmot G., *The Names, as far as can be ascertained of the Officers who served in the South Carolina Regiments of the Continental Establishment.* See *Year Book—1893. City of Charleston, So. Ca.,* 208-237.

Dictionary of American Biography, 20 vols. (New York, 1928-1936).

Dictionary of National Biography, 63 vols. (London, 1885-1900).

Neither this nor any other standard biographical work in England contains a sketch of Colonel John Maitland.

Douglas, Sir Robert, *The Peerage of Scotland*. As revised by John Philip Wood, 2 vols. (Edinburgh, 1813, 2nd. ed.).

Elbert, Samuel, "Order book of Samuel Elbert, Colonel and Brigadier General in the Continental Army, October 1776, to November, 1778," in *Collections of the Georgia Historical Society*, V, Part 2 (Savannah, 1902). The original is in the Georgia Historical Society.

Elzas, Barnett A., *The Jews of South Carolina From the Earliest Times to the Present Day* (Philadelphia, 1905). Contains information about Jewish participants in the Siege of Savannah.

Gamble, Thomas. The Gamble Scrapbooks in the Savannah Public Library include the accounts of the Siege contributed by Mr. Gamble to the *Savannah Press* and *Savannah Morning News* during the period of the sesquicentennial of the event. A newspaper clipping inserted by Mr. Gamble in one of these Scrapbooks states that the "Grenadiers' Marching Song" was composed in commemoration of the part played by the Sixtieth or Royal American Regiment at Savannah. Correspondence by the author with the Director of the Music Room of the British Museum and research elsewhere in England fails to substantiate this claim. A compilation of fife music in 1805 mentions "The Georgia Grenadiers' March" by a Mr. Alexander.

Garden, Alexander, *Anecdotes of the American Revolution* (Charleston, 1828); and *Anecdotes of the Revolutionary War in America* (Charleston, 1822).

Gardiner, Asa Bird, *The Order of the Cincinnati in France* (Newport, 1905). Considerable information about the French participants in the Siege of Savannah is found in this work. In a number of instances, however, it is unreliable as to who served or did not serve there.

Gibbes, Robert W., *Documentary History of the American Revolution; consisting of Letters and Papers relating to the Contest for Liberty, chiefly in South Carolina*, 3 vols. (New York, 1853–1857).

Gilman, Caroline, ed., *Letters of Eliza Wilkinson* (New York, 1839). A contemporary description of General Lincoln is found in one of the letters.

Gordon, William, *The History of the Rise, Progress, and Establishment, of the Independence of the United States of America*, 3 vols. (New York, 1789).

Gordon, William W., "Count Casimir Pulaski" in *The Georgia Historical Quarterly* (Savannah, 1917), XIII (September, 1929), pp. 169–227.

Gregg, Alexander, *History of the Old Cheraws.* . . . (Columbia, S. C., 1925 ed.). Contains excerpts from Reverend Evan Pugh's diary concerning the memorial sermon for those killed at Savannah on October 9th.

Remains of Major-General Nathanael Greene, The, A Report to the General Assembly of Rhode Island (Providence, 1903).

Harden, William, *A History of Savannah and South Georgia,* 2 vols. (Chicago and New York, 1913).

Heitman, Francis B., *Historical Register of Officers of the Continental Army During the War of the Revolution* (Washington, D. C., 1893). In the back of this book is a list of the officers who served in America with the French armies.

Hough, Franklin B., ed., *The Siege of Savannah, by the Combined American and French Forces, under the Command of Gen. Lincoln, and the Count d'Estaing, in the Autumn of 1779* (Albany, N. Y., 1866).

Howe, Robert, "Proceedings of a General Court Martial . . . the Trial of Major General Howe December 7, 1781," in *Collections of the New York Historical Society for the year 1879,* pp. 217-311. The court martial grew out of the British capture of Savannah in December, 1778. The testimony is of value here by way of topographical and other information about Savannah.

James, William Dobein, *A Sketch of the Life of Brig. Gen. Francis Marion and a History of his Brigade* (Charleston, 1821). Reprint by Continental Book Company of Marietta, Ga. (1948) with introduction by A. S. Salley.

Johnson, John Archibald, "Beaufort and the Sea Islands. Their History and Traditions." A typewritten copy of this series of articles which appeared in the *Beaufort County Republican* in 1873 is in the Charleston Library Society.

Johnson, Joseph, *Traditions and Reminiscences Chiefly of the American Revolution in the South* (Charleston, 1851).

Johnson, William, *Remarks, Critical and Historical, on an Article in the Forty-seventh Number of the North American Review, Relating to Count Pulaski* (Charleston, 1825). A portion of this answer to Captain Bentalou's article deals with the controversy that developed over the circumstances under which General Pulaski fell at Savannah.

Johnson, William, *Sketches of the Life and Correspondence of Nathanael Greene, Major General of the Armies of the United States, In the War of the Revolution,* 2 vols. (Charleston, 1822).

Johnston, Edith Duncan, *The Houstouns of Georgia* (Athens, 1950).

Jones, Charles C., Jr., *The History of Georgia,* 2 vols. (Boston, 1883).

Jones, Charles C., Jr., *History of Savannah, Ga.* (Syracuse, 1890).

Jones, Charles C., Jr., "Casimir Pulaski." Address delivered before the Georgia Historical Society. *Collections of the Georgia Historical Society* (Savannah, 1875), III, 385-410.

Keltie, John S., *A History of the Scottish Highlands, Highland Clans and Highland Regiments*, 2 vols. (Edinburgh, 1885).

Konopczynski, Wladyslaw, *Casimir Pulaski*. Translated from the Polish by Irena Makarewicz (Chicago, 1947). This biography contains a catalogue of the Pulaski papers in the Polish Roman Catholic Archives and Museum at Chicago. The work contains a reproduction of a French painting depicting the return of Pulaski's riderless charger to the place where the Allied commanders were gathered after the battle.

Lebey Family History (typewritten) in Savannah Public Library. If six Lebey brothers fought at Savannah they were not members of any of the regular French regiments whose rosters have been examined by the author.

Lee, Henry, *Memoirs of the War in the Southern Department of the United States* (New York, 1870, revised edition).

Lefferts, Charles M., *Uniforms of the American, British, French, and German Armies in the War of the American Revolution 1775–1783*, edited by Alexander J. Wall (New York, 1926).

Léger, J. N., *Haiti, Her History and Her Detractors* (New York, and Washington, 1907).

Lodge, Henry Cabot, *The Story of the Revolution*, 2 vols. (New York, 1898). Cited because of the painting of the storming of the British lines on October 9, 1779.

Lossing, Benson J., *The Pictorial Field-Book of the Revolution*, 2 vols. (New York, 1852).

MacLean, J. P., *An Historical Account of the Settlements of Scotch Highlands in America Prior to the Peace of 1783* (Cleveland, 1900).

McCall, Hugh, *The History of Georgia, Containing Brief Sketches of the Most Remarkable Events up to the Present Day*, 2 vols. (Savannah, 1811, 1816).

McCrady, Edward, *The History of South Carolina in the Revolution*, 2 vols. (New York, 1902).

Mason, F. Van Wyck, *Rivers of Glory* (New York, 1942). Mr. Mason's novel contains an interesting and colorful account of the Siege of Savannah, the research for which was based on orthodox sources only.

Meng, John Joseph, *D'Estaing's American Expedition 1778–1779* (New York, 1936). This pamphlet-size work presents the expedition only in outline.

Moore, Frank, ed., *Diary of the American Revolution. From Newspapers and Original Documents*, 2 vols. (New York, 1863). In addition to Anthony Stokes' description of the Siege reprints of contemporary newspaper accounts of the event are found in this work.

Moultrie, William, *Memoirs of the American Revolution, So far as it related to the States of North and South Carolina, and Georgia*, 2 vols. (New York, 1802).

National Portrait Gallery of Distinguished Americans, The, 4 vols. (Philadelphia, 1835–1839). Sketches of Thomas Pinckney, Benjamin Lincoln and Lachlan McIntosh.

New England Historical and Genealogical Register, The (Boston 1847–   ) VIII (1854), 189–190. Contains reminiscences about the French at Boston in 1778, including references to d'Estaing and Bougainville.

Pettengill, Ray W., *Letters from America 1776–1779, Being Letters of Brunswick, Hessian, and Waldeck Officers with the British Armies During the Revolution* (Boston and New York, 1924). This work is a translation of letters published in Schlözer's *Briefwechsel, meist Historischen und politischen inhalts,* 10 vols. (Göttingen, 1776–1782).

Pinckney, Rev. Charles Cotesworth, *Life of General Thomas Pinckney* (Boston and New York, 1895).

Preston, John Hyde, *Revolution 1776* (New York, 1933).

Ramsay, David, *The History of the Revolution of South-Carolina, from a British Province to an Independent State,* 2 vols. (Trenton, 1785).

Ribaut, Jean. *The Whole & True Discouerye of Terra Florida* (Deland, 1927). A facsimile reprint of the London edition of 1563.

Richardson, John, letter written by on March 15, 1779, from "Savannah River in Georgia on Board the Vengeance," *The American Historical Review,* VII (1902), 293–294. Richardson was a British privateersman.

Russell, Peter, "The Siege of Charleston; Journal of Captain Peter Russell, December 25, 1779, to May 2, 1780." *The American Historical Review,* IV (1899), 478–501. Captain Russell who was at Savannah on February 3–4th, 1780, visited the British works at Spring Hill.

Sabine, Lorenzo, *Biographical Sketches of Loyalists of the American Revolution,* 2 vols. (Boston, 1864).

Salley, A. S., Jr., *The History of Orangeburg County, South Carolina* (Orangeburg, 1898).

Salley, A. S., Jr., ed., *Journal of the Commissioners of the Navy of South Carolina July 22, 1779—March 23, 1780* (Columbia, S. C., 1913).

Savannah Morning News, October 9th, 1879. A special edition on this date was entirely devoted to the Siege of Savannah. It featured a lengthy account by C. C. Jones, Jr., which was largely a rewrite of the chapters on the subject in his *History of Savannah, Ga.* and his *History of Georgia.*

Skelly, Francis, "Journal of Brigade Major F. Skelly." Edited by Charles C. Jones, Jr., in *Magazine of American History* (New York, 1877–1893), XXVI (1891), 152–154, 392–393. The journal covers the period of the British raid on Charlestown in 1779 during which

Skelly had "the pleasure" of serving under Colonel Maitland in the Seventy-First Regiment.

Skinner, Allan Maclean, *Sketch of the Military Services of Lieutenant-General Skinner and his Sons* (Stafford, 1863).

Sparks, Jared, *The Library of American Biography*, 25 vols. (Boston, 1834–1848), IV. Sketch of General Casimir Pulaski. Francis Bowen's biography of Benjamin Lincoln is in Vol. XIII (2nd. series, 1847).

Stedman, Charles, *The History of the Origin, Progress, and Termination of the American War*, 2 vols. (London, 1794). Stedman, who served in the British army in the Revolution, was a warm admirer of Colonel Maitland.

Stevens, William Bacon, *A History of Georgia, from its First Discovery by Europeans to the Adoption of the Present Constitution in MDCCXCVIII*, 2 vols. (New York, Philadelphia, 1847, 1859).

Stewart, David, *Sketches of the Character, Manners, and Present State of the Highlanders of Scotland: With Details of the Military Service of the Highland Regiments*, 2 vols. (Edinburgh, 1882).

Stone, Edwin Martin, *Our French Allies* (Providence, 1884).

Story, D. A., *The de Lanceys, A Romance of a Great Family* (London, 1931).

Uhlendorf, Bernard A., *The Siege of Charleston With an Account of the Province of South Carolina: Diaries and Letters of Hessian Officers From the von Jungkenn Papers in the William L. Clements Library* (Ann Arbor, Michigan, 1938).

Watson, Elkhannah, *Men and Times of the Revolution or Memoirs of Elkhannah Watson* (New York, 1861, 2nd. ed.). Watson visited Savannah in 1778 when the Americans were in possession of the town.

Weems, M. L., *The Life of Gen. Francis Marion* (Philadelphia, 1809).

White, George, *Historical Collections of Georgia* (New York, 1854).

White, George, *Statistics of the State of Georgia* (Savannah, 1849).

Wilkes, Laura E., *Missing Pages in American History Revealing the Services of Negroes in the Early Wars in the United States of America 1641–1815* (Washington, 1919).

Williams, Henry, *An Address Delivered on Laying the Corner Stone of a Monument to Pulaski in the City of Savannah, October 11, 1853* (Savannah, 1855). This pamphlet includes a paper written by William P. Bowen, Sr., about Pulaski's burial place and contains documents supporting his contention that General Pulaski died at Greenwich plantation and was buried there. The other side of the issue is presented by the Rev. Father Mitchell in the *Savannah Press* on August 19, 1929, in an article entitled "Savannah's Unknown Soldier."

Wilson, Adelaide, *Historic and Picturesque Savannah* (Boston, 1889).

Year Book—1885. City of Charleston, So. Ca., 344–345. Brief account of German Fusiliers of Charleston at the Siege of Savannah.

MAPS

British:

"Plan of Attack and the Fortifications at Savannah in the Revolution as described by Capt. A. C. Wylly, who was present." John S. Bowen, Del. (1779?). 17½ x 19¼ inches. De Renne Collection, University of Georgia. Alexander Campbell Wylly was an officer in the King's Rangers. Following a lengthy exile, during which he became Royal Governor of New Providence, he returned to Georgia, where he died in 1833.

"Plan of the French and American Siege of Savannah in Georgia in South [sic] America under command of the French Gener. Count D'Estaing The Britt: Commander in the Town was General August Prevost." A photolithograph is in the Thomas Addis Emmet Collection. This map was reproduced in Jones' *History of Georgia* and also in *The Siege of Savannah, in 1779, as Described in Two Contemporaneous Journals of French Officers in the Fleet of Count d'Estaing.* The map is believed to have been of Hessian origin.

"Plan of the Town of Savannah, With the Works constructed for its Defence, Together with the Approaches & Batteries of the Enemy, and the Joint Attack of the French and Rebels on the 9th of October 1779. From a Survey by John Wilson, 71st Regt., Asst. Engineer." Clinton Map No. 325. 37½ x 28½ inches (Original in color). The legend contains Moncrief's signature. The map is in the William L. Clements Library, University of Michigan. It is reproduced as an endpaper in this book.

"Plan of the Siege of Savannah, with the joint Attack of the French and Americans on the 9th October 1779." Engraved for Stedman's *The History of the Origin, Progress, and Termination of the American War, op. cit.*

French:

Map prepared by the French engineer, Captain Antoine O'Connor, showing the British and Franco-American lines and route of the attacking Allied columns. It contains a detailed legend. A copy is in the Library of the Service Hydrographique de la Marine, Paris. It is reproduced as an endpaper in this book.

Map by O'Connor showing lines and the various phases of the French retreat from Savannah. Library of the Service Hydrographique de la Marine, Paris.

Manuscript map in the Public Library of the City of Boston showing the operations at the Siege of Savannah in 1779 by the French and American forces with names and data in French. 15½ x 23⅞ inches. This map is the same as the first of the O'Connor maps mentioned above.

"*Caroline Meridionale et Partie de la Georgie*," a map illustrating the coast of Georgia and the operations at the Siege of Savannah. 24¼ x 21⅝ inches. It is in the Public Library of the City of Boston.

The following French maps relating to the Siege of Savannah are in the Karpinski Collection in the William L. Clements Library, University of Michigan, Ann Arbor:

No. 256. Showing lines of the siege of Savannah and apparently based on O'Connor's maps referred to above.

No. 409. Similar to No. 256.

No. 432. Same except as to size.

No. 559. Map of entrance to Savannah River showing depths, October, 1779. Prepared by "M^r. le C^e. de Chastenet Puisegur."

No. 747. A rough sketch of the lines and the environs of Savannah containing O'Connor's name.

Index

Aboukir Bay, Battle of, 143, 144
Adams, John, 146
Agénois Regiment, 13, 18–19, 25, 32, 55, 167
Agincourt, 17
Albert de Rions, Comte d', M. de Suffren praises, 10; unable to block Port Royal, 47; beaten by Revolutionists at Toulon, 140; captures H.M.S. *Experiment*, 158
Amazone, 11, 22, 157, 181
American artillery, 24, 61–62
American battery, 61–62, 83
American generals, d'Estaing's comments on, 75
American press, d'Estaing's opinion of, 21; lauds d'Estaing, 131
American Revolution, vii, viii, 5, 114, 116
Americans, mentioned, 34, 60; d'Estaing on faults of, 62; relations with French at Savannah, 72–74; French impressions of, 74–75; mentioned, 93, 114, 125; losses on October 9th, 107, 116, 160, 178; strength of army, 22, 24, 55, 158
Anecdotes of the American Revolution (Garden's), 55, 108, 111
Annibal, 9, 156
Antoinette, Marie, mentioned, 15, 17, 136, 138
Archives Nationales, ix, 183
Ariel, capture of, 11, 156, 181
Armagnac Regiment, 13, 31, 55, 138, 167
Artois, Count d', 136
Augusta, 24, 59, 92
Augusta Road, 1, 91

Austerlitz, 112
Austrian Succession, War of, 19
Auvergne, 15, 125, 175
Auxerrois Regiment, 13, 19, 25, 55
Avignon, 185

Bahamas, 149
Baillie, George, 34
Baillie, Jourdina Cunningham, lends Count d'Estaing a horse, 34; demands its return, 123
Baillie, Robert Carnabie, 95, 107
Baker, Colonel John, 24
Balch, Thomas, 191
Barracks at Savannah, 3, 52, 84, 158, 175
Barras, Louis, Comte de, 10
Barrett, Samuel, criticizes French for abandoning siege of Newport, 60, 199
Bart, Jean, 66
Bartram, John, 3
Bay Street, 1, 78, 159
Beaufort, 8, 11, 25, 26, 29, 31, 39, 45, 46, 47, 73, 156, 157
Beauharnais, Josephine, 137
Beaulieu, mentioned 2; French land at, 31; described, 31–32; mentioned, 33, 53, 58, 61, 65, 157
Beauvais, General, 18
Belfield, Captain of Virginia Dragoons, 24
Belleville, Dr. Nicholas, his recollections of Pulaski, 188
Bellona, 20
Bemis's Heights, 71
Bentalou, Captain Paul, 33, 110, 118, 167

207

INDEX

Berand, Captain Matthew, mortally wounded on October 9th, 107
Bertrand, Count, marries Fanny Dillon, 137
Bethesda (Orphan House), d'Estaing visits, 34; French depredations at, 35; mentioned, 124
Béthisy, Jules-Jacques-Elenore, Vicomte de, 18, 96, 105, 140
Blandat, Lieutenant Mathieu, killed on September 24th, 1779, 19
"Blue" Party in French navy, 12, 65
Bonaparte, Napoleon, 136, 139, 142, 143, 144
Bonaventure, damaged by French, 124
"Bonnie Prince Charlie," finds refuge in Thirlestane Castle, 27
Borda, Jean-Charles, Chevalier de, 12, 87, 191
Boscawen, Admiral Edward, threatens to put d'Estaing in chains if captured, 16; mentioned, 27
Boston, French at, 87, 142
Boudeuse, frigate, 13, 89
Bougainville, Louis-Antoine de, humorous allusion to Captain MacKenzie's defense of the *Ariel*, 11; career of, 12–13; mentioned, 16, 67, 86; animadversions on Vice-Admiral d'Estaing, 88; d'Estaing's confidence in, 88, 128; angered by requisition of his cannon and cannoneers, 90; allusion to d'Estaing's wounds, 122; opposes retreat to Charlestown, 128; sarcastic entry in his Journal about d'Estaing's departure, 132; narrowly escapes death in French Revolution, 139; mentioned, 158
Bougainvillea plant, named in honor of M. de Bougainville, 13
Bougainville Island, 13
Bouillé, Marquis de, 67, 138
Bouvines, Battle of, Dieudonné d'Estaing sacrifices self to save Philip Augustus, 14
Bowen, Francis, 178
Bowen, Jane, aids French, 124
Boyce, Lieutenant Alexander, killed on October 9th, 107
Brandywine, Battle of, 51
Brazil, 144
Brest, d'Estaing's cool reception on arrival at, 135
Brétigny, Colonel, describes conditions in South Carolina, 21; mentioned, 48, 58; has words with d'Estaing, 126; mentioned, 160
Brewton Hill, d'Estaing watches Maitland's troops enter Savannah by water, 52; mentioned, 157, 160
Bricole, 77, 81, 157, 180
Brier Creek, 51
Brisson, Pierre-Raymond de, 143
British army, strength at Savannah, 8, 54–55, 171; casualties, 116, 160, 178
British battery at Spring Hill, 97, 106, 174
Broad River, 47, 156
Brooke, Francis T., description of social life at Savannah, 3–4; mentioned, 163
Brooks, Governor John, on character of Benjamin Lincoln, 71
Broughton Street, 5, 6, 77, 159
Broves, Rafelis, Comte de, 12, 88, 161
Browne, Colonel Thomas (Tory), 92
Browne, Major Thomas, (Dillon Regiment), drinking habits of, 69; opposes attack, 93; mentioned, 97; killed, 106
Brown's Volunteers, 54
Bruneau, Lieutenant James, mortally wounded on October 9th, 107
Bruyères-Chalabre, Comte de, 12
Bryan, Jonathan, 35
Buck Island, British vessels anchor at, 49
Buffington, Moses, 188
Bunker Hill, 116
Bush, Lieutenant John, 107, 108
Butler, Major Pierce, 22
Byron, Admiral John, 7, 38, 66, 89, 156

"Cabal," first Duke of Lauderdale "1" in, 27
Calignon, M., Adjutant, killed, 111
Callibogue Sound, 46, 49
Cambis, Vicomte de, quotes a line from Molière after release, 53
Cambresis Regiment, 13, 55, 132
Camden, Battle of, 181
Campan, Jeanne Louise Henriette, *Memoirs* of, 139
Campbell, Colonel Archibald, mentioned, 4; his estimate of Prevost, 41

INDEX 209

Capellis, Chevalier de, 12
Cap François, 18, 55, 155
Casabianca, 144
Catherine the Great, 18
Causton's Bluff, French embark from, 129, 160
Central Railroad, excavations by at Spring Hill, 175
Cérès, 158
Cervantes, 32
César, 9, 12, 133, 143
Chabert, Joseph-Bernard, Marquis de, 12
Champagne Regiment, 55
Charles II, 17, 27
Charlestown, S. C., mentioned, 7, 8, 20, 21, 46, 47, 59, 74, 86, 87, 115, 118, 127, 128, 129, 133, 148, 150, 151, 155, 156, 160, 178, 180
Charlestown Fusiliers, 110, 205
Charlestown militia, d'Estaing's description of, 25; mentioned, 97; d'Estaing comments favorably upon conduct of, 108
Charlestown press, 21, 47, 151
Charlotte, Fort, 36
Cheraws District, funeral sermon for dead, 116
Cherokee Hill, 157
Cherokee Indians, 6, 32, 81, 100, 157
Chesapeake Bay, 133, 161
Chimère, 81, 133, 180
Choiseul, Duke de, opinion of d'Estaing, 57, 172
Chouin, André-Michel-Victor, Marquis de, 25
Christ Church, 3, 77, 159
Christophe, Henri, 18, 164
Clay, Joseph, 49, 61, 62, 192
Clinton, Sir Henry, ix, 7, 28, 39, 48, 90, 100, 115, 133, 148, 151, 156, 169
Cockspur Island, 161
Colbert, Édouard-Charles-Victurnin, Comte de, 12, 140
Coleman, Kenneth, 190
Colomb, Pierre, 3, 41, 197
Colvill, Reverend Robert, author of "Savannah," 30, 56, 149, 151, 152, 193
Combahee, 156
Comet, 50
Condé, Dragoons of, 142
Condé ("the Great"), 35
Condé, Prince of, 140

Continental Congress, 10, 44, 70, 127, 130, 160
Continental Line of South Carolina, described, 23-24
Continental Line of Georgia, 24-25
Continental troops, described, 24-25; French compliment, 74, 107-108; losses among, 116, 160, 178
Cornwallis, Lord, 146
Costebelle, Pastour de, 170
Court House, occupancy of by British troops at Savannah, 3
Creek Indians, 6, 100, 157
Crouch, Mrs., publishes Charlestown *Gazette,* 150
Cruger, Colonel John Harris, mentioned, 39; quoted on Franco-American relations at Savannah, 72; brilliant defense of Ninety-six, 149; claims British always determined to defend Savannah, 168
Cuba, death of Vicomte de Noailles in, 139
Culloden, Battle of, 27
Curry, James, reputed to have betrayed Allies, 97-98, 176
Cuyler, Telamon C., 169

Dallemagne, Claude, 19, 142
Dampierre, Chevalier de, 67
Dancing Assemblies, Savannah, 6
Danton, 137
Darien, 2
Dauphin Royal, 9
Davis, Jefferson, 73
Davis, John, describes Savannah, 199
Davis, Sam, father of Jefferson Davis, 73
Dawfuskie Island, 46, 49, 157
De Grasse, François-Joseph-Paul, Comte, 10, 67, 132, 133, 181
De Lancey, Mrs., lines in memoriam of Colonel Maitland, 152, 182
De Lancey, Stephen, 6, 149, 182
De Lancey, W. H., 149
De Lancey's Brigade, 54, 78
Delaware River, Maitland's raid on, 27
DeSaussure, Lieutenant Louis, killed on October 9th, 107
Desmoulins, Camille, 137
Desmoulins, Lucile, dies on scaffold with Count Dillon, 137
DeSoto Hotel, site of barracks, 175
d'Estaing (see Estaing)

INDEX

De Treville, Lieutenant John LaB., captures Prevost's dispatch to Maitland, 29
Diadème, 9, 156, 161
Dillon, Arthur, his family, 17; mentioned, 18, 67, 72; opposes attack, 93; leads right column on October 9th, 97; reaches entrenchments, 105; anecdote about his offer of reward to troops, 120; mentioned, 122, 123; signs protest as to place of French embarkation, 128; premonition of violent death, 137; anecdotes concerning his execution, 137; mentioned, 158, 160, 168, 181, 182
Dillon, Comtesse de, 17
Dillon, Édouard (*"le beau Dillon"*), 17
Dillon, Fanny (Countess Bertrand), 137–138
Dillon, Théobald-Hyancinth, in Dillon Regiment at Savannah, 17; wounded on October 9th, 106; massacred by his troops in French Revolution, 138
Dillon family, 17, 182
Dillon Regiment, 13, 36, 129, 168
Dolomieu, Deodat de, 191
Doniol, Henri, quoted on d'Estaing, 125
Donnom, Captain William, killed on October 9th, 107
D'Oyley, Captain Daniel, 82
Doysié, Abel, x
Dubois, Captain David, killed on October 9th, 107
Duguay-Trouin, 66, 112
Du Petit-Thouars, Aristide-Aubert, on d'Estaing's secretiveness, 20–21; his opinion of the Vice Admiral's seamanship, 66; sees Savannah afire from river, 78; quoted as to effect of shell-fire on British fortifications, 83; describes condition of French fleet, 87–88; heroic death of, 144–145; mentioned, 174
Dunkirk, 149
Duquesne, Abraham, Marquis de, 66
Durumain, Chevalier Trolong, commands flotilla sent up Savannah River, 50; mentioned, 77, 91; amphibious attack of fails to get started, 112; mentioned, 159, 160, 171

Ebenezer, 22, 156, 157
Ebenezer Road, 1, 108, 148
Eden, William, mentioned, 176
Elbert, Samuel, 24, 192
Elholm, Augustus C. G., participates in ruse leading to surrender of Sunbury detachment, 117, 159
Elliott, Mrs. Susannah, 108
Émeriau, Maurice-Julien, 143
Erneville, Chevalier d', leads French vanguard, 104; anecdote about his death, 120–121; mentioned, 179
Estaing, Charles-Henri, Comte d', mentioned vii, ix, 6, 7; recommends M. de Suffren for command, 11; appearance of, 14; career, 15–16; character, 15–16; his talent for writing, 15; ambitious nature of, 15–16; captured and paroled in India, 16; compliments Colonel de Noailles and writes to Vicomte's parents about him, 16–17; complains to Ministry about delivery of mails, 19; secretiveness of and criticism of American newspapers, 20–21; lands at Beaulieu, 31; quoted on difficulties of landing his troops, 32; meeting with Pulaski, 33; stops at Bethesda where he sees portrait of Lady Huntingdon, 34; demands surrender of Savannah, 35–36; refuses to propose terms, 36; mentioned, 37; orders M. d'Albert de Rions to block Port Royal, 47; exonerates Fontanges from blame for junction of Beaufort troops, 48; realizes importance of preventing British junction, 48; mentioned, 50; consents to truce, 51; watches last of Colonel Maitland's troops enter Savannah, 52; mentioned, 53; Choiseul's opinion of, 57–58; his reasons for failure to attack immediately, 58–59; justifies his decision to stay on at Savannah, 60; asserts no formal siege of city intended, 61; quoted on sanguineness of Lincoln and Americans, 62; observations on French Negro "musketeers," 65; unpopularity of in navy, 65–66; quoted on characteristics of English, 66–67; on American grog, 67; reprimands Major Browne of Dillon

INDEX

Regiment for drinking while on duty, 69; incident of his descent on Tybee Island, 69–70; opinion of Lincoln, 71; quoted on plain fare of Southern generals, 71–72; writes to and hears from Colonel Laurens, 72; blames Americans for Maitland's entry into Savannah, 73–74; his admiration for George Washington, 75; mentioned, 77, 80, 83, 84, 87; feeling against in French fleet, 87–88; Bougainville's animadversions on, 88–89; his ideas as to locale of attack, 91; curtness to those who opposed him, 93–94; imagines himself a martyr to America, 94; his arguments in favor of an attack, 93–94; Pulaski sends a proposed plan to, 95; Pulaski justifies himself in letter to, 96; desires to take British by surprise, 97; mentioned, 98; aware of desertion among Americans on night of October 8th, 101; mentioned, 102; hears Scotch bagpipes prior to assault, 103; his reasons for not calling off attack, 103; mentioned, 104; wounded in arm, 105; complains of lack of ardor of all but vanguard, 105; mentioned, 106, 107; wounded second time and rescued by Lieutenant de Truguet, 109; quoted on conduct of de Noailles' corps of reserve, 111; comments on reasons for failure of Durumain's river attack, 112; anecdote about Captain Lynch's retort, 120; remains in actual command after being wounded, 122; harassed by details of retreat, 123; suffering of, 124; blames M. de Brétigny for bringing French to Georgia, 125–126; receives grant of land and citizenship from State of Georgia, 126; his reply to American suggestion that his honor required him to stay on and take Savannah, 127; Dillon and de Noailles write to protesting the plan of retreat, 128; threatens to supplant his young Colonels, 128–129; praised by General Lincoln and American press, 130–131; America's debt to, 131; blames American pilots, 133; reason for Colonel de Noailles' visit to Savannah, 133–134; hardships encountered on voyage home, 134–135; sends report to M. de Sartine upon arrival at Brest, 135, 161; reception of in France, 135–136; his course during French Revolution, 136–137; testifies in trial of Marie Antoinette, 136; guillotined, 137; mentioned, 139, 140, 141, 142, 143, 155, 156, 157, 158, 160, 161, 164, 167, 170, 171, 172, 173, 175, 182, 183, 184, 191, 196

Estaing, Comtesse d', sues husband for separation of property, 15

Estaing, Dieudonné d', saves life of King Philip Augustus, 14

Étiquette, Madame (Comtesse de Noailles), 17, 138

Ewensburg, 2

Experiment, capture of, 85, 86, 158

"Fairfield Hero," General George Garth, 85–86

"Fair Lawn," Tattnall's home burned, 43, 169

Falkland Islands, Bougainville colonizer, 12–13

Fantasque, 9, 156

Farrar, Lieutenant Field, killed on October 9th, 107

Fendant, 9, 10, 133, 161

Few, William, 146

Fier Rodrigue, 9

Filature or Old Silk House, 3

Findlater and Seafield, Earl of, 27

Five Fathom Hole, 50

Flag of Second Regiment of S. C., 108–109, 199

Flanders Regiment, 137

Foix Regiment, 13, 25, 55, 88, 173

Fontanges, François, Vicomte de, mentioned, 18; mission to Charlestown, 20, 155; mentioned, 47; d'Estaing exonerates, 48; reports arrival of Beaufort troops to d'Estaing, 51, 52; mentioned, 70; has words with Colonel Laurens, 73–74; wounded, 106; mentioned, 116, 155, 170

Fontenoy, Battle of, 13, 41

Fouquier-Tinville, 136

Fourberies de Scapin, Les, line from quoted by M. de Cambis, 53, 171

Fowey, 44

Franche-Comté, 19

Frederick the Great, 18

INDEX

French, Captain Thomas, 117, 159
French army, foot-soldiers of era, 13–14; favoritism to nobility in, 18, 64; strength at Savannah, 55, 158; heterogeneous make-up of at Savannah, 64; mentioned, 67; positions given to regiments according to seniority, 102; losses on October 9th, 116, 160; desertions, 129, 160; reputed panic of French troops before embarkation from Georgia, 134
French batteries, 61, 75, 83, 84, 158, 159
French navy, preference to nobility in, 9–10; plight of sailors, 19; nobility in, 64; reputed failure of some of French naval officers to co-operate with d'Estaing, 66, 172; mentioned, 67; lack of supplies in and sickness in fleet off Savannah, 87–88; condition of d'Estaing's squadron, 89–90
French Revolution, 18, 19, 136, 137, 139, 140, 141, 142, 143, 144
Fuser, Lt. Colonel Lewis V., 168, 176, 181, 190

Gamble, Thomas, 200
Gantheaume, Henri, 144
Garden, Alexander (*Anecdotes*), 38, 55–56, 108, 111
Garrett, Thomas, anecdote of about Pulaski, 177
Garth, General George, 85–86, 158
Gaston, Lieutenant Robert, killed on October 9th, 107
Gazette de France, 130
Gazette of the State of South-Carolina, 20, 23, 28
Gâtinais Regiment, 13, 25, 55, 104, 176
Genville, Levert de, first to reach British entrenchments, 104
George III, viii, 1, 3, 8, 148
Georgia, ix, 1, 2, 3, 9, 11, 22, 24, 41, 126, 146, 147, 148
Georgia Gazette, 6, 28, 39, 43, 44, 81–82, 92, 110, 150, 153, 195
Georgia troops, 24–25
Gérard, M., d'Estaing writes to, 175
Germain, Lord George, ix, 22, 42, 43, 113, 148, 151
Germain, 190
German Fusiliers of Charlestown, 110, 205

Géronte, character in Molière, 53
Gervais, John Lewis, mentioned, 62
Gibbes, William Hasell, 83, 147, 192
Gibbons, Mrs. Sarah, Pulaski stops at plantation of (Sharon?), 168
Glascock, Thomas, his reputed rescue of Pulaski from battle-field, 118
Glasier, Major Beamsley, 92, 107
Glen, John, attitude of toward Loyalists, 40, 169
Goldesbrough, Lieutenant, 49
Godoy, 64, 83
Good Hope, Cape of, 134
Governor's House, 3, 4
Graham, Colin, leads British sortie, 68, 158
Graham, James, refugees flock to plantation of on Hutchinson Island, 81
Graham, John, Lieutenant Governor, 77, 78, 147, 153, 159
Grasse, Comte de (see de Grasse)
Gray, Lieutenant James, 107, 108
Greene, General Nathanael, quoted on abandonment of the siege of Newport, 60; on anti-d'Estaing faction in fleet, 66; buried in Graham vault, 153
Greenwich, tradition of Pulaski's burial at, 118, 204; owner furnishes provisions to French, 124; d'Estaing convalesces at, 124, 180
Grenada, mentioned, 15, 17, 35, 58, 66, 69, 102, 133
"Grenadiers' Marching Song," 200
Grimké, John Faucheraud, 72–73, 86, 146
Grog, d'Estaing's opinion of, 67
Guadeloupe, 55, 149
Guale Indians, 1
Gudin, Jean, painting of M. de Noailles' naval exploit, 139
Guerrier, 9, 13, 88, 89, 90, 132
Guiton, Duke de, aids Pulaski, 96
Gustave III, 18, 107, 191–192
Gwinnett, Button, mentioned, 24

Habersham, Major John, 3
Habersham, Colonel Joseph, 24, 146, 190
Habersham plantation ("Silk Hope"?), Pulaski writes from, 33
Haddington Borough, John Maitland represents in Commons, 27
Hainault Regiment, 13, 19, 25, 55
Haiti, 18, 177

INDEX

"Half Moon Bluff" (Greenwich), 124
Halifax, 21
Hamilton, Colonel John, 92
Hamilton, Paul, his reaction to American defeat, 116; Governor of S. C. and Secretary of Navy, 147; mentioned, 192
Hammond, Samuel, 146–147
Hancock, John, presents d'Estaing with a portrait of General Washington, 75
Hawes, Lilla M., x
Hayne, Isaac, records death of William Jasper, 117
Hector, 9
Henry, Captain John, 27, 144, 169
Hervilly, Louis-Charles, Comte d', mentioned, 18; death of, 140
Hessians, 5, 6, 26, 30, 54, 175
Heyward, Thomas, Jr., 22
Hilton Head, 49, 85, 158
Hinrichs, Captain Johann, his Journal quoted, 30, 42, 83, 97, 148, 166, 193
Hispaniola (San Domingo), d'Estaing confides his plans to Governor of, 21
Hobkirk, Battle of, 98
Holmes, John Bee, his reputed rescue of Pulaski from battlefield, 118
Horry, Colonel Peter, mentioned, 22, 59; denies Weems' account of colloquy with Sergeant Jasper, 117; comments on John Newton and Jasper, 147; his criticism of Weems' book, 172; mentioned, 176, 187
Houdon, Jean-Antoine, his bust of Count d'Estaing, 14
Houstoun, Governor John, 4, 24, 98
Houstoun, Sir Patrick, Sixth Baronet, explains his presence among American militia at Savannah, 98
Howe, General Robert, 4, 29
Huger, General Isaac, 22, 112
Hugues de Bouville, 139
Hume, Lieutenant Alexander, 107, 108
Huntingdon, Selina, Lady, 34, 123, 168
Huntington, Samuel, 22, 130
Hutchinson Island, 81, 82
Hyder Ali, 11

India, 10, 11, 16

Indian Ocean, 11
Indians, 1, 5–6, 32, 46, 81, 100, 157
Iphegénie, 10, 140
Irish troops, desertions in Dillon Regiment, 129
Ishmael, servant of Major Jones, 87

Jackson, James, mentioned, 24; on legal ability of Charles Price, 39; tells of Major Jones' and Lieutenant Baillie's premonition of death, 95; anecdote about Lieutenant Lloyd, 118–119; later career, 146; mentioned, 187
Jacksonborough, S. C., 173
Jamaica, 149
Jasper, William, Weems' story of his rescue of colors, 108–109; account of Sergeant Jasper's deathbed colloquy with Horry denied by latter, 117; Colonel Hayne records death of, 117; Horry on honesty of, 147
Jay, John, 43
Jefferson, Thomas, d'Estaing writes to, 126; mentioned, 146
Jerseys, Major Maitland in, 27
Jewish burial ground, 111
Jockey Club, 6
Johnson, Judge William, quoted, 115, 189
Johnston, Elizabeth Lichtenstein, opinion of American Revolution, 5; mentioned, 81; describes incident of bombardment, 82; mentioned, 171, 194
Johnston, Mrs. Lewis, sends her young sons into lines, 82
Johnston, William Martin, mentioned, 171, 194
Jones, Charles C., Jr., 164, 191
Jones, Major John, describes effect of Allied bombardment, 78; predicts destruction of Savannah by fire, 78–79; alludes to hardships undergone by Mrs. Lachlan McIntosh, 80; believes Allied attack necessary, 84; mentioned, 87; has premonition of death, 95; killed on October 9th, 107; letter from his wife, 114; mentioned, 173, 187
Jones, John Paul, quoted on favored position of nobility in French navy, 9–10; opinion of d'Estaing, 15; mentioned, 199

INDEX

Jones, Mrs. Polly, 87, 114, 173
Jourdan, Jean-Baptiste, 19, 142
Journal d'un officier de la Marine, quoted, 66, 73, 94, 103, 191

Kehoe, Barbara B., x
Keppel, Admiral, 125
Keppel, brig, 50
Kersaint, Gui-Pierre de Coëtnempren, Comte de, 10, 140
Kervéguen, Gaultier de, 142-143
King's Rangers, 92, 205
Kinnill, Lieutenant Joseph, killed on October 9th, 107
Knowles, Captain, 79

Labarre, Lieutenant, 142
Lafayette, Marquis de, vii, 75, 125, 131, 138
La Galissonière, Athanase Scipion de Barin, Marquis de, 12
Lagos Bay, Spain, Maitland in sea battle, 27, 179
La Motte-Piquet (see Motte-Piquet)
Languedoc, ix, 9, 13, 14, 40, 75, 132, 133, 155, 156, 160, 161, 184
La Pérouse, Jean-François de Galaup, Comte de, 11-12, 144, 156
La Rochefoucauld-Liancourt, Duke de, 197
Lauder, Scotland, 27
Lauderdale, Charles, Sixth Earl of, viii, 26-27
Lauderdale, first Duke of, 27
Lauderdale, Seventh Earl of, 153
Lauderdale, Fifteenth Earl of, 179, 195
Laurens, Henry, mentioned, 131
Laurens, John, mentioned, 22; writes letter welcoming d'Estaing, 72; M. de Fontanges addresses warm words to, 73-74; leads American column on October 9th, 97; becomes separated from part of his command, 109; Weems' story of his reaction to order to retreat, 111; mentioned, 118; writes to his father about Siege, 131; mentioned, 172, 173
Lebey brothers, 106, 202
Lee, General Henry, quoted, 15, 48, 59, 107, 148
Leeward Isles, 160
Legaré, Lieutenant James, 108
L'Enfant, Pierre-Charles, wounded on October 9th, 147; attempts to set abatis on fire, 159

Le Peley, Georges-René-Pléville, 142
Lichtenstein, Elizabeth (see Johnston)
Lincoln, General Benjamin, mentioned, 4, 22, 24, 33, 47, 48; d'Estaing describes reaction of to junction of Beaufort troops, 52; mentioned, 57; informed of truce by Count d'Estaing, 59; optimism of, 62; irritated at Count for sending summons in name of King of France, 70; d'Estaing's opinion of, 71; plain fare served at his table, 71-72; O'Dune blames Lincoln for refusal to grant safe conduct to women and children, 80; mentioned, 83, 94, 98, 101, 122, 123, 126; tries to persuade d'Estaing to stay on at Savannah, 127; praises French commander in report to Continental Congress, 130; mentioned, 146, 155, 157, 158, 160, 167, 178, 187, 199
Livingston, Governor, 43
Lloyd, Lieutenant Edward, anecdote about, 118-119
Lloyd, Mr., acts as guide, 166
Lock, Lieutenant, reconnoiters French ships off Tybee, 7
Lodi, Battle of, 142
Lomel, Pulaski writes from, 165
London, viii, x, 60, 113, 140
Louis XVI, vii, 13, 15, 18, 136, 137, 139, 140, 141
Lynah, Dr. James, 118, 179
Lynah, J. H., 179
Lynch, Isidore de, anecdote about, 120; in Battle of Valmy, 142

McArthur, Major Archibald, leads sortie, 173
McCall, Hugh, quoted on Colonel Maitland's death, 150
McDonald, Sergeant, 108
McGillivray's Plantation, 158
McIntosh, Lachlan, 24, 40, 59, 80, 95, 97, 109, 157, 158-159
McIntosh, Mrs. Lachlan, undergoes hardships during Siege, 80
McIntosh, Captain Roderick, 115
MacKenzie, Thomas, Captain of the *Ariel,* 133, 181
McLean, Andrew, explains his presence at Savannah in American militia, 40

INDEX 215

McPherson, Lieutenant Henry, killed in sortie on September 24th, 173
Madras, d'Estaing captured at, 16
Magnifique, 9, 89, 90, 160
Maham, Hezekiah ("Maham Tower"), 22
Maitland, John, mentioned, viii; commands troops at Beaufort, 26; career of, 27–28; friendship with General Washington, 28; mentioned, 29; leaves Beaufort, 30; mentioned, 36, 39, 46, 48, 49; reaches Savannah, 51; dramatic appearance before Council of War, 55–56; outspoken opposition to any idea of capitulation, 56; mentioned, 57, 78; commands British right flank, 92; praise of by General Henry Lee, 107; orders counter-attack on October 9th, 111; mentioned, 125; death of, 149–150; story that he died of excessive drinking, 150; Prevost reports death of to General Clinton, 151; praised by contemporaries, 151–152; poems commemorating his death, 152; burial at Savannah, 153; mentioned, 156, 157, 159, 160, 165, 168, 179, 190, 195
Maitland, Right Honourable Ian Colin, 179, 195
Maitland family, 26–27
Maps of Siege of Savannah, 205–206
Marigny, Bernard, Comte de, 12, 133, 161, 181
Marigny, Charles-René, Vicomte de, 181
Marines (British), 44, 54, 104
Marines (French), 55, 112
Marion, Colonel Francis, mentioned, 22; describes appearance of troops, 23–24; his reputed strictures on truce, 59; mentioned, 117, 147, 172, 187
Marseillais, 79, 167, 185
Martinique, 55, 135
Maryland, 133
Meehan, Norma Berry, x
Melvin, Captain George, takes part in ruse leading to surrender of Sunbury detachment, 117, 159
Meriwether, David, 24, 146
Meyronnet de Saint-Marc, describes incident of French landing, 32–33; quotes British deserters as to effect of Colonel Maitland's arrival, 57; quotes d'Estaing on prospect of success at Savannah, 58; mentioned, 65; sees conflagration at Savannah, 79; on Georgia weather, 86; quotes d'Estaing as to necessity of attack, 93; on Tories in American militia, 98; mentioned, 99; French aware of American treachery before attack, 101; describes confusion on October 9th, 106; praises Continental troops, 107–108; tells of exchange of words between Colonel Brétigny and d'Estaing, 125–126; his journals, 167, 185
Michaud, Joseph-François, quoted on d'Estaing's role in French Revolution, 136
Midway, 2
Militia (American), 23, 25, 40, 55, 98, 107–108, 112
Militia (British), 44, 54, 55
Militia (French), 64
Millen's plantation, Americans camp at, 157
Minden, Battle of, 13
Minis, Philip, recommends Beaulieu for place of French landing, 31
Minis house, French at, 35
Missiessy, Édouard de, 143
Mitchell, the Reverend Father Joseph D., 204
Môle St. Nicolas, 138
Molière, M. de Cambis quotes line from *Les Fourberies de Scapin*, 53; d'Estaing uses allusion from *L'Avare*, 135
Moncrief, Captain James, wins "immortal honour" at Savannah, 43; promises successful defense in event of a formal siege, 63; mentioned, 84; death of, 148–149; mentioned, 156, 157
Mons-en-Puelle, 139
Montcalm, Marquis de, 12, 89
Montgomery, Fort, 51
Montgomery, General Richard, 43
Montpellier, 30, 166
Moore, Major T. W., property of destroyed in bombardment, 77; mentioned, 79, 99; describes battle-ground after Allied repulse, 115; mentioned, 194

Morel, Mrs. John, 35, 168
Morel plantation, 32, 35
Motte, Major Charles, killed on October 9th, 107
Motte-Piquet, Toussaint-Guillaume, Comte de La, 10, 160
Mouchy, Duke de, 17, 138
Moultrie, General William, 23, 28
Mowbray, Captain J., 190
Mulryne, Colonel John, 124
Mulryne, Mrs., damage to her home at Bonaventure, 124
Murray, John, affidavit concerning John Glen, 40

Napoleon (see Bonaparte)
National Guard of France, 136
Negroes, labor on Savannah defenses, 43; casualties among in bombardment, 77, 79
Negro troops, 18, 55, 64–65, 81–82, 129, 157, 177
Newfoundland, 21, 149
New Hebrides, 11
New Jersey, 27, 100
Newport, French at, 35, 60, 66, 131
New York, mentioned, viii, ix, 6, 7, 26, 85, 100, 113, 149
Nile, Battle of, (see Aboukir Bay)
Ninety-six, Cruger's defense of, 149
Noailles, Louis-Marie, Vicomte de, described, 16; d'Estaing praises 17; mentioned, 18, 67, 69, 72, 75, 77, 87; his reply to Count d'Estaing's comment on his views about proposed attack, 93; placed in command of reserves, 97; conduct of his rear guard on October 9th, 111, 177; mentioned, 123; urges retreat by way of Charlestown, 128, 160; visits Savannah, 133, 160; d'Estaing divines purpose of his visit, 134; his reputed statements to English while at Savannah, 134; emigrates during French Revolution, 138; death of, 139; mentioned, 140, 171, 181
Noailles, Comtesse de, celebrated as *Madame Étiquette*, 17; guillotined with her husband and daughter, 138
North Carolina Loyalists, 54, 92, 104

O'Connor, Antoine-François-Térance, mentioned, ix; d'Estaing's tribute to, 60–61; quoted on conduct of French reserve, 111; Journal of, 165, 176; maps by, 205–206
O'Dune, Thadée-Humphrey, 68, 80
Oeil-de-Boeuf, 35
Ogeechee Ferry, 168
Ogeechee River, 47, 116, 159
Ogeechee Road, 2, 33, 158
Ogilvy, Elizabeth, Lady, 27
Oglethorpe, James Edward, mentioned, 1, 113
O'Moran, Joseph, delivers d'Estaing's summons, 36, 157; guillotined, 138; mentioned, 168
Orangeburg, 23
Ossabaw Sound, 32, 157
Oxford, 68

Pacific Ocean, 12, 89, 144
Panthéon, 138, 142
Paris, x, 35, 60, 137
Parr, Captain in S. C. Royalists, 188
"Pechot," *nom de plume* of Jean-Rémy de Tarragon, 167, 186
Pérouse, La (see La Pérouse)
Petit Trianon, viii, 17
Philadelphia, 87, 130, 131, 138
Philip Augustus, King, 14
Philip the Handsome, 139
Pierrevert, Marquis de, 144
Pinckney, Charles Cotesworth, mentioned, 5, 22; criticizes guides, 102; remains optimistic despite defeat on October 9th, 127; later career of, 146
Pinckney, Eliza Lucas, mother of C. C. Jr. and Thomas Pinckney, 188–189
Pinckney, Thomas, mentioned, 22, 34; recounts incident of d'Estaing's descent on Tybee Island, 69–70; anecdote about, 82–83; mentioned, 94; describes confusion on October 9th, 109; mentioned, 110; reputed exhortation of his troops during retreat, 111; later career of, 146; mentioned, 177, 181, 188–189
Plombard, M., 48, 74, 170
Pollard, Ensign, killed, 78, 159
Pompadour, Madame de, 12, 15
Pondevaux, Marquis de, 18, 93
Pontèves-Gien, Jean-Baptiste-Elzéar, Marquis de, 12

INDEX

Pontgibaud, Chevalier de, 10, 25, 198
Porbeck, Lieutenant Colonel von, field officer of the day on right flank, 92
Port au Prince, 55
Port Royal, 26, 47, 126, 170
Port Royal River, 48, 170
Port Royal Sound, 46, 47, 156
Prévalaye, Pierre-Dimas, Marquis de, 10, 140
Prevost, General Augustin, mentioned, viii, 5; ideas as to objective of French fleet, 7; writes to Admiral Byron, 7-8; quoted on size of French fleet off Savannah, 9; mentioned, 28, 29, 30, 32; stalls for time, 36; pessimism of, 38; exhorts his troops, 38-39; appearance and character, 41; effect of age and service on health, 41; mentioned, 43, 46, 48, 51, 53, 55; refuses to surrender, 57; surprised at d'Estaing's delay in attacking, 58; mentioned, 62; proposes that non-combatants be permitted to leave Savannah, 80; mentioned, 81, 84, 91, 99; reports his victory to Lord Germain, 113; mentioned, 120; last years of, 148; informs Clinton of Maitland's death, 151; mentioned, 156, 157, 159, 166, 168, 169, 171, 173, 178, 194, 199
Prevost, Mrs. Augustin, 41, 80
Price, Charles, accompanies Americans to Savannah, 39-40
Propaganda, British, 99, 130
Provence, 9, 135, 156, 161
Pugh, Reverend Evan, memorial service for dead, 116
Pulaski, Casimir, mentioned, viii; message to Count d'Estaing, 24; mentioned, 25; d'Estaing writes to, 33; meets General d'Estaing, 33-34; suggests plan of attack, 95; justifies himself to Count d'Estaing, 96; mentioned, 97, 106, 107; circumstances of his fatal wound, 109-110; d'Estaing attributes death of to Pulaski's advancing prematurely, 110; British strictures on, 110; Dr. Lynah removes grapeshot, 118; death of and burial, 118; movements on September 14, 1779, 167-168; mentioned, 156, 159, 160, 174-175, 177, 178-179, 189, 193, 204
Pulaski's Legion, 25, 110, 167
Purysburg, 22, 157
Puysegur, Antoine-Hyacinthe-Anne, Comte de Chastenet de, mentioned, 12; ascends Savannah River, 50; commands *Truite*, 77; accompanies Durumain on October 9th, 112; mentioned, 140; commended by d'Estaing, 170; his chart of Savannah River, 206
Puysegur, Bernard-Jacques-Hubert, Comte de, 186

Quash, slave, 4
Quebec, Prevost at, 41

Ramsay, Dr. David, mentioned, 22; on spirit of money-making in South Carolina, 23; mentioned 110, 114, 193
Recollections of a Georgia Loyalist 82, 194
"Red" party in French navy, 12
Rhode Island, 7, 126
Ribaut, Jean, 46, 47-48
Richardson, John, describes Savannah, 2, 163
Rigaud, André, 18
Rions, Comte d'Albert de (see Albert de Rions)
Rivington, James, (Rivington's *Royal Gazette*), 113, 166, 195
Robespierre, 139
Robuste, 9, 67, 89, 132, 134
Rochambeau, General de, vii, 115
Roche-Fontenilles, Marquis de, 18
Rochefoucauld-Liancourt (see La Rochefoucauld-Liancourt)
Rogowski, Major, asserts that Pulaski fell while leading cavalry charge, 109-110, 193
Roman de Lisle, Major, 102, 176
Rose, 158, 174
Rossbach, Battle of, 13
Rouvray, Laurent-François, Marquis de, 18, 68, 129, 140, 166
Roux, Captain Albert, mortally wounded on October 9th, 107
Royal American Regiment, 107
Russell, John, d'Estaing describes his portrait of Lady Huntingdon, 34
Russell, Peter, describes Savannah, 2; on defenses of city, 148, 203

218 INDEX

Rutledge, galley, Negroes recruited for service aboard, 81; captured, 174
Rutledge, Hugh, 146
Rutledge, John, mentioned, 22, 48, 58; d'Estaing writes to, 126; urges French to stay on at Savannah, 128, 160

Sablière, M. de, 112
Sagittaire, 9, 47, 149, 158
St. Augustine, 5, 38
St. Augustine Creek, 158
Saint Christopher, 138
Saintes, Battle of the, 135, 138, 149
Saint Helena, 137, 144
St. James, Santee, 119
Saint James Square (Telfair), 199
Saint Lucie, 67, 138
Saint Vincent, 58
Salley, A. S., 187
San Domingo, 18, 55, 64–65, 69, 138, 149, 155, 175
Sans Souci, Henri Christophe's citadel, 18
Saratoga, 101
Sartine, Antoine-Raymond-Jean-Gualbert-Gabriel de, Minister of Marine, mentioned, 17, 21, 48, 66, 71, 112, 134, 135, 161, 182
Savage, Thomas, plantation of, 116
Savannah, mentioned, vii, viii; appearance in 1779, 1–3; society in, 3–4; strategic importance of, 4–5; turf events and dancing assemblies at, 6; mentioned, 7, 8, 19, 22, 23, 25, 29, 31, 34; French march on, 34–35; British despair of successful defense, 38–39; Americans confident of capture of, 40; storming of by British in 1778, 40–41; state of defenses before Siege, 42; British work on defenses, 43–44; Maitland's arrival at, 50–51; Lincoln's army reaches environs of, 57; American description of defenses, 58; Allies decide upon siege of, 60; shelling of, 76–80, 159; incendiary bombs thrown into, 78; damage in, 79; progress of British in fortifying, 84; British supplies in, 86; mentioned, 98, 100, 105, 113, 114, 115, 116, 117, 120, 124, 126, 127, 130, 131, 134, 138, 140, 141, 142, 143, 144, 146, 147, 148, 149, 153, 155, 156, 157, 158, 159, 160

"Savannah," poem by Robert Colvill, 30, 56, 193
Savannah River, mentioned, 1, 10, 24, 47, 50, 52, 59, 97, 134, 156, 157, 158, 159, 161, 170, 171
Saxe, Marshal de, 14, 35
Schwerin, General von, grandfather of Colonel Stedingk, 18
Scotland, 26
Scots Magazine, 41, 56
Scourge, galley, 26
Scurvy, in d'Estaing's fleet, 19
Sea Island Road, 2
Séguier de Terson, Philippe de, his Journal quoted, 32, 33, 36, 52, 67, 70, 85, 102, 104, 109, 122, 134, 140, 167, 192
Ségur, Count de, anecdote about Isidore de Lynch, 120
September massacres, 141
Seventy-first Regiment, 8, 26, 28, 29, 54, 92, 103, 153, 176, 204
Seven Years' War, 16, 19
Shaffer, George W., reminiscences concerning Central Railroad's excavations at Spring Hill, 175
Shaw, Captain Alexander, aide-decamp to Prevost, 5
Shav's Rebellion, Lincoln quells, 146
Sheftall, Levi, acts as guide, 166
Sheftall house, 199
Sheppard, Captain Charles, killed on October 9th, 107, 111
Sigoier, M. de, praised by d'Estaing, 173
Sixteenth Regiment, 68, 149
Sixtieth Regiment (Royal American), 5, 44, 54, 92, 107, 176, 199
Skelly, Major Francis, 203–204
Skinner, Colonel, 54
Skinner, Lieutenant John, 68, 149, 173
Skirving, Colonel William, 115
Skull Creek, 29, 46, 156
Smith, Chief Justice William, on importance of British victory at Savannah, viii, 113
South Carolina, ix, 2, 5, 21, 22, 28, 81, 100, 115, 146, 156
South Carolina Fifth Regiment, 97
South Carolina First Regiment, 97
South Carolina militia, 23, 25, 156
South Carolina Royalists, 188
South Carolina Second Regiment, 23, 108, 109, 118, 199

INDEX

Spanish Wells (Hilton Head Island), 46
Sphinx, 156
Spring Hill redoubt, 91, 95, 96, 97, 102, 104, 105, 106, 107, 108, 141, 159, 160, 174, 175, 176
Stedingk, Curt-Bogislaus-Louis-Christopher, Count von, described, 18; mentioned, 32; quoted on American army and people, 74; criticizes place chosen for attack, 93, 94; leads column on October 9th, 97; mentioned, 102; wounded, 105; reaches entrenchments, 106–107; praised by d'Estaing, 107; his anecdotes of the attack on October 9th, 119–120; mentioned, 137, 191
Stedman, Charles, quoted, 51, 152, 204
Stedman, Lieutenant James, 119, 179
Stevens, W. B., 188
Stokes, Chief Justice Anthony, mentioned, 3; on strategic importance of Savannah, 4–5; mentioned, 39; opposes surrender, 42; praises defenders of city, 44; description of bombardment, 76, 77; loses several slaves and his books in fire, 79; quoted on Siege, 113, 114; mentioned, 124, 159, 163, 194
Steele, John, 174
Stono, Battle of, 28, 51
Suffren, Pierre-André de, commands *Fantasque*, 10; wins fame in Asian waters, 11; criticism of d'Estaing's seamanship, 66
Sullivan, General John, 34–35, 60
Sunbury, 8, 39, 47, 117, 156, 159
Surinam, 149
Swiss Guard, M. d'Hervilly transmits king's order to, 140

Tabago, 103, 113
Tarragon, Anne-Claude de, 103, 143
Tarragon, Jean-Rémy de, his Journal quoted, 31, 32, 35, 64, 68, 70, 78, 83–84, 101, 102, 105, 111, 116, 128, 143, 167, 170, 186
Tarragon, M. Rémy de, 187
Tattnall, Josiah, his home burned by British, 43, 169
Tawse, Thomas, stationed near Spring Hill redoubt, 92; throws his troops into battle, 104; heroic death of, 105
Teneriffe, 12
Terson, Séguier de (see Séguier de Terson)
Thermopyles, Les, tragedy by M. d'Estaing, 15
Thirlestane Castle, 27
Thomson, Colonel William, 23
Thomson, Mr., death of daughter of in bombardment, 77
Thunderbolt, 61, 118, 122, 123, 124, 128, 129, 158, 160, 180
Tonnant, 9, 144, 161
Tonyn, Governor Patrick, 39, 92
Tories, 5, 40, 98, 147
Toulon, 19, 124, 140, 185
Toulon squadron, 67, 155
Tour du Pin, Marquise de la, daughter of Count Dillon, 137
Tourville, Admiral de, 66
Trafalgar, 143
Trenches, Allied, 60–61, 68, 93, 112, 175
Trogoff, Jean-Honoré, Comte de, 140
Truguet, Laurent, Comte de, 65, 87, 109, 141
Truite, 50, 77, 81, 157, 158, 159, 170, 180
Trustees' Garden, 2, 158
Tuileries, 139, 140
Turenne, General de, 35
Turf, spirit of the, at Savannah, 6
Twiggs, Colonel John, 24
Tybee bar, 6, 156, 161, 170
Tybee Island, 5, 7, 9, 14, 20, 29, 50, 69, 78, 155, 156, 172, 174
Tybee Roads, 49

Vaillant, 9, 143
Valbel, volunteers of, 55
Valmy, Battle of, 142
Vardy, Captain, captured with dispatch to Maitland, 29
Vaudreuil, Louis-Phillipe de Rigaud, Marquis de, 10, 133, 140, 141, 161
Vély, Abbé, 139
Vence, Jean-Gaspard, 104
Vengeur, 9
Vergennes, Comte de, 18
Vernon River, 13, 31, 156
Versailles, 15, 17, 103, 135
Vigilant, 26, 46, 49
Villeneuve, Pierre-Charles de, 143–144

INDEX

Villiers, Barbara, Duchess of Cleveland, 17
Vindictive, galley, 26
Viper, 174
Virginia, equipment of troops, 24
Virginia Light Dragoons, 24
Virginia militia, 24, 108, 177
Vleland, Lieutenant Cornelius Van, mortally wounded on October 9th, 107; anecdote about, 118

Wallace, Anne, Lady, daughter of Governor Wright, 85
Wallace, Sir James, 85, 149
Wall's Cut, 49, 50
Walsh Regiment, 55
Walton, George, 4
Warren, Samuel, anecdote, 119, 179
Warrior, 149
Washington, D. C., laid out by Major L'Enfant, 147
Washington, George, mentioned, 28, 41, 67, 74, 75, 88, 127, 133, 146
Washington, J., 167
Washington, Captain Thomas [?], 167
Waterloo, 149
Watson, Elkhannah, 3, 204
Wattignies, Battle of, 142
Weems, M. L., account of Jasper's rescue of flag, 108–109; Peter Horry on Weems' "inventions," 117; mentioned, 147; story of the circumstances of Maitland's death, 150; mentioned, 172, 187
Wellington, Duke of, mentioned, 149
Wereat, John, transmits offer of grant of land to d'Estaing from Georgia, 126
West Indies, 7, 10, 18, 58, 64, 67, 81, 88, 100, 112, 133
Westminster Abbey, Sir James Wright buried in, 148
White, Colonel John, mentioned, 24; his extraordinary ruse on October 1, 1779, 117, 159, 178
White Bluff Road, 67
Wickham, Captain (Sixtieth Regiment), 104
Wickom, Lieutenant John, killed on October 9th, 107
Williamson, General Andrew, 23, 112
Wilson, Adelaide, quoted, 175
Windward Isles, 86, 120
Windward Passage, 8
Wise, Major Samuel, killed on October 9th, 107
Wissenbach's Hessians, 5
Wolfe, General James, 41, 149
Wright, Sir James, returns to Georgia in 1779, 4; receives word of arrival of French fleet, 6; mentioned, 39, 41; opposes surrender, 42; quoted on importance of outcome of Siege, 42; praises Captain Moncrief, 43; describes joy at Savannah upon Maitland's arrival, 51; mentioned, 76, 78, 85; opinion of result of defeat of Allies, viii, 113–114; declares day of Thanksgiving, 114; George III sends message of commendation to, 148; death of, 148; mentioned, 159, 161, 169, 194–195
Wright, James, Jr., 148
Wylly, Captain Alexander Campbell, map of Siege, 205
Wylly, Colonel Richard, 192

"XYZ Affair," 146

Yamacraw, 2, 45, 76, 97, 170
Yamacraw Creek, 106
Yamassee Indians, 46
Yorktown, 10, 133

Zélé, 9, 12
Zubly, Rev. John Joachim, 44
Zubly's Ferry, 2, 59, 157, 160

www.ingramcontent.com/pod-product-compliance
Lightning Source LLC
Chambersburg PA
CBHW012333230426
43664CB00044B/2899